Leading by Coaching

"Amidst the avalanche of books on leadership in recent years, this one stands out as offering something different and of real practical value. Leadership is a fluid concept and there are many authentic and valid leadership styles but *Leading by Coaching* offers a pathway to what may well come to be seen as a core skill for all successful leaders. In a business world bedevilled by short-termism, *Leading by Coaching* sets—out how talent can be nurtured and developed by leaders in a way which helps to genuinely build and sustain organisations over the long-term."

—Peter Large, *Executive Director, ACCA*

"If you want to be a true leader then all you need to do is to get people to follow you. Nick Marson has accumulated an unparalleled understanding of what it takes to be able to achieve this. Having coached dozens of global business leaders his book brings together decades of study, insight and experience to give the reader everything they need to know about how to become a respected and successful leader."

—David Ross, *Director, Weber Shandwick*

"What I love about Nick's approach in this book is that it highlights to need to 'put the hard work' into leading, as he says, 'one conversation at a time'. There is no crash diet answer; people are all individuals and if you can't be bothered to care about them or listen to them, the days are gone when you will be able to lead them effectively and sustainably."

—Sian Fisher, *CEO, The Chartered Insurance Institute*

"Leadership is in large part seeing something in others that they don't yet see in themselves. There is not a more powerful approach to identifying and helping bring awareness to untapped potential than coaching. In *Leading by Coaching*, Nick Marson will provide you with a complete and practical framework for unleashing the potential of those in your charge—one conversation at a time."

—Anthony Iannarino, author of *Eat Their Lunch: Winning Customers Away from Your Competition*

"A book that inspires you to think, to reflect and to self-evaluate. Helping leaders to create silence, listen well and to have the confidence to be themselves."

—Victoria Brackett, *Chief Executive for Business Legal Services, Irwin Mitchell LLP*

"I love the way Nick has woven his story and deep, personal experience into this book. With care, wisdom, and practical guidance, Nick inspires us to look within and find our authentic, brilliant and best selves, and then he challenges us to consciously and humbly bring what we find to our every inter-action, so we too can change the world for the better, one conversation at a time. A recommended and mind-opening read!"

—Ben Emmens, *author of* Conscious Collaboration *and Director,*
The Conscious Project

"This excellent and insightful book is definitely worth a read and a pause for thought if you want to be a better leader and coach—it makes you take a step back and focus on the power of silence and taking the time to truly listen and engage."

—Ingrid Waterfield, *Director KPMG*

"I really liked the style of the book. It's powerful stuff, powerfully put across. It's clear and to the point, and explains difficult concepts (e.g., the structure of the brain) very accessibly. I like the way it addresses the learner personally, via a step-by-step approach, with regular pauses to summarise and to ask the reader to reflect and apply what has been said to his/her own experience... So many things of interest and value—the different styles of leadership, the real-life examples, the emphasis on listening and on positive feedback."

—Dr. Keith Wren, *formerly Vice-Chancellor of Chaucer College and Lecturer*
in Comparative Literary Studies at the University of Kent

"I like the way Nick has found a balance between structure and substance, and how he manages to address a complicated and complex topic in a way that is interesting and lively and sometimes truly entertaining. I very much like the Pauses for Thoughts. And I think the Prologue is a brilliant way to start. Nick offers a clear structure from the beginning, so readers know up front what they can expect, when and where. And again, he does it in a way that is not too dry but with a light touch. In short, fascinating topics—but at the same time a really good read!"

—Hans von der Linde, *formerly General Counsel, Downstream at Shell*

Nick Marson

Leading by Coaching

How to deliver impactful change one
conversation at a time

palgrave
macmillan

Nick Marson
Parallel Mind
London, UK

ISBN 978-3-319-76377-4   ISBN 978-3-319-76378-1   (eBook)
https://doi.org/10.1007/978-3-319-76378-1

Library of Congress Control Number: 2018951553

This Palgrave Macmillan imprint is published by the registered company Springer Nature Switzerland AG
The registered company address is: Gewerbestrasse 11, 6330 Cham, Switzerland

This book is dedicated to my wife Christiane who has, more than she can ever know, made me who I have become, helped me grow and nurtured the development of The Parallel Mind. She has been a major source of inspiration, research and feedback for my book. Thank you for the belief you have shown in me and your unwavering support. Without you this book would never have been written.

Nick Marson
December 2018

Foreword

I am delighted and honoured to have been invited by Nick to write the foreword to his excellent book, *Leading by Coaching*. I met Nick when I was Chairman of Eversheds Sutherland, a global law firm with 66 offices. He coached senior members of the management team in communication skills. I found his approach and methods intriguing. His book provides a deep understanding of the scientific principles of leading and coaching. Nick's book has the resources you need to fully appreciate why *Leading by Coaching* works, what it involves, and how this leadership style can be used to improve individual and organisational performance. *Leading by Coaching* contains a wide-ranging and detailed academic study of how the brain works, underpinned by the latest neuroscience research findings. Nick uniquely explains the science behind the Gestalt coaching method and why it brings about accelerated learning and change.

Many of Nick's insights resonate with my own experience of moving from being a student to working as a lawyer and eventually becoming the elected leader of the firm. The power of silence, that he strongly advocates, is a learning I was fortunate to gain in my first week of University. My tutor had on his wall the following quote from Viktor E. Frankel:

> Between stimulus and response there is a space. In that space is our power to choose our response. In our response lies our growth and our freedom.

I have followed this learning throughout my career. Rather than reacting instantly, this space allows a considered response, the time to reflect and to seek other views. Your response time can be as long or as short as you wish. The use of silence as a window of self-discovery is a recurring theme in Nick's book. Resonating with my own experience, Nick advocates the instrument of coaching is the coach, and their most powerful tool is silence. The coach controls the silences to allow individuals the space to gain a deeper understanding of themselves through thinking about their thinking.

When I started my career the leadership style was command and control. The first senior partner I worked under had been in the military and his style was to send out orders which the rest of us were obliged to follow. When I became the Chairman of the firm, however, I soon realised that the only way I could have influence was through engaging in an authentic and sincere way. New age leaders, as Nick says, are values-based, humble, mindful, inclusive, good listeners, empathetic and imbue their followers with a strong sense of purpose. In my post-Chairman life at the firm, I have been coaching younger lawyers, helping them to develop their careers. New soft skills have to be learnt which require deep personal insights and this can be best achieved through everyday coaching conversations. Only through using a *Leading by Coaching* style, as advocated by Nick, can leaders help talented individuals grow personally to fulfil their potential and develop into our future leaders.

The guiding principles in Nick's book are brought to life through the wise words captured from the conversations he had with a diverse range of senior leaders he interviewed for his book. Equally the organisation case studies in *Leading by Coaching* provide practical insights into how leaders can have more impact as change agents.

I thoroughly recommend this book as a comprehensive and very timely personal guide for today's leaders who want to inspire and develop tomorrow's leaders to be ready to take full advantage of the opportunities that a rapidly changing world provides.

Leeds, UK   Paul Smith
                                    Former Chairman, Eversheds
                                    Sutherland. Consultant and author

Preface

Leading by Coaching is an ambitious research led project into what motivates people to follow and go on a journey with their leaders. *Leading by Coaching* brings together the multiple disciplines of neurobiology, gestalt psychology, sociology, and philosophy and applies them seamlessly to the business of leading impactful change, *one conversation at a time.*

Leadership used to be about telling people to go where you sent them—now it is about persuading them to come with you. Old leaders needed to create an artificial persona of infallible authority to issue orders that were obeyed—today's leaders need to uncover their own authentic leadership personality and bring that open and honest self to conversations that inspire others to willing and lasting change. Enlightened leaders want to engage and develop, not control and direct. Tomorrow's leaders will demand and deserve no less.

My book is a conversation with you the reader. It is written in a discursive style. I want to provoke your thinking about how you lead and give you the opportunity to reflect on your authentic leader signature presence.

My book is not designed like a camera manual. It will not give you precise step-by-step instructions. It will, however, give you a scientific framework for coaching, powerful principles to follow, and some tips and techniques to help you on your way. It will open up a wide-angle view, so that you can focus on the areas that interest you.

A coach, like the lens on a camera, paints with light in the dance with the client. Like the film in a camera, each conversation is a snapshot capturing your client's feelings and thinking. Every conversation is another picture of the client's current reality. Only when the pictures come together does the story emerge. The camera, like the coach, is an instrument in the search for truth, constantly capturing, developing and illuminating, providing new ways of seeing, new realities, new choices, and new opportunities to develop.

The only way you can become a better coach is to practise your coaching. You develop your coaching skills by attending a specialised training programme where you can see your performances on video and get expert feedback from professional coach trainers. Professional coach supervision is also an essential tool for developing yourself as a coach. Learning by reflecting on your experiences defines your unique coach signature presence. Helping the next generation of leaders to shine requires passion and commitment.

Much of life involves seeking permission from others. My greatest piece of learning on my life journey is that you need to give yourself permission to be yourself. Who you are is enough in itself: it is enough to change the world one person at a time, one conversation at a time, and enough to give permission to your followers to be, and express, who they truly are. Before we can give ourselves permission, we need to believe in ourselves, and that requires others to believe in us. Belief gives us the confidence and energy to act, to reach out to other kindred spirits and inspire them to follow us in our common purpose and shared passion.

Trusted leaders all have one common characteristic: they choose to care. They listen carefully. They know, like Haemin Sunim, the Zen Buddhist teacher, that *knowledge wants to talk, and wisdom wants to listen.* That is why they are followed. Trust is not something you do, it comes from who you are, from knowledge about yourself and about your humanity. Trust is driven by the power of empathy and nurtured by compassion. It is about sharing a common identity, a common purpose and a common story.

The essential truth is that we change one conversation at a time. The people around us also change with us and in this way, organisations also change one conversation at a time, one person at a time. Leaders change people's thinking and change their organisations by having more effective conversations.

Coaching is the gift of you, that you bring to your clients. Use it with care and with joy, as there is no better way for you to leave your leadership legacy. Life's journey is profoundly a search for truth, and that truth starts deep within us all. Only when we find our authentic voice can we begin our work to improve the human condition and make the world a happier place to live and work. Our task as leaders is to hold the space for others to develop and grow. We must clear the path and get out of the way, so that their light can shine brightly. I hope this book gives you inspiration to do so.

My book has been designed to be entertaining as well as informative. It is full of conversations to bring to life its central ideas. You will find many questions to awaken your curious mind and challenge you to do things differently. It is my sincere wish that *Leading by Coaching* inspires you on your journey to lead impactful change, *one conversation at a time.*

London, UK   Nick Marson

Acknowledgements

My book has been inspired by and grown out of many conversations and sources. This diverse collection of voices has resulted in a unique richness. *Leading by Coaching* aims to capture this eclectic collection of human experiences into something meaningful and purposeful for you, the reader.

My business partner Derek Benton introduced me to the fascinating world of Neuroscience. The research into our brain at work is the scientific underpinning of *Leading by Coaching, one conversation at a time.* It helped me to understand the importance of conversation in our everyday lives, how it shapes our thinking, informs our relationships and drives our actions.

The Chair of The Parallel Mind Ltd, Neil May, has been a constant source of encouragement and wisdom. His unwavering support and cool head have kept this book project alive when my energy reserves were getting low. He understands the human dimension of change in organisations. He has a remarkable ability to see through a mass of complex information and has edited the book with great diligence and deep reserves of business acumen.

I am grateful to Paul Barnett of Strategic Management Forum for introducing me to Stephen Partridge, Business Editor of Palgrave Macmillan. And I am grateful to Stephen for giving me the opportunity to publish. Thank you both for your support and the wonderful gift of letting my voice be heard by a wider audience.

My friend Hans von der Linde has been an enthusiastic supporter of my book project and a source of great leadership wisdom. I met Hans when I interviewed him for this book at the Shell headquarters in London when he was Global Counsel for their Downstream business. From the first moment, his intelligence and humanity shone through. I feel blessed to know him. Our conversations enlighten my thinking with fresh perspectives and interesting new avenues to explore.

I learned about receiver-driven communication when I was working with John Miers of Black Isle Consultants in Hong Kong. John is the former business partner of Lee Bowman Jr. who was the communication skills coach to Presidents Bill Clinton and Barack Obama. Lee Bowman Sr. was the Public Speaking coach to Ronald Reagan, the great communicator. The big revelation from the technique I was taught was that communication takes place in silence, not when we are talking. Silence, it turns out, is the key to effective communication and also the key to effective coaching.

David Ross, who was Director of Communication at the Chartered Insurance Institute when I worked with him, strongly encouraged me to write a book. He never wavered from his insistence that I finish my book and get it published. Thank you, David, for your personal support and constant nagging!

Dr. Keith Wren, formerly Vice-Chancellor of Chaucer College and Lecturer in Comparative Literary Studies at the University of Kent gave me invaluable guidance on the nuances of the English Language.

I am also indebted to my colleagues at the University of Munich where I ran a programme for Inter-Cultural Communication. Their support and willingness to impart their knowledge has deepened my understanding and provided me with a wonderfully solid academic foundation for cultural studies.

Finally, I would like to thank all my clients and contributors, far too many to mention, for giving me such a varied and rich collection of inspiring stories—a deep ocean of insights to stimulate my thinking. Their authenticity, wisdom, compassion and personal leadership journeys illuminate the core messages in the text. They provide the colour and context to *Leading by Coaching, one conversation at a time.*

Contents

List of Figures

Prologue

It is 5 a.m. high in the Himalayas. The first light of the day gently brushes the ancient stone walls of the Tibetan monastery. All you can hear, if you listen carefully, is the dawn chorus of animals and birds stirring in the valley below. A monk strikes one gong, followed quickly by another, and the dawn quiet is pierced like the sound of thunder claps. More gongs follow to announce the dawning of the new day. The monastery begins to stir: the quiet shuffling of soft footsteps and the rustling of clothes. There are no voices, just the silence of the monastery and the silence of not speaking.

It is 5 a.m. in Canary Wharf. The street cleaners are polishing the marble steps to the cathedrals of capitalism. Inside the shiny facades computers lie quiet, waiting to be powered into the money-making machines that they are. Waiting for the office workers travelling in their thousands on an underground telephone exchange of spaghetti lines like a swarm of bees bringing their neural nectar to the hive. How they yearn for the peace and solitude of the monastery far away in a distant land. How they long for the silence of the monastic life. Or do they?

Silence is scary! The silence of noise-cancelling headphones as the tube clatters silently beneath the busying streets of the City above is reassuring. There is nobody to bother you and nobody to have to listen to. The silence of not speaking is poignant but the silence of not listening is no less poignant. Quiet is difficult. We need the constant stimulus of the internal noise of social media and the external noise of real people. We spend our lives just reacting to our hectic environment. We don't have time to listen. We don't make time to think about what is really important. Silence scares us because it asks us the questions, we would prefer not to ask ourselves.

Silence reveals the truths we don't want to hear. Maybe that is why we fill our lives with noise. Maybe that is why we don't listen. Being busy insulates us from ourselves and from caring about others. It is much easier not to take the trouble to really listen and understand another human being rather than reaching out to them. A chance to share our fragile humanity, and build a deeper bond, is lost. Not listening shuts out the thoughts of others just as noise-cancelling headphones shut out our own thoughts.

As a leader and a coach our duty is to listen in silence, so that our client can hear themselves. Communication takes place in the silences, in the silent moments that transcend the words. Like music without notes or a play without words, silence forces us to think, to imagine, to dream. The unsaid has a voice of its own. Tibetan monks talk very little but say a lot. Silence is the voice of compassion. Silence is the voice of art. Silence is the voice of human consciousness. Silence is the beginning of everything. Silence forces us to listen to ourselves and creates a space to hear others.

Why do I start my book with silence? Because silence is the key to you becoming a better person, a better coach and a better leader. Silence creates a space for you to reflect, for you to be more aware of your thinking, to be more conscious, more awake. Your brain is working hard in between all the noise but without that external noise, your brain is forced to listen to what's going on inside of it. If it does, it can self-reflect, make connections and learn. Your brain is a bit like the deep sea, still beneath the turbulent waves on the surface. Silence nourishes your brain. Greater consciousness makes you more human.

We don't need to transport ourselves to a monastery to find silence; we can find it within ourselves. Stillness is essential, it is not empty. Our subconscious mind is that part of our brain which is on the fringe of consciousness and contains material of which it is possible to become aware by redirecting attention. Literally thinking about our thinking.

The Dalai Lama encourages us to develop and master the power of silence. We dream in silence. We listen in silence. We reflect in silence. Silence has a powerful presence. Silence is good for our brains. In the hippocampus, the main part of the brain associated with learning and memory, silence heightens awareness. The silence of the pause in conversations creates space for us to grow and develop. It gives us space to think, to let our subconscious, (the part of the mind which is on the fringe of consciousness and contains material of which it is possible to become aware by redirecting attention) or unconscious brain, (the part of the mind containing instincts, impulses, images and ideas that are not available for direct examination), talk to our conscious mind and raise the level of our thinking required to solve the complex problems that tomorrow's leaders will face. Silence allows us to use our Parallel Mind.

The silences in your *Leading by Coaching* conversations will allow you to connect on an emotional level. Listening deeply shows you really care, and so silence builds trust. And you lead and coach impactful change at the speed of trust and *one conversation at a time.*

Pause for thought

How consciously aware are you of the noise around you?
How consciously aware are you of the silences in your day?
When in your day can you allocate some time for your brain to relax and reflect?

Theme I

Looking in—*Reflecting*

Overview

Exciting findings from emerging neuroscience research are illuminating different parts of the brain that until now have been shrouded in mystery and darkness. There are, however, still many parts of the brain that we do not fully understand. Neuroscientists, neurobiologists and psychologists are all trying to unravel the story of the brain and its language to map the neural networks that drive the technology of our mind.

Understanding how your brain works is your "killer app" for *Leading by Coaching* one conversation at a time.

There are many books and scientific journals for those of you who want to immerse yourselves, as I have done, in the detail of this ongoing investigation. And there is not always agreement amongst the scientists on exactly how the brain works. My purpose in this book is to translate what is known and generally agreed. I will give you sufficient information for you to be more conscious of your thinking and what is motivating it, to literally *think about your thinking*. When you are more consciously aware and mindful you will be better able to understand, show empathy and lead those around you.

In Theme I of *Leading by Coaching* you will discover the biological limits that underlie your mental performance.

Understanding how your emotional brain works helps you master your mind and take over the controls. You will be able to use your unconscious mind and conscious mind together—your Parallel Mind. You can then "ride your elephant" to resist your hard-wired habits and the power of others.

My Neuro-Leadership Intelligence (NLI) Model, that strings together the other intelligences—emotional, social and cultural, allows you to lead and coach in a brain-friendly way.

In Theme I, I hold up a mirror and invite you to look in and reflect on the critical question: *why would anyone want to be lead and coached by you?* Who are you? What do you believe in? What is important to you? What change do you seek? What are your strengths?

I will guide you to find your authentic voice as a person, as a leader and as a coach. To discover the power of you. To see yourself as others see you. To master yourself, so you can be trusted to lead others.

And you can check your progress with your Leader's Check List.

1

Your Parallel Mind

Introduction

Your brain is amazing! And if you know how it works you can have better conversations with more impact as a leader and as a coach. This scientific understanding of how your brain works is the bedrock for *Leading by Coaching*.

Here, in this my first chapter, I look inside your brain, how it is built, how it functions unconsciously and consciously, as well as emotionally and logically. Before you can control your mind, you need to understand how your brain controls you. Your unconscious brain will decide just about everything if you let it. I then move on to explore your emotional brain, your social brain and your learning brain.

Here, in Your Parallel Mind, I investigate your conscious thinking brain before examining how you can listen to your unconscious brain but make decisions with your conscious mind.

And here, in this chapter, I conclude by looking at how you can operate more effectively as a whole system, using your parallel mind. Your brain is a self-organising emergent system. If you don't organise your thinking, your brain will do it for you!

Inside Your Parallel Mind

Inside your beautiful brain are all your thoughts, emotions, languages, memories, awareness and consciousness. An entire human life resides inside the three-pound lump of gooey grey matter that pulsates inside your skull, an

© The Author(s) 2019
N. Marson, *Leading by Coaching*, https://doi.org/10.1007/978-3-319-76378-1_1

extraordinarily powerful organ powered by a mere 20 watts of electricity, equivalent to a small and dim light bulb.

Inside your beautiful brain is a supercomputer that has roughly 100 billion nerve cells, called *neurons*, connected in labyrinthine ways by 100 trillion *synapses*, more than the data pumped out in a year by the Large Hadron Collider, the particle smasher at CERN near Geneva, Switzerland. Your brain is the most complex thing in the known universe. The processing speed, 120 metres per second, of the resulting network is staggering. Counting each connection at one per second would take you at least 30 million years.

What makes *neurons* special is that they have long filamentary projections called *axons* and *dendrites* which carry information around in the form of electrical pulses. *Dendrites* carry signals into the cell. *Axons* carry signals to other cells. The junction between an *axon* and a *dendrite* is called a *synapse*. Information is carried across *synapses* by chemical messengers called *neurotransmitters*.

Apart from specialised nerve cells, there is a lot of anatomical specialization in the brain itself. Three large structures stand out: the *cerebrum*, and its outer layer, the *cerebral cortex*, the *cerebellum*, for movement and posture, and the *brain stem*, for keeping the heart and lungs working. In addition, there is a cluster of smaller structures in the middle. These are loosely grouped into the *limbic system*—the emotional centre of the brain—and the *basal ganglia*—the multi-connected automatic pilot sequencing system of the brain. The brain structure is paired. In particular, the *cerebrum* is divided into two hemispheres connected by the *corpus callosum*.

The *cerebral cortex* forms 80% of the human brain and is truly mankind's distinguishing feature. It is divided into *lobes*, four on each side. The rearmost lobe, called the *occipital*, handles vision, then come the *parietal* and *temporal* lobes which deal with language and movement. At the front is the *frontal lobe*. This is humanity's "killer app", containing many of the cognitive functions associated with being human.

Jeffrey Hawkins explains why our brains are prediction machines in his book, *On Intelligence*. Our brains are constantly working out our odds of surviving and thriving. When to advance and when to retreat. When to walk and when to run. There is a growing number of reductionist scientists who argue that the brain is just an algorithm programmed machine. Mark Lee, a Professor in the Department of Computer Science at Aberystwyth University, suggests, however, that "To call the brain a machine is to ignore the complex and social nature of human intelligence". The changing nature of water in all its manifestations cannot be explained by saying it is made of hydrogen and oxygen. Explaining the sea as a mass of H2O without reference to the forces that power tides and waves is the same as explaining the brain as a machine without factoring in the influence of other brains and the situational context of its working environment on its behaviour.

> **Pause for thought**
> Is your brain just a machine or a dynamic embedded living organism? What do you think?

In the age of Artificial Intelligence robots can change the world but they can't win at darts, as *The Times* columnist, Matthew Syed points out with his usual acuity.[1] Machines can now diagnose cancer, play chess and drive cars but struggle to play most sports. Even the mechanical action of throwing a dart cannot be replicated by the most sophisticated machine aided by highly developed algorithms. These movements require vast computational sophistication that happens in humans below conscious awareness. Elite sport is the expression of our motor intelligence at its most sublime, requiring the interface of mind and body.

Think about the grace and movement of Roger Federer when he hits a tennis ball. The flawless processing power of the brain expressed through graceful movement and immaculate timing. Sport expresses human ingenuity in its most vivid form and elevates the human brain above the machines it creates.

Our brains are stranger than we think. Our lives are woven into the fabric of our brains. Every one of us has a unique encounter with the world and our brains guide us through the maze, miraculously giving us the conscious ability to witness our journey from, somehow, outside our brain.

As far back as Plato man has been coming to terms with the idea of the brain as the seat of the human soul, that somehow our human identity is connected to the brain. Our ability to feel love and sadness, in our own unique way, is what makes us human. And yet it is our brain that, by some miracle, constructs our unique personality. Your brain knows about itself.

And when it comes to the brain, according to Helen Thomson, in her 2018 book, *Unthinkable*, we should look at people with extraordinary abilities of memory and perception as marvels of humanity rather than eccentrics

---

[1]Syed, M. (2018, February 6). Artificial intelligence will change the world, but it can't win at darts. Retrieved from https://www.thetimes.co.uk/article/artificial-intelligence-will-change-the-world-but-it-wont-replace-sport-even-darts-0l9gp8pzb.

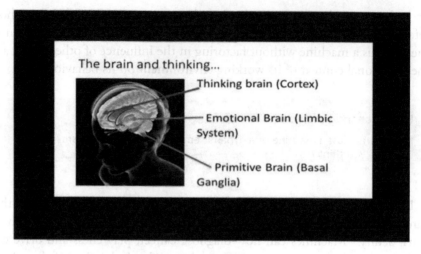

Fig. 1.1 The Parallel Mind Brain and Thinking Model

or freaks. Nothing is unthinkable because we all have an extraordinary brain. So, the question is how do we harness the power and magic inside this remarkable feat of neural engineering?

There is still a long way to go before we can fathom the mysteries of the brain entirely, especially the puzzle of consciousness, but what follows is a map of the known brain, the cartography of the human mind (Fig. 1.1).

Your Unconscious Primitive Brain

The *hindbrain* is located at the base of the skull, just above the neck. It was the first brain structure to evolve. It is made up of three structures: the *medulla oblongata, pons* and *cerebellum*. The *medulla oblongata* is responsible for many of the automatic behaviours that keep us alive, such as breathing, regulating our heartbeat, monitoring our blood pressure and sleeping. The *pons* plays an important role in the control of facial expressions and in receiving information about body movements. The *cerebellum* is the most prominent part of the *hindbrain* and is richly supplied with sensory information to enable the body to carry out complex fine-motor skills and movements.

The *midbrain* plays a role in many of our physical actions. One of its central structures is the *substantia nigra* which is a rich source of the transmitter *dopamine*, essential for oiling the wheels of motion. *Dopamine* is also the reward *neurotransmitter* and is necessary for many forms of learning, compulsive behaviour and addiction. Other regions of the *midbrain* are responsible for hearing, visual information processing and the regulation of mood.

Many of our uniquely human capabilities evolved in the **forebrain**. It includes the *thalamus*, a relay station that directs sensory information to the *amygdala* for quick assessment and reaction and to the *cerebral cortex* for slow processing for conscious awareness; the *hypothalamus*, which releases hormones into the bloodstream; the *amygdala*, which deals with emotion; and the *hippocampus*, which plays an important role in processing memories. The *thalamus, hypothalamus, amygdala,* and *hippocampus* are all part of the *limbic* system, the emotional centre of the brain. The *basal ganglia* is the part of the deep structure of the brain responsible for routine actions. It is the *cerebral cortex*—our conscious thinking brain, with its 20 billion non-linear *neurons*—that makes us human. The brain is a very large complex system with feedback loops from its two trillion interconnections. It should be noted that the brain has an average number of connections per neuron of about 1000 compared to a computer with around five. If our brain was so simple that we could understand it, we would be so simple that we couldn't. We would need a brain the size of the universe to understand the most complex known structure in it!

Your *basal ganglia* in your *forebrain* is a collection of mechanisms that perform functions like walking, dancing, driving a car and any habitual behaviour on autopilot so that you don't have to think consciously. It is your automatic pilot that allows us to do a multitude of things without thinking in a low energy consumption way. It wants to make everything you do automatic and safe. That is why habits are so difficult to break. Your primitive *basal ganglia* brain is working hard in the background to stop you changing anything that is working. It is hardwired to resist change. To overcome this resistance, using the analogy of an elephant and its rider, you need to ride your elephant!

The *basal ganglia* is multi-connected to other parts of the brain and is brilliant at picking up and remembering patterns—events, ideas, language and sensory information like taste. Once you repeat a sequence a few times your *basal ganglia* will remember it and allow you to repeat the sequencing automatically next time you need to complete this task. It develops and embeds your daily routines, so you are free to think of other things you can do. It makes you take the same familiar route to the station in the morning, it directs you around the supermarket shelves without realising, even picking up the same branded goods that your brain knows you like.

Your *basal ganglia* is the unconscious automatic pilot system of your brain. Your unconscious brain records everything your conscious brain thinks and does, processing up to a million bits of information a second. It is like a movie camera permanently stuck in recording mode. It is recording your life and storing everything for your future recall. When you think, you slow the recording down, so that you can focus on the footage you want to examine. When you decide to do something and then do it, you are in single frame mode—quite literally taking one step at a time. Buddhist teaching uses an analogy that thinking is like a waterfall. We see a curtain of water, but the reality is just tiny drops of water. If you suspend your flow of thoughts, and think about your thinking, you can see those tiny drops of thoughts that make up your waterfall!

Your Emotional Brain

The system we call emotion (from the Latin verb emovere, "to move away"), works with speed and power to motivate our behaviour. We have emotions because they get us out of trouble quickly. Emotion is an instinctive response aimed at self-preservation. It comprises a series of muscular changes in the body preparing us for action. Interestingly, when life-threatening situations are perceived, the fight or flight mechanism kicks in and our rational brain is shut down. This can save our life if the perceived threat is real. The nervous system is firing on all cylinders, chemicals flood the body. Stress releases *cortisol*, a chemical hormone, into the blood. That steroid invades the *hippocampus* and interferes with its work of providing access to memory or learning. We feel before we think. Our brain is designed that way, so it can respond to dangerous threats without wasting precious time thinking about what to do. As a result, most people are incapable of performing any, but the simplest of tasks under stress. They cannot remember the most basic things. In addition, stress (or any strong emotion) erodes the ability to perceive. *Cortisol* and other hormones released under stress interfere with the working of the *prefrontal cortex*. All of these bodily changes happen outside our consciousness. Emotion doesn't always serve us well.

A series of air crashes in the 1970s highlighted a psychological blind spot that when cognitive load is high, decision-making can be compromised. "Situational awareness" is the term used to describe the capacity of a crew to keep track of everything going on in an emergency situation inside the cockpit of a commercial airliner.

On 29 December 1972, Eastern Air Lines Flight 401 took off out of the bitter cold of New York travelling to Miami. As it made its descent into Miami International the pilot noticed that the light to indicate the landing wheels were lowered had failed to light up. Frantically trying to locate and test if the bulb had blown, the entire crew failed to notice that the autopilot system was switched off, and an alarm bell was ringing in the cockpit to signal that the plane was losing height rapidly. This inattentional blindness killed 101 people as Flight 401 crashed into the Everglades.

According to Matthew Syed, in his book *Black Box Thinking*, cognitive dissonance occurs when mistakes are too threatening to admit to, so they are reframed or ignored. Looking for a scapegoat to blame is easier than confronting the reality that pilots are part of a complex interdependent system. Sometimes the system is to blame, not the person who is making decisions based on incomplete or incorrect information.

Learning is about making mistakes and discovering better ways to do things. The airline industry responded to the air crashes in the 70s by leading a reformed approach to teamwork, the introduction of checklists, and a range of other changes including strategic checks and balances. Air transport is safer as a result. In 2017 there was not a single aircraft crash.

Maybe Carillion plc, a British multinational construction company, went into compulsory liquidation on 15 January 2018 as a result of a fatal combination of a lack of situational awareness, inattentional blindness and cognitive dissonance.

The human brain cannot process any information consciously and logically without first processing it unconsciously and emotionally. Your emotional experience is connected to a large brain network called the *limbic system*, which is the emotional centre of your brain. This is where you experience emotions. You cannot engage your thinking brain until your emotional brain has processed its response to the environment that you are in.

Emotions may seem to be conscious feelings, but they are in fact responses to stimuli, designed to push us away from danger and towards reward. Emotions are generated constantly, although most of the time we are unaware of them. Emotions are generated in the *limbic system*, beneath and connected to the *cortex* with a two-way traffic system allowing emotions to be consciously processed. In this way, the brain generates a fight or flight fear response to ready us for a survival reaction. This primitive, automatic response mechanism is still at the heart of emotion.

The *limbic system* tracks your emotional relationships to your thoughts. It drives your behaviour largely unconsciously. The *amygdala* is the alarm bell in the system. It goes off when it senses danger. It served us well when, as cavemen, vigilance in the forest kept us alive. The breaking of a twig set the brain into a high alert system to be aware of a club-wielding threat lurking in the bushes somewhere. It is the *amygdala* that triggers a panic attack.

You know that moment when you step onto the stage to deliver your big presentation. Your heart is beating faster; you are in a high state of alert. Your reputation is on the line in front of your peer group. It is time to get those butterflies all flying in formation, to take control of your emotions and concentrate on the main actor on the stage, you!

What is going on to cause this massive alert? It is a chemical reaction. It is back to the basic "towards" or "away" decision the brain is constantly making, based on its prediction of the safety of the environment it is scanning continuously. When it senses a reward coming, the brain releases *dopamine*, the neurotransmitter of desire. It drives the "towards" response. Positive expectations play a huge part in how we experience something. This is the power of suggestion used by advertisers to lure us to buy their products. Conversely, when we experience something threatening, whether physically, emotionally or socially, the neurotransmitter *cortisol* is released, and levels rise to make us feel more anxious. *Cortisol* is the neurotransmitter of fear, the "away" response of the brain.

The term *amygdala* means almond in Latin. It consists of two almond-shaped groups of cells—one group on each side of the brain—located deep within the *medial temporal lobes*. It becomes activated by strong emotional reactions to prepare you for fight or flight. It is linked to responses to pleasure as well as fear. Evaluation of an event takes place in the *amygdala*, part of the *limbic system*, and creates an emotional stimulus as the result of this evaluation. An emotional signal is sent to the *prefrontal cortex* via the *thalamus* and the *hypothalamus* where a decision is made on an appropriate bodily response. Combined emotions create feelings. And feelings mixed with experience create meaning. Meaning defines human existence.

People with higher than normal activity levels in their *amygdala* have higher levels of stress and are more prone to cardiovascular disease according to Dr. Ahmed Tawakol of Harvard Medical School.

It is important to be able to label your emotions, so that you can deal with each one consciously. Rationality allows us to analyse our emotions and gives us answers to the question of why we feel a certain way. Emotional control enables you to interact more successfully with yourself and the world.

Why hasn't evolution long since made emotions irrelevant, if they lead us to bad decisions? The answer is that, even though they may not behave in a logical manner, our emotions frequently lead us to better, safer, more optimal outcomes. There is logic in emotion and emotion in logic, it seems.

Plato understood that emotions could override reason and that to operate effectively we have to use the reins of reason on the horse of emotion. The intellect without the emotions is like the jockey without the horse.

Emotions can, however, be a positive experience! Your *limbic system* next to the *amygdala* is responsible for feelings of pleasure, like watching your football team scoring. Anticipation of pleasure is influenced by the reward circuit. This acts on the *hypothalamus* and *amygdala*, secreting *dopamine.*

The *amygdala* is the conductor of emotions in the brain. The emotions of fear, anger, sadness, and disgust are all linked up with other parts of the brain by the *amygdala* during the processing of emotions. Joy, for example, involves the *amygdala's* neighbour, the *hypothalamus. Serotonin-based* and *dopamine-based neurons* are both important for emotional responses. The emotions of embarrassment and guilt are, however, handling in the *cerebral cortex*, rather than in the *limbic system.*

One of the most famous cases relating to the brain is the tragic case of a railway navvy Phineas Gage whose brain was damaged in a railway accident involving explosives on 13 September 1848, when a metal pole went through his skull removing a slice of his *frontal lobe.* His personality changed from being a sober, industrious individual to be a foul-mouthed drunkard. The accident damaged the connection between the *frontal cortex*, responsible for social cognition and decision-making, and the *limbic system*, the emotional brain centre. As a result, he was unable to moderate his social behaviour or make decisions based on any emotional processing of the social situation he found himself in.

We are emotional beings. Our primitive *limbic system* is in control and coats everything with emotional significance. Every time we think, we are being influenced by feelings based on our emotional experiences. This is why emotional regulation for a coach and a leader is important to create predictable behaviour that allows the trust necessary to build, maintain and develop relationships.

Whilst we can't control when we feel anger, or fear, we can gain some control over what we do while in their grip. It only takes six seconds to take control of our emotions and respond rationally rather than let our primitive brain react with sometimes life-changing consequences.

Our emotional brain is hard-wired to react emotionally when it senses there is lack of respect, or lack of freedom, fairness, appreciation or empathy.

The Dalai Lama encourages us to develop and master our inner radar for emotional danger. We should question destructive mental habits and stop beating ourselves up. We should be more self-compassionate and forgiving of our human failings: and we should be more compassionate and forgiving of the failings of others. We should be kinder to ourselves and value ourselves more. Only if we are more comfortable with ourselves can we be more considerate with others.

The most important thing for me is that we are always on the side of compassion. Without compassion there can be no collaboration and without collaboration there can be no progress. A compassionate leader shares the suffering of their followers but keeps enough distance to give them objective advice and support.

Pause for thought

Stop and think for a minute: when did you feel emotionally violated and what reactions did your *amygdala* provoke?
Reflect on what you could have done differently if you had counted "six seconds" and engaged your *prefrontal cortex* thinking brain?
Think of the damage you cause by your inability to self-regulate your emotional brain.

Your Social Brain

We are wired to be social. Our social brain is linked to our emotional brain. Our social brain regulates our emotions so that we can maintain the relationships required to collaborate with other human beings, essential to our survival as a species. We operate in an emergent non-linear system that is constantly changing. We have a need to constantly adapt, and to adapt we need context. Systems are self-organising: there is a natural order. Humans are social and defined in mind by relationships with other "minds".

According to Daniel J. Siegel, MD, the Self has three elements: the brain, the mind and its relationships to others. A healthy mind integrates the three elements through the exchange of energy and information via social relationships and networks. We are driven by relationships. When our brains are relaxed, we start thinking of ourselves and other people in our social networks. We are social animals, strongly dependent on our social standing in our social groups to survive and thrive. The brain has a social network that enables one human being to get resources from another. Your brain needs social connections. Collaborating with others is what human beings do.

In the absence of positive social cues, such as smiling, it is easy for people to fall back into the more common mode of human interactions, namely distrusting others. When we distrust someone, the *limbic system* is aroused. The primitive fight or flight survival reaction is activated: friend or foe, "towards" or "away"? Conversely when we listen to someone, when we really pay attention—listening with our heart, eyes and ears—we build trust. Connection leads to collaboration. The human being has a fundamental desire for relatedness, connectedness and cohesiveness. Co-operation and collaboration is what makes us human.

Recently discovered circuitry in the brain lets us tune into and resonate emotionally with each other during a face-to-face interaction. Video conferences can't replicate this human connectedness: if it is important, get on that plane! Your social brain is a mirror. The networks in your brain that light up when you perform an action also light up when you see someone else perform the same action. The way these networks "mirror" the behaviour of others gives them their name: *mirror neurons*, first discovered by Giacomo Rizzolatti at Parma University in Italy. This important discovery of *mirror neurons*, that fire when we witness another person's suffering, gives a scientific basis to empathy. Without this ability to feel empathy and compassion, human beings would simply not be able to collaborate. Empathy is the basis of rapport and trust. *Mirror neurons* create the personal closeness that build relationships. Sensing what another is feeling without them saying so, captures the essence of empathy. Empathic concern is a key attribute of successful leaders. Your capacity for empathy is what sets you apart as an inspirational leader. Empathic literacy, explicit understanding of what someone else feels and thinks at any given moment, is the key skill for leaders of change.

Neurobiology of Empathy

For much of human history, up until the advent of agriculture around 12,000 years ago, our ancestors appear to have lived in tribal bands typically no larger than 150 members competing with others for scarce resources, avoiding predators, constantly searching for food. In that harsh environment those who were able to collaborate typically lived longer and left more offspring. Those who were better at teamwork usually beat those whose teamwork was weak. It is their genes we have mainly inherited. This evolutionary process that shaped our neurobiological mechanisms gave rise to neural networks that allow us to empathise with others. Empathy became the oil in a civic society. Before this social lubricant there was only competition for power and control. The danger we face now in our data-driven world is that social media is destroying our capacity for empathy, the very thing that stops us killing each other and allows us to collaborate instead.

We have the capacity to sense and to simulate within our own experience other people's actions, their emotions and their thoughts. We can see with our heart as well as our eyes. We can build on your natural ability to empathise by being more aware, more mindful and noticing micro-expressions.

Pause for thought

Next time you have a coaching conversation
notice the behaviour of others
tune into your own feelings and sensations
watch the other person's face and eyes
notice their fleeting micro-expressions
attend to your own thoughts
actively imagine the thoughts of the other person
check back and stay open

Oxytocin, also known as the "cuddle hormone" plays a key role in social behaviour including sexual arousal, recognition, trust, anxiety and mother–infant bonding. As a leader ask yourself: do you have what Kets de Vries of Insead calls the "teddy bear factor"—people feeling comfortable with you and wanting to be close to you? According to research from Cardiff University, presented at the Society for Endocrinology's 2016 annual conference, people suffering from medical conditions causing low levels of *oxytocin* can also develop problems in their emotional lives.[2] *Oxytocin* is produced by the *hypothalamus*, the area of the brain controlling mood and appetite.

The *cingulate cortex*, the part of the *cortex* closest to the *limbic system*, is where we experience intense emotions like love and anger. It is active when mothers hear their babies cry. It is the area of the brain responsible for detecting how others feel and react to their emotions. It has been identified as a key part in monitoring conflicting information and ambivalence, and *oxytocin* assists with this.[3]

---

[2]Drain, K. (2016, November 8). Retrieved from http://www.medicaldaily.com/empathy-test-can-low-oxytocin-levels-impact-someones-feelings-sympathy-403762.

[3]Preckel, K., Scheele, D., Eckstein, M., Meier, W., & Hurlemann, R. (2014). The influence of oxytocin on volitional and emotional ambivalence. Social Cognitive and Affective Neuroscience, 10(7), 987–993. https://doi.org/10.1093/scan/nsu147. https://www.ncbi.nlm.nih.gov/pmc/articles/PMC4483569/.

Your Learning Brain

Your brain is a self-organising emergent system. Every day, hundreds of thousands of *synapses* are released into the brain as a free learning resource to make new connections. The brain is constantly adapting to a changing environment in search of wholeness, to find a natural order.

Learning is an emotional experience: we learn best when we are engaged. The *hippocampus*, responsible for memory, sits inside the *limbic system*, the emotional centre of the brain. Optimal learning is a social activity: we learn best when we are in small groups. This suggests leaders should create a multitude of informal opportunities for followers to learn together.

Social learning is a powerful tool for creativity. Shared purpose is the driver for social learning.

Informal learning, from social networks (clients and colleagues), is the engine of innovation. "Wiring and Firing" together builds powerful neural networks. By paying conscious attention to what is emerging, valuable insights can be captured.

Warm-heartedness makes us more intelligent! We should aim to solve our problems through meaningful dialogue, choosing "we" rather than "me". Responding mindfully should be a natural part of our thinking and a genuine smile can change conflict into collaboration. Choosing to care about our fellow human beings makes a vital difference.

We need to learn emotionally: to learn to trust our hearts and to deal with our destructive emotions. We need to master our emotions. We need to increase our awareness of our unconscious mind, to analyse our subconscious thoughts and what is driving them, and to use the dual processing power of our Parallel Mind. If we are more emotionally intelligent we will become more socially intelligent. By balancing our emotions and finding our inner peace of mind we become a force for good as a leader and a coach. Finding our emotional balance is a journey, not a destination.

The secret of getting older gracefully is learning to forget our bad memories. MRI scans highlight that in the over-60s, the *ventromedial prefrontal cortex*, which is involved in higher thought, is telling the *amygdala*, a brain region involved with negative emotion, to reduce its activity. To forget, or at least put to the back of our mind, our bad experiences. In the younger adults scanned, however, the *amygdala* became more excited. From an evolutionary point of view, it appears that present-oriented goals such as living a happy life and feeling good are being prioritised. Our brains, it seems, are ring-masters full of illusionary tricks to keep us sane in our golden years.

Facilitation of insight is real learning. Insights change the brain. Learning takes place when there is coherence, congruence and consistency, a clear weave. Connecting components in a network. Emotional engagement makes connections stronger in the *limbic system*. But to see the connection you need a map. That is why the human brain always looks for patterns and meaning. Always looks for the answer to the question *why*. Always searches for purpose. Central threads make clear connections based on *neurons* "firing and wiring" together. A single brain cell can grow 15,000 connections to help it communicate with its neighbours.

Context is personal—people find their own meaning and relevance. Learning is emotional and social—driven by a sense of shared purpose.

Before we explore the conscious mind, let me make one more important observation. Our unconscious brain is not just an unthinking autopilot incapable of rational thought; it is far more than that. It is our subconscious thought that makes the human mind so special. Our higher consciousness alone is not what sets us apart from other animals. Subconscious thought processes play an important role in many uniquely human activities, like music, art and language. It is the subconscious, creative mind that gives us the gift of learning.

Unconscious learning and adapting takes place beyond the realm of reason, based on our experiences. When we have an emotional experience, our brains learn by strengthening electrochemical transmissions among *neurons* and creating new sites at which *neurons* can communicate with each other. *Axons*, the fibres that send signals, grow and form new branches and *synapses*. Memory is the result.

Without memory you could not learn. Without learning your conscious brain would have nothing to think about. Our Parallel Mind integrates cognition and emotion into a unified system that makes us human. The other you, your subconscious mind or *synaptic* self, should not be dismissed lightly (Fig. 1.2).

Your Conscious Thinking Brain

Let me start the tour of your conscious brain with an illuminating example of its incredible processing power by explaining how we see—the magic of visualisation.

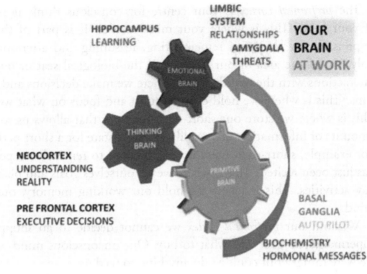

© The Parallel Mind Ltd 2016

Fig. 1.2 The Parallel Mind Your Brain at Work Model

The *retina* of the eye consists of approximately 130 million cells known as *cones* and *rods*. They process 100 million information sequences as you catch sight of an image. This enormous amount of data is processed in a split second and passed through the *optic nerve* at a rate of 9 million information sequences per second. The data arrives at the *thalamus* where the information reaches the *occipital lobe* which is found at the back of the brain. This *visual cortex* then processes and analyses all the data which is passed on to the *prefrontal cortex* where it is ultimately stored in the *hippocampus*. At this point, the person in question sees and understands the visual object. Thus, although it seems to take no effort whatsoever to look at an object, it requires the work of billions of *neurons* for this to happen, not forgetting that all this transpires in a nanosecond.

How are the striking developments taking place in neuroscience, cognitive science, and artificial intelligence helping us understand consciousness? Can irrational thoughts be controlled by consciousness? Are we our thoughts? Or are our thoughts us? What part does self-awareness play in directing our thoughts to our actions? Let us continue our short tour of the brain with the thinking part of our brain, the *cerebral cortex* which consists of the *neocortex* and the *prefrontal cortex*.

The *prefrontal cortex* is your centre for conscious thinking at the front of your head. This is where your mind resides. It is part of the *neocortex*, responsible for thinking, remembering, reasoning and attention. It covers only 5% of the area of our brain. It is the biological seat of our conscious interactions with the world. This is where we make decisions and solve problems. This is where we hold our attention and focus on what we are doing. This is where we store our short-term memory that allows us to hold small amounts of information in a readily available state for a short period of time. For example, short-term memory can be used to remember a postcode that has just been recited. This is where we set ourselves goals and plan our everyday activities. This is where we hold our working memory, our conscious mind.

Without our *prefrontal cortex* we cannot decide to go shopping, which supermarket to visit and what to buy. Our unconscious mind would know we were hungry but couldn't do anything to feed us.

Critically our *prefrontal cortex* controls our impulses. This is where we regulate our emotions. For example, when we feel the strong urge to hit out at someone who makes us really angry, it is only the voice of reason of our thinking brain that tells us that is not a good idea. On a more positive note, our *prefrontal cortex* allows us to visualise future scenarios, to think creatively, to be human.

To use David Rock's stage metaphor, from his book "Your Brain at Work", the stage is what you focus on at any given time. Actors represent information you hold from your outer world at any one time, such as your shopping list. They enter the stage from the side. Members of the audience also come on to the stage. These represent information from your inner world. Your *prefrontal cortex* makes the connection between your inner and outer world to make value judgements. Distractions from the audience make it more difficult to focus on the central actor on the stage. This process of inhibition, of keeping certain actors off the stage, requires a lot of effort and energy. The stage needs a lot of lighting to function. That is why you use a lot of energy when you are thinking hard to solve a problem. The stage is small and can only hold a small number of actors at a time. We need to clear our mind and shine the spotlight on the main actor.

If you want to get your shopping list done, switch off the television and stop thinking about your football team's next match. One idea at a time works best, one conversation at a time. The conscious mind can only pay attention to very limited number of things at a time, perhaps no more than four, so choose carefully. Immediate or short-term working memory is stored in the *thalamus* region of the brain, and can only remember a few items at a time, with suggestions that three may be an optimal number. We have a mechanism in our brain that filters all incoming signals and only those considered important come through. It would be impossible to function without this mechanism. This unconscious automatic selection process means you don't have to think. If you choose to think, however, you can feed your brain with what to select. This allows you to prioritise the importance of tasks, for your focus of attention in your working memory. Working memory even has an automatic retrieval system built in. Even if your ears are not being stimulated by external sounds your brain's auditory centre remains active. If your favourite song cuts out, your brain cuts in to retrieve the memory of the song's musical lyrics, creating an illusion of sound.

Working memory is attention or conscious thought. Our brain, as we saw with our shopping trip, can only hold small amounts of information at a time. And this information can be directed by a magician without us even being aware of what is going on. The magician doesn't do the trick, your brain does! The magician directs or misdirects you, so that you pay attention to what they want you to pay attention to, or they distract you when they don't want you to pay attention and see what they are doing. Working memory is what we choose to focus on, or someone else chooses us to focus on. It is the "executive function of the brain" and without it we couldn't hear a conversation in a noisy pub. This is your conscious centre of attention at any given moment.

Your brain is not very good at multitasking. Although we think we're doing several things at once, multitasking, this is a powerful illusion created by the brain, according to Earl Miller, a neuroscientist at the Massachusetts Institute of Technology, and one of the world's experts on divided attention.[4] Learning information while multitasking, according to Russ Poldrack, a neuroscientist at Stanford, causes the new information to go to the wrong part of the brain. If students study and watch television at the same time, for example, the information from their schoolwork goes into the *striatum*, a region specialised for storing new procedures and skills, not facts and ideas. Without the distraction of television, the information goes into the *hippocampus*, where it is organised and categorised to make it easier to retrieve. Asking the brain to shift attention from one activity to another causes the *prefrontal cortex* and *striatum* to burn up *oxygenated glucose*, the same fuel

---

[4]Holohan, M. (2016, January 27th). How to do one thing at a time: The secret to improving your focus. Retrieved from Today: https://www.today.com/series/one-small-thing/multitasking-doesn-t-work-why-focus-isn-t-just-ho-cus-t69276.

they need to stay on task. And the kind of rapid, continual shifting we do with multitasking causes the brain to burn through fuel so quickly that we feel exhausted and disoriented after even a short time. This leads to reduced cognitive performance and increased anxiety that causes a build-up of the stress hormone *cortisol*, which in turn can lead to impulsive and aggressive behaviour. By contrast, staying on task is controlled by the *anterior cingulate* and the *striatum*, and once we stay on task we use less *glucose*: we are burning our brain fuel more efficiently.

Pause for thought

How effective are you at multitasking?

Thinking with Your Parallel Mind

The gift of consciousness is what makes our brains so beautiful. It gives us the chance to examine our lives. Back in 1759 Adam Smith, the leading Scottish philosopher, wrote about "the man within" in his book, *The Theory of Moral Sentiments*. His idea was that we all have an impartial spectator who allows us to witness our actions, thoughts and emotions not as an involved participant but as a disinterested observer.

Our biggest mystery, as a human race, is that we can actually think about our thinking. We can consciously think about our consciousness. Can the brain ever truly know itself? Is the concept of self a self-deception of the brain? According to Antonio R. Damasio, Rene' Descartes (1596–1650) made an error when he said, "I think; therefore, I am". What Descartes meant by this, is that our essential being is in the action of thinking. Damasio says he was wrong to believe that mind and consciousness drive brain function. Damasio, a neuroscientist, saw mind and consciousness as a side-effect of the brain's synaptic functioning. He thinks that the brain is systemic, the organ of information and government, and does its job through unconscious learning. So, by deduction, self is a concept constructed by the brain, "I am; therefore, I think". This trick of the brain is the supreme paradox of thought. The paradox is that it takes a conscious mind to wonder why it is conscious.

Consciousness helps us be more self-aware, to self-select, and self-regulate. In coaching, self-awareness is needed to help us focus and direct attention on the person in front of us, and away from ourselves. A depth of understanding of the brain, mind and thought helps us to witness our shared humanity on the one hand, and our unique personality on the other. The paradox is that we are self-organising organisms but we each have a mind of our own. Our brains work in the same way, but no two minds are the same. Like trees, we are shaped by our life experiences to make us uniquely who we are. Nature and nurture go hand in hand to define us.

You are not your brain; you are more than your brain. But your unconscious mind is running the show and you need to know how it is operating, so that you can override it using your conscious thinking brain. Understanding how your emotional brain works will help you make better decisions as a leader. Understanding the brain at work will help you be a better coach. Using both sides of your brain together, your Parallel Mind, will help you lead impactful change, one conversation at a time.

The most fundamental thing about consciousness is the fact you are one person—a unity of many attributes of human consciousness: laughter, music, poetry, sentiment, nostalgia and self-awareness. Through all these human attributes, and many more, we experience a unity of self.

Christof Koch and Francis Crick discovered a thin layer of tissue underlying the *insular cortex* in the brain, that doesn't have any known function but is connected to all parts of the brain. This tissue, named the *claustrum*, is sending and receiving signals from all the regions including the *amygdala* in the *limbic system*, the centre of the emotional brain. There is a chapter detailing their exciting findings in the 2013 book, *Thinking*, by John Brockman. The fact that you are one unified unique person, as the fundamental principle of consciousness, makes the *claustrum* a strong candidate for the seat of your conscious brain. According to Koch and Crick the *claustrum* is ideally suited for a unifying role.

Consciousness originates in the *medial prefrontal cortex* where the impulses of over 10 billion *neuronal* cells of the brain's nervous system unite. The brain is such a complex organ that each one of these billions of neurons has up to 10,000 connections to other neurons. When you acquire a piece of information from the outside world it is passed from *neuron* to *neuron* so that it eventually forms an electrochemical impulse which is basically the language of the nervous system that causes your body to react.

To better understand this amazing capacity of the brain just think of what has to happen for you to view an object as explained earlier. Your brain is truly amazing!

Einstein explained his ability to better understand the universe as due to his "thought experiments", or what we might colloquially call day-dreaming. The unconscious mind is a world of dreams that surface in your thoughts and motivate your actions. The conscious mind takes over to make decisions and act. Your brain has two systems working in parallel, a binary system and a fuzzy logic system. We inhabit, in our mind, a world of "clocks and clouds".

The mind and the body are one. Thinking is a bodily function, as are emotions and feelings. The brain is an integral part of the body, responsible for regulation in respect of the changing state of the environment. It reads the outside world and directs the body in reacting to it.

Your conscious, logical mind is like a general on top of a platform looking at the landscape from a distance, analysing everything linearly, thinking in data and speaking in prose. Your unconscious, emotional mind is like a million little observers running all over the landscape sending back a continuous flow of information, generating instant responses, expressing everything in images, stories and music.

Your unconscious mind can be likened to a deep-flowing stream. Events deep down in the stream throw up bubbles on the surface of the stream into your conscious mind. Interpreting these events in a balanced way allows you to use your Parallel Mind in a harmonious and healthy way. You need to be aware and pay attention to what is surfacing. Your unconscious mind is always talking to your conscious mind. But you need to be awake, slow down and pay attention to hear it.

Unconscious biases are the root cause of discrimination. The best way to tackle these underlying behaviours is to consciously think about the issues and to welcome inclusion and diversity with open arms. We need to monitor our unconscious prejudices that surface, understand what is driving them and override our instinctive behaviours.

The Evolution of the Conscious Mind

The development of the long-term memory in primitive man was crucial in the evolution of consciousness because it was this mental mechanism that helped him to imagine the future. Once language came into being, so did the first abstract thoughts and the ability to plan and organise activities collectively. Consequently, we can surmise that our ancestors began to develop the ability to express mental representations that two persons or more could attain together. This caused another social factor to come into existence: co-operation. Once our ancestors understood the concept of co-operation and collaboration they could then form communities.

In his book, *Hierarchy in the Forest: The Evolution of Egalitarian Behaviour* (1999), Dr. Christopher Boehm, a specialist in ancient tribes, concludes that primitive mankind functioned in a structure that was essentially hierarchical like chimpanzees, based on submission and dominance. This was a form of co-operative individualism that allowed mankind to live in an organised collective society where any individual who tried to gain an advantage would be removed from the community. As Charles Darwin put it in *The Descent of Man*,[5] "ultimately our moral sense or conscience becomes a highly complex sentiment—originating in the social instincts, largely guided by the approbation of our fellow-men…" Like Plato before him, Darwin believed that the development of reputation was the social glue of trust, essential for all collaboration.

Beyond egalitarianism, social glue and consciousness lie the area of philosophy and physics of The Conscious Universe, the notion that we only exist as part of a bigger whole. Human cells develop a kind of social identity according to their immediate context and what is needed for the health of the larger organism. If mass and energy are interchangeable, connected as in Einstein's equation $E = mc^2$, then is every living creature in itself energy? And is it all connected?

A number of physicists have written about this, from Professor Stephen Hawking to Henri Bartoft and Sir James Jeans, but returning to teachings from religions such as Buddhism we can take the message that everything is interdependent, nothing exists without a cause and effect and we tend to cling on to impermanent things. We need to learn to let go.

Pause for thought

How consciously aware are you of:
Being yourself
Controlling your emotions
Being empathic
Communicating with sensitivity?

Using Your Parallel Mind

Mankind's consciousness is the result of conscious and unconscious mechanisms out of which thought arises in the brain. Consciousness involves awareness, intuition, experience, dreams, emotions, memories, and a sense of a "self" in our own personal world. This is the essential Spirit

[5]Darwin, C. R. (1871). The descent of man, and selection in relation to sex (1st ed., Vol. 1). London: John Murray. http://charles-darwin.classic-literature.co.uk/the-descent-of-man/ebook-page-89.asp.

of Man, the *psyche* of the Swiss psychiatrist Carl G. Jung. Critically our mind enables us to think rationally. We can internalise our thoughts and express them verbally. This process of making internal sense of our external world is based on perception. The Latin *perceptio* means interpretation of the human senses. This process of perception is called transduction and always begins with an object, or in Gestalt coaching terms, a figure in the ground (see Theme II, Chapter 4). This becomes the focus of attention that allows us to think about our thinking and find a way to better fit into our circumstances.

Using our energy and marshalling the energy of others efficiently is a challenge. The more positive energy there is individually, the better the performance collectively. Sounds simple doesn't it? So, what gets in the way, who is the villain? Step forward the chimp, or to be more precise, the Chimp Brain. In his brilliant book, *The Chimp Paradox*, Professor Steve Peters talks about two minds consisting of the Chimp and the Human.

The Chimp is the primitive unconscious, emotional or limbic side of the brain. It is Peters' description of the *limbic system*. The Human is the more sophisticated rational, conscious side of the brain. And guess who is running the show? Yes, you guessed it, the Chimp is. The Chimp is directing your emotions and, therefore, your behaviours and performance based on the same gut reaction that keeps you safe from people you don't quite trust. This reactionary behaviour serves you well in many situations, especially when you need to make snap decisions, but holds you back from being able to use the processing power of your Human brain. You can have the ultimate control over your thinking and actions. The Chimp should be your servant rather than your master. You should *ride your elephant* to use another metaphor.

Our brains have evolved biologically to work unconsciously and consciously together as one Parallel Mind. Sometimes we use our unconscious mind to think fast to assess the threat level and alert the body to respond to any perceived danger. Your unconscious mind is fast-thinking—the intuitive brain is tuned into pattern detection and biases. Sometimes we need to slow down our thinking to use information in our memory to think through a problem step by step. Your conscious mind, on the other hand, is slow-thinking—the reasoning brain is tuned into data analysis and linear logic. The skill is to know when to override your gut feeling. But careful, your gut is linked to your unconscious brain and is often right! (Fig. 1.3).

	AMYGDALA	HYPOTHALMUS
FAST	ASSESSES THREAT LEVEL AND EMOTIONAL SIGNIFICANCE	HORMONAL CHANGES BODY RESPONSES
UNCONSCIOUS		
SLOW	SENSORY CORTEX PROCESSES CONSCIOUS AWARENESS	HIPPOCAMPUS INFORMATION ENCODED FORM MEMORIES
CONSCIOUS		

Fig. 1.3 The Parallel Mind Emotional Stimuli Processing Model

The Organisation Is a Mirror of the Brain

Organisations are collections of individual brains and behave collectively like a giant brain. Fundamentally organisations, like the brain, are self-organising organic systems. They are both deeply social and emotional. The personality or culture of the organisation will reflect the personality of the dominant individuals' brains.

The organisation will seek a strong sense of purpose just like your brain does: purpose in the organisation and in your brain, drives passion. Organisations behave like brains. They are driven by seeking reward and avoiding threat. Organisations have *amygdala* attacks and act irrationally and impulsively when a sudden shock hits them. An organisation is ultimately a human community of brains. That is why the power of others, as discussed later in Chapter 2, is so powerful. Peer group pressure has an iron grip. Emotional contagion can spread quickly when there is a crisis.

Maybe organisations should be more consciously aware of their unconscious brain. Maybe they would make better collective decisions if they learned to *ride their elephant* and let their thinking brain take charge. Conscious Awareness should be a collective practice. This would result in better quality collaborative conversations that lead to better outcomes (see Theme II, Chapter 6).

Pause for thought

Take a few minutes to think about some major events in your organisation, such as a merger, difficult trading conditions or winning a major new client.

Remember what you noticed about the behaviours of the people around you. Could you see their primitive chimp brains at work? Could you see the emotional contagion taking place? Could you see the emotional reactions taking place?

Intentions v Behaviour—*Riding Your Elephant*

Our unconscious emotional brain craves safety. However, to embrace change, we need to focus our conscious brain. Firstly, we intend to do something. Secondly, we pay attention to what we want to do. Thirdly, we do it. Then, we repeat the process. Attention density changes the brain. Every time you pay attention to something, the neurons in your brain fire and your neural paths rewire. The brain is plastic, wired to change to meet the challenges of a constantly changing environment.

But if we want to be in charge, we need to be mindful. Attention is the key that unlocks our free will: it is the gatekeeper of our awareness. Consciousness acts as a "bright spot" on the stage, directed by the selective spotlight of attention. Mindfulness can activate wilfully directed attention. For Buddhists, it is the moment of restraint that allows mindful awareness to take hold and deepen. Directed mental force stops the grinding machines of the unconscious. Mindfulness is falling awake, getting out of our own way and paying attention.

There is a gap between our conscious intentions and our unconscious behaviour. The unconscious mind is hardwired to resist change. Habits are hardwired into our brain. The unconscious mind is a lot bigger and stronger than the conscious mind and has been honed over millions of years of evolution. Our brains, as mentioned before, are driven by basic responses towards pleasure or away from pain, based on external stimuli processed by the *limbic system*, the emotional centre of the brain. When it senses a threat, the *amygdala* hijacks our conscious brains. This primitive knee-jerk reaction puts us in automatic fight or flight mode; we are hijacked by fear which often isn't rational. We need to take over the controls and override our autopilot which is our *basal ganglia* and engage our thinking brain, the *cortex* by expanding our conscious awareness.

Being mindful means taking control of your elephant, of your unconscious mind. You can be the "rider" and take the controls, but it needs discipline and energy. The "elephant", the *basal ganglia*, responsible for habitual actions, is much more powerful than you are, and habits are hard to change as they are hardwired into your brain. The brain will rewire itself if you fire it enough times by concentrating your attention through the power of focus and repetition.

Choice begins the moment you become present. Until you become present you are being conditioned by the memories of your unconscious mind. When you surrender to what is happening now, you become fully present, your past ceases to have any power. This is the *Power of Now* put forward by Eckhart Tolle in his book of the same name. Being present in the now is the essence of the Gestalt coaching system covered in Chapter 4.

To be human is to be creative. Creativity is an inherent human capability and an evolutionary advantage that has set us apart from all other species. We will need to exploit this innate creativity if we are to survive and thrive in an increasingly complex and challenging future world: expressing ourselves, pushing possibilities, creating more with less, thinking the unthinkable.

Our brain has an almost unlimited capacity to help you. Scientists suggest that we currently only use a tiny proportion of the brain's capacity. The figure is debatable, but it is beyond argument that there is a lot of spare mental capacity in the grey matter between our ears! The challenge for the next stage in human development is to raise conscious awareness and tap into all that unused processing power, connecting our unconscious mind with our conscious mind. If we do so, then the twenty-first century will be defined by our ability to use our Parallel Mind.

In Summary

In this chapter I have considered how remarkable your brain is, and how adept it is at protecting you from all kinds of harm and building bonds with others.

You process information unconsciously and emotionally before it becomes available to your conscious mind. This means you are in danger of justifying backwards what has already been decided.

We are emotional beings. Every time we think, we are being influenced by feelings based on our emotional experiences. It only takes six seconds to take control of our emotions and respond rationally. If we are to master ourselves and master our conversations we need to first master our emotions. We need to be present in the moment and be mindful.

Our capacity to feel empathy and to show compassion is what makes us human, the social lubricant that allows us to collaborate.

We humans are social creatures. We want to feel connected to our group. *Oxytocin* is a key hormone that gives us a sense of well-being when we are relaxed and socialising. In the absence of positive social cues our unconscious mind will automatically be wary of a threat. *Cortisol* is a key hormone in relation to stress.

Your conscious brain is poor at multitasking: rather than running several tasks at once it burns energy oscillating between them. You will be more effective if you limit the number of actors on the stage and if you ring-fence time to do the harder thinking tasks when you are fresh.

The organisation is a mirror of the brain, deeply social and emotional. Change requires you to be mindful, to have high awareness, if you are to bridge the gap between conscious intentions and unconscious behaviours.

Your brain is made up of many interconnected parts, but the conscious thinking parts are only a small proportion. The unconscious rest, including the *basal ganglia*, has great strength like an elephant: you need to learn how to become the rider who is in control of the elephant.

Pause for Reflection

Silence forces thinking. You capture your thoughts by thinking about your thinking. Like freezing a waterfall to reveal the tiny droplets of water.

To LISTEN you need to be ......? Rearrange the letters to find out!

For how long can you hold the silences in a coaching conversation?

2

Looking in Your Mirror

Introduction

My second chapter moves on from investigating the brain and mind to helping you investigate <u>your</u> mind. You will be challenged to stop, think and reflect on who you are as a person, as a leader and as a coach. And the difference you want to make. What do you stand for? What do you believe in? What is important to you? How do you like to be treated? How do you see the world? What motivates you? What makes you tick? Who you are as a person is who you are as a leader and who you are as a coach.

In expanding your self-awareness, and experimenting, you are encouraged to move outside your comfort zone. The chapter includes a number of different models for you to explore because how you see yourself matters: so, does asking others how they see you because, at this moment, your self-awareness might not be accurate.

In becoming more self-aware you will consider what you reveal as well as what you conceal. When you look in the mirror, do you see your true reflection, or do you see your brain's carefully constructed self-image? In learning how to lead in an intelligent way, this chapter builds on the neuroscientific background of Chapter 1. You will notice that the chapters are building a picture, a systemic view, an interconnected patchwork of what it is to be human—my *theory of everything* that makes us who we are. I look at habits, how they are formed and why they are so hard to break. Habits hard-coded in our brains make change so difficult even when we know we need to change.

Emotions are considered in a wider context than covered before, and you will have the opportunity to score your emotional intelligence. This will help

© The Author(s) 2019
N. Marson, *Leading by Coaching*, https://doi.org/10.1007/978-3-319-76378-1_2

you to be more aware of your emotions, to manage them better and improve your emotional resilience.

You will have the chance to reflect on the power of others over you and how to develop your own social intelligence. I investigate the power of empathy and why it is the key factor in establishing rapport and building high trust relationships. You will have the chance to find out what your default social style is and how it drives your leadership style.

I also look at different dimensions of cultural intelligence—how you can connect better across national cultures and in the distinct culture of an organisation.

I introduce for the first time the Parallel Mind Neuro Leadership Intelligence (NLI) Competency Model. NLI uniquely helps you lead with your brain in mind. NLI is about using and adjusting your EI, SI and CI together, so that they are in sync with each other and the leadership situation you are facing. My NLI competency model requires a comprehensive understanding of the brain at work—the science behind what motivates people's behaviours and how they make decisions.

Whatever your experience as a leader, this chapter will challenge you to be a better leader. You can look in your mirror to see your true reflection, if you dare to.

How you see yourself is how others will see you. It's time to look in the mirror.

Self-Awareness

Who am I? We have been asking ourselves this question from the beginning of civilisation. The ancient Greeks had the words "know thyself" inscribed on the Temple of Apollo at Delphi. But can we ever answer this question? Is it possible to gain a true picture of our self that corresponds with the reality of others? We are within ourselves, so any attempt to build a full picture is naturally fraught with our own cognitive biases and problems of self-reference. Even the miracle of language cannot help us articulate accurately who we really are.

Our brains create our own reality, a reality full of contradictions. This is sometimes referred to as the epistemic self, that is, the self that knows about itself and underlies mindfulness and meditation.

What I want you to get from reading my book is a greater awareness and ability to control what you are feeling, thinking and doing. But in assessing your capacity for self-knowledge, you may suffer from a grand delusion: that your Self somehow exists apart from your material body. Most philosophers and neuroscientists today think that this sort of "ontological" self is a fantasy: there is no self, separate from the brain that interacts with it. The "I" that we feel is an outcome of the material processes that constitute our brain and body. The brain is the physical embodiment of the mind. It is shaped by our sensory experiences and thought patterns because the life we lead leaves its mark in the form of enduring changes in the complex circuitry of the brain. This means our minds can change our brains through the power of volition and attention: you might say we literally become our thoughts. Our thoughts become our actions, and our actions become our legacy. It also means that we are all one of a kind. We are unique human personalities. Each one of us is a package of our genes and the multidimensional experiences our brain has enjoyed and endured on our spinning planet called Earth.

In this chapter, I want to give you a starting point for reflecting on your journey of self-discovery, rather than seducing you into putting yourself neatly into a human typology box, however comforting that may be. The truth is there are no types; humans are irreducible one-offs. And in the age of robots and Artificial Intelligence let's celebrate and leverage this wonderful human diversity!

However, there is a fundamental barrier to self-reference: we cannot achieve complete knowledge about the universe because we ourselves are part of it. Knowledge may be everything, but we're stuck working out whether everything is knowledge!

Who you are determines what you see and how you see it. People unaware of who they are, and how they behave, often damage relationships with others. What we don't like about others is very often connected to something we don't like about ourselves. What isn't part of ourselves doesn't disturb us. We see things as we are, not as they are.

Pause for thought

What do you most value about yourself?
Write down three things that make you who you are.
1.
2.
3.

Developing yourself as a leader and as a coach starts with knowing yourself. The **Johari Window** is a useful tool to raise self-awareness, to understand better your relationship with yourself and others. It consists of an imaginary two-by-two matrix, mapping what you know and what others know.

Start by looking into this mental map at what is known to you and what you have disclosed to others, by being transparent and behaving authentically. This self-disclosure, including selectively showing your human vulnerability, is the foundation for building trust as a leader. This is your **Open** window.

What you know but are hiding from others is your **Hidden** window. This is your opportunity to disclose who you really are, imperfections and all. This will help you build trust by being more real and accessible. People don't want perfect leaders, they want to believe in real people.

What is unknown to yourself but known to others is your **Blind** spot. It is your window of opportunity. By asking for feedback and being coached, you can increase your knowledge of yourself. This will tell you what impacts your leadership behaviours are having on the people you lead. Asking for feedback requires courage: after all, you might not enjoy hearing the truth. But courage gives you a competitive advantage as a leader. Feedback helps you grow as a person, as a coach and as a leader.

What is not known to you, and not known to others, is your **Unknown** window. Coaching is the most powerful tool to open this window, by creating the space for insights to emerge. Coaching provides a wonderful, and unique, opportunity for self-enlightenment.

As Manfred F. R. Kets de Vries of INSEAD put it in *The Leader on the Couch:* "Peel back the layers of self-deception and you reveal how your inner personality – largely hard-wired since early childhood - affects the way you lead and manage others".[1]

Your Intelligent Mind

Your mind is a wonderful gift, a multitude of intelligent thought systems. My car analogy can help illuminate how your intelligent mind works. Your intelligence quotient is your engine, it powers your reasoning ability. Your social intelligence is your wheels, keeping you grounded and in touch with people. Your cultural intelligence is your four-wheel drive system, enabling you to navigate other cultures socially. Your emotions are the fuel that drives

[1]Kets de Vries, M. F. (2012). *The leader on the couch: A clinical approach to changing people and organizations.* San Francisco, CA: Wiley.

you, your motivation to propel you on your journey. Emotional Intelligence is the gears and brakes to control your emotions so that you don't go out of control. NLI, my new model introduced for the first time in this book, is the computerised control system that is monitoring all the functions of your brain so that you can drive along safely. Conversational intelligence is the lubricant that provides a smooth ride, getting the feedback that allows you to make adjustments to your leading and coaching. You not only need power to get you there, but you also need to control your power to get you there safely.

IQ is not enough. Researchers now believe that intelligence is a blend of abilities, skills and personality traits.

Being clever is not enough. You need to be smart, to be "Neuro Leadership Intelligent", leading with the brain in mind. You need to be emotionally intelligent. You need to be socially intelligent. You need to be culturally intelligent. These intelligences will all help you be conversationally intelligent. You can only make real progress with the help of others. You need to be able to motivate others.

Leading with an understanding of how your brain works means you need to be aware of the rewards and threats your brain, and the brains of others, seek and seek to avoid. You also need to know how you can successfully control and help others control those impulses.

How aware are you of your emotions in the moment? How aware are you of your emotionally significant memories? How do they influence your thinking?

NLI is about using and adjusting your intelligences, so that they are in sync with each other and the leadership situation you are facing. My NLI competency requires a comprehensive understanding of the brain at work—the science behind what motivates people's behaviour and how they make decisions (Fig. 2.1).

Do you see yourself as others see you? You need to be aware of your behaviours and the impact they are having with others in social settings. "Knowing others is intelligence; knowing yourself is true wisdom. Mastering others is strength; mastering yourself is true power"—Lao Tzu 604 BC.

People make decisions in different ways. Some may have a predominant thinking style that is pragmatic. Some like to take decisive action, others like to pause, while others seek creative options.

My chapter will increase your awareness of the strategies you typically use to make decisions by using a variety of different exercises that will open your intelligent mind to new ways of thinking.

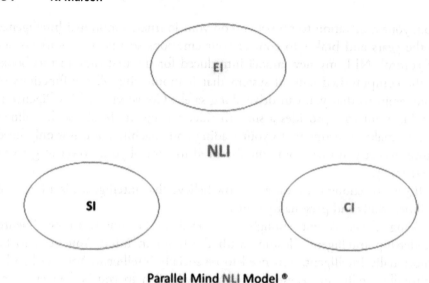

Parallel Mind NLI Model ®

Fig. 2.1 The Parallel Mind Neuro Leadership Intelligence Model

Exercise

This is a quick psychological test to help you get a handle on how you think. Just choose intuitively the left-side box(s) or the right-side box(s): e.g. do you prefer blue or red?

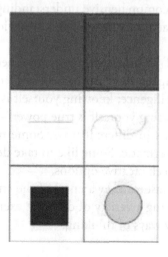

What do your choices suggest? If you chose blue, you tend to be rational when making decisions. If you chose red you are more emotional and impulsive. If you chose the straight line, you are likely to be a pragmatic thinker. If you chose the squiggly line, you are likely to be a creative thinker. If you chose the purple square, you are likely to be decisive. If you chose the yellow circle, you are likely to prefer to think about your options before deciding what to do.

In reality, our minds work in parallel, so we operate in all six boxes seamlessly. The test is designed to give you a starting point about your preferred or default styles of thinking. The most important thing is to recognise habitual behaviour and check in with yourself, so that you can choose a different behaviour when appropriate.

What about your decision making in situations of higher stress? To survive we need to be able to take the controls. In, *Deep Survival - Who Lives, Who Dies, and Why*, Laurence Gonzales gives us his rules. Test yourself on his rules of survival.

Exercise

If your plane came down in the Andes how would you react?

Tick the boxes

Believe you will pull through ☐

Stay calm ☐

Get organised ☐

Focus on small and manageable tasks ☐

Be bold and cautious ☐

Take joy in completing tasks ☐

Be grateful you are alive ☐

Play ☐

See the beauty in the ordinary ☐

Let go your fear of dying ☐

Do whatever is necessary to live ☐

Never give up ☐

How many boxes did you tick? Gonzales suggests survivors do all or most of the above dozen things. If the vast majority of people freeze in panic, then what makes the small percentage stay focussed and alive? They face their situation with courage and plan. Their logical conscious, *cortex* brain takes control over their fearful unconscious, *limbic* brain.

Habits

What am I?
I am your constant companion
I will compel you to success
Or drag you down to failure
I am completely at your command
If you are firm with me I will place the world at your feet
If you are easy with me I will destroy you
I am Habit—The body is a good servant but a bad master. Anon

All our lives are but a mass of habits. Most of the choices we make each day may feel like carefully made decisions, but they aren't. They are habits. Habits can be changed if we know how they work. The *basal ganglia*, the primitive autopilot deep in the centre of your brain, is treading its familiar paths just like an elephant in the jungle. The paths have proved to be safe. The elephant uses up less precious energy if it does not need to think about how to get through the jungle.

So how can you make the elephant go a different way? Your brain needs triggers to make actions routine, so that they become habits. Patterns work within our lives, at home, at work and in society.

The neurobiology of free will is in the habit loop.

To modify a habit, you must decide to change it. But before you can decide, you must be aware of it. And what craving or need is driving it. Then you can redirect the flow and find an alternative routine.

Charles Duhigg, the author of *The Power of Habit*, suggests the following framework:

Identify the routine
Experiment with rewards
Isolate the cue
Have a plan

So, you want to give up your favourite chocolate bar. Well, not entirely, but to resist buying it every time you go to your usual supermarket! First of all, accept your craving is real but manageable. The cue to pick up the sugary treat is the confectionery aisle in the supermarket. It is at the far end of the supermarket next to the cereals aisle which you normally go to at the end of your shopping routine. You will need to give your brain a reward for not stopping by the chocolate bars and picking up your usual treat. Maybe you will buy yourself a magazine on every third shopping trip to the supermarket. Maybe you will give the money you save to your local village charity box.

You can experiment with rewards to see which reward is the most effective at reducing your chocolate consumption. Next, you need to isolate the cue and change the routine you use to navigate your way around the supermarket. Start at the opposite end of the supermarket and even consciously decide to skip the confectionary aisle. Repetition of the new routine causes your plastic brain to fire and rewire its decision, making new circuits. You can stop drinking, stop smoking, and stop gambling if you really want to, and if you find alternative ways of providing the benefits that you are getting from those activities.

Your conscious volitional mind can override your unconscious craving mind. It is hard to ride the elephant! The elephant always wants its own way. And it is very powerful. You could of course disorientate your elephant completely and go to a different supermarket that your brain has no mental map of! The important thing is to have a plan and stick to it. Don't be afraid to change your plan if it is not working. When you fail, don't give up. Just pick yourself up and try again. Failure and success are symbiotic. You need to be patient with yourself, to work *with* yourself through change rather than trying to force action.

As Mark Twain wrote in *Pudd'n Head Wilson*, "Habit is habit, and not to be flung out of the window by any man but coaxed downstairs one step at a time".[2]

> **Pause for thought**
> What habits will you change?

---

[2]Twain, M. (1894). *Pudd'nhead Wilson* (1st ed.). New York: Charles L. Webster & Company. Retrieved from https://americanliterature.com/author/mark-twain/book/the-tragedy-of-puddnhead-wilson/chapter-6.

Emotions

Emotions are an expression of our needs. Emotions are your brain's best guesses for what your body sensations mean, based on the situation you find yourself in. Your brain is a prediction-making machine producing emotions outside your sphere of awareness to keep you safe. The emotional brain, I referred to in Chapter 1, is our survival mechanism.

For centuries, famous thinkers like Aristotle, Darwin and Freud, have tried to explain emotion using common sense. But the human brain creates memorable sensations, as diverse as joy and sadness, without revealing how it is doing its magic. And your incredible brain makes meaning from the identical sensation in diverse ways, depending on the context, past experience and body balance.

In the Disney film *Inside Out*, the main characters are the emotions of sadness, anger, fear, disgust and joy. It takes place largely within the brain of Riley, an 11-year-old girl who is unsettled by her family's relocation from Minnesota to San Francisco. Joy delivers daydreams on the train of thought and is custodian of Riley's memories. She is in a constant battle with sadness. The goal of *Inside Out* is for Joy finally to discover the point of sadness—the revelation is that unhappiness is a vital and valid emotion.

To a neuroscientist, the human brain has not changed since the Stone Age. We still have a deep-seated tribal instinct, a sense of "us and them" that can explode in a fraction of a second when our primitive rage circuit is ignited. Brexit and the Donald Trump phenomena are both modern examples of tribalism. People voted against the establishment because they were angry that they didn't feel heard. The neural circuit of rage was forged on the open plains of Africa as a primitive survival mechanism to combat tribes competing for limited food resources. As Einstein, a lifelong pacifist, wrote in 1946 after the creation of the atomic bomb, "Everything has changed – except the way we think".[3] Our thinking is still driven by our *limbic system*.

The language of our brain's unconscious threat-detection circuitry is communicated to our conscious awareness by multicoloured emotions that convey very specific messages about the threat. Emotions are powerful motivators of behaviour: the emotion of anger prepares us to fight. Every emotion comes with a variety of flavours, for example:

---

[3]Einstein, Albert. (2012, April). Retrieved from https://atomictrauma.wordpress.com/the-scientists/albert-einstein/ and Krauss, L. M. (2013, January 15). Deafness at Doomsday. Retrieved from https://www.nytimes.com/2013/01/16/opinion/deafness-at-doomsday.html.

Emotion: Intensity

Angry: annoyed, offended, disgusted
Sad: disappointed, dismayed, disillusioned
Anxious: stressed, confused, bewildered
Hurt: aggrieved, betrayed, abandoned
Embarrassed:confused, ashamed,isolated
Happy: pleased, excited, elated

Pause for thought

Think of a situation that made you feel emotionally very positive or very negative. Run through the list of emotions above and label the emotion(s) you felt. Then decide on its/their intensity.
It is important to label the flavour of your emotions to understand what is driving them, so you can deal with them better.

As Eleanor Roosevelt wrote in *Footprint In Your Heart:* "to handle yourself, use your head; to handle others, use your heart".[4] And as Maya Angelou put it: "people will forget what you said, people will forget what you did, but people will never forget how you made them feel". The question here is, how often do you stop to reflect on how do you make other people feel?

It is important to be able to label your emotions, so that you can deal with each one consciously. Our rational brain allows us to analyse our emotions and gives us answers to the question of why we feel a certain way. You can analyse your feelings by breaking them down into the following emotional components:

The situation
Your feelings
Your thoughts
Your body systems
Your behaviour
Reflective learning

You will remember a time when you sat an important exam. Perhaps even a life defining exam. You arrived maybe two hours early at the examination centre. You remember feeling anxious and a little stressed but not confused

---

[4]Dedes, J. (2017, February 18). Footprints in Your Heart, Eleanor Roosevelt's Wisdom Poem. Retrieved from https://jamiededes.com/2017/02/18/footprints-in-your-heart-a-poem-by-eleanor-roosevelt/.

and certainly not bewildered. You felt you were well prepared and confident of success. Your thoughts turned to the exam questions. What would come up? Would there be any questions that you couldn't answer? Would the paper be overall a fair one? Would you run out of time and not complete all your answers? As time got closer to the start of the examination you could feel your pulse quicken, the palms of your hands getting sticky. Your body system was in a threat state. You consciously calmed your body down. You thought to yourself that you could not be better prepared. Well maybe you shouldn't have gone to see your local football team play an important match. Maybe you shouldn't have gone to the cinema with your friends. Maybe you shouldn't have … Just maybe!

Well, it is too late now to change anything. You are probably as ready as anyone. The important thing, you tell yourself, is to relax. Get into the zone. Not to panic. To focus on the questions. Read them slowly. Think carefully about the key points of your answers. Write them down on the margin of the exam paper and afterwards, the traditional exam post-mortem. Did I miss the point on question three? Did I answer all the questions? Did I get enough marks to pass? Did I pass with the distinction I worked so hard for?

And after the result you will have time to reflect. If you have passed with the grade you were hoping for then perhaps you will trust that your unconscious learning brain has done its job, in remembering the pieces of the jigsaw, and your conscious brain has done its job, in focussing on directing your knowledge to answering the questions. Your joined-up parallel mind seamlessly getting you over the line!

In the marshmallow test experiment, four-year-olds from the Stanford University preschool were brought to a room and sat in a chair in front of a marshmallow on a table. They were told they could eat it now or get two if they were willing to wait until the experimenter came back from a small errand.

We now know that when we get an impulse to do something, but then don't act on it, we can thank the *dorsal front-median cortex*—an area just above and between the eyes. A failure in this circuitry may be at play in disorders ranging from attention deficit to addictions. In the marshmallow test, impulse control turned out to predict how well those kids were doing in high school. Those who waited, compared to those who scoffed, were more popular with their peers and achieved higher grades at graduation. Self-control is an important trait for effective leaders too!

Developing Your Emotional Intelligence

Emotional intelligence (EI), also known as your emotional intelligence quotient (EIQ), is the capability of individuals to recognise their own emotions and those of others, distinguish between different feelings and label them appropriately, use emotional information to guide thinking and behaviour, and manage and/or adjust emotions to adapt to environments or achieve one's goal(s). Although the term first appeared in a 1964 paper by Michael Beldoch, it gained popularity in the 1995 book, Emotional Intelligence, written by the author, and science journalist Daniel Goleman.

Daniel Goleman's HAY Emotional Intelligence framework is a helpful model and suggests four key aspects:

Self-awareness—*Knowing me*
The fundamental principle of emotional intelligence is that you must connect first with yourself before you can connect with others. Be comfortable with who you are, and you will be able to see the best in others.

Self-management—*Managing me*
You need to tune into your emotional state—to be consciously aware of your feelings—so that you can control and adjust your behaviour. Your impact on others is then likely to be more positive.

Social awareness—*Knowing others*
Showing empathy is the key to establishing rapport and building trust.

Relationship management—*Connecting with others*
You should try to understand what makes the other person tick so that you can adjust your behaviour and make more sense to them.

Emotional connectivity is a two-way process of giving a bit of yourself, showing your feelings and absorbing feelings from others. It occurs when two people can express, share, appreciate and understand their genuine feelings. To connect emotionally, you need to tune into the emotional state of the person you are talking to. Mirror their body language and tone. Tune into their frequency so that they see themselves and hear themselves speaking.

Exercise
For an initial assessment of your current E I, score yourself honestly on below:

RELATIONSHIP **SELF**
LOW 1 2 3 4 5 HIGH

I am comfortable with who I am
I take responsibility for my own happiness
I use internal dialogue to drive my emotional states
I reflect on negative feelings effectively
I regroup quickly after a set-back
I understand the feedback others give me
I develop new and more productive behaviours
I can incorporate my feelings into my decision making
I guide my feelings, so I can focus on what is important
I reflect regularly to resolve internal emotional conflicts
I recognise the links between my emotions, thoughts and behaviours
I can relax after a difficult day

RELATIONSHIP **OTHERS**
LOW 1 2 3 4 5 HIGH
I communicate my emotions effectively
I ask others how they feel
I show empathy to others
I help others manage their emotions
I make others feel good about themselves
I develop consensus
I achieve win/win outcomes
I respond rather than react when people try to undermine me
I choose my words carefully
I listen deeply to understand others
I show compassion to others
I am a coach to others
Look at the pattern of your scoring. What does this suggest you might do to improve your relationship with yourself and with others?

Here are six things you can do to be more emotionally intelligent.

1. Know that trust is the issue. Being authentic builds trust. Know who you are, be who you are and, above all, don't be afraid to show who you are.
2. Start labelling your feelings, rather than labelling people or situations. Say "I am afraid", rather than "you are driving like a lunatic". Distinguish between thoughts and feelings because all actions are motivated by feelings. Emotions put us in motion, so express them so that others can understand you better.
3. Validate other people's feelings. Show empathy, understanding, and acceptance of other people's feelings. Ask people how they are feeling. Listen deeply to people's needs. Show genuine empathy and compassion for others.
4. Demonstrate a healthy curiosity without being intrusive. Have a learning frame of mind. Recognise that people are different so treat them differently.

5. Give yourself the credit you deserve. Don't beat yourself up when things go wrong but instead challenge negative self-talk. Be an inner coach, not an inner critic. Never let others undermine your self-esteem and dent your confidence. Stand tall: we are all born to shine.

6. Show yourself some compassion. Self-compassion protects you against the consequences of self-judgement: because you recognise your interconnectedness and equality with others, you accept you are not perfect and that is OK.

Relationships

It has been said that success is built one relationship at a time. Relationships are the core of life. Every relationship is unique and based on conversations, experiences and perceptions. Trust is the glue that holds relationships together, so developing long-term trust should be the aim. There is an essential fluidity in relationships; they are dynamic and shifting all the time as events unfold. Relationships are difficult to capture and to define. Relative positions are always changing. Negotiation is taking place continuously to find a balance of power and interests. Ebbs and flows in relationships are natural. There must be mutual respect. No relationship is perfect, but it needs to be consciously purposeful. There are needs and wants that must be satisfied, both parties need to feel appreciated, not taken for granted. There must be effective communication, a good positive tone. Conversations must be honest, with assumptions shared, and roles plus contributions agreed. Every relationship should have an overall vision with specific objectives and underlying values. Listening to the needs of the other is vitally important. Empathy is essential because compassion builds the human bond. Accept people for who they are.

And a sense of humour helps!

Pause for thought
Considering the above, how would you describe your work relationships? How would you describe your personal relationships?
What could you improve?

The Power of Empathy is the power to understand and imaginatively enter into another person's feelings. Empathy allows us to build rapport and establish trust. It allows us to establish more personal relationships with our colleagues and clients. Empathy is one person's drive to understand another, their thoughts and feelings—who they are and what motivates them.

It operates in the moment—the here and now—and is experienced by the other person through the sensitive but honest responses given.

Empathy gives people the power to express themselves openly and without fear. It takes us deep into the truth of the other person, giving us the insights and understanding to know where their reality ends and ours begins. Empathy tells us who we can trust and who we should avoid, how to protect and defend ourselves, when to move forward and when to hold back. It tells colleagues and clients that we care about them as fellow human beings. Empathy brings people closer to us, it is the great enabler. Empathy is the lifeblood of influence.

According to Daniel Goleman, there are three levels of empathy.

1. Cognitive empathy is when you can understand intellectually someone's predicament.
2. Emotional empathy is when you can feel their pain.
3. Empathic concern is the ability to sense what somebody needs from you. I will add a fourth.
4. Compassionate empathy is reaching out and trying to help people in whatever way you can. It means witnessing them. Talking to a colleague whose partner or child is seriously ill acknowledges they exist and that you chose to care about them.

Empathic listening is the key to being influential. The power of reciprocity is that people will listen to you once they have been fully heard and understood. What does everyday empathy sound like?

To the courier delivering your parcels on a freezing cold day, it could be "Thank you for coming out on such a cold day". It doesn't cost anything, but it might make their day and a smile can make all the difference. Mindful empathy accelerates the speed of trust.

It is about tuning into the feelings of others to show you care about them. It starts with noticing the behaviours of others. Noticing their fleeting micro-expressions. Checking in with your own thoughts and feelings. Looking for a human connection. Try to imagine what it might be like to be in their shoes. Show some compassion.

Pause for thought

Here is a very short course in human relationships:
The three most important words in a relationship are…?
The two most important words are?
The single most important word is?

I suggest the answers are: I was mistaken; thank you; and we. How often have you used those words today? How often have your colleagues used them today?

Developing Your Social Intelligence

Imagine yourself at a social gathering with people you don't know. How are you feeling? You will be feeling many emotions for sure. Your *limbic* brain will be in overdrive looking for threats. Will they like me? Can I trust them? Am I looking ok, will I fit in? Am I enjoying the conversation or am I going to find an excuse to leave early. Introverts will be dreading the thought of new people while extroverts will be positively energised.

Social intelligence is the skill to be aware of your minute-by-minute emotions in a social setting and manage them in real time, so you can make a positive impact. Social awareness is the ability to read the social setting you are in and tune into the emotional frequency of others. You can then behave in a trustworthy way that signals to the other persons they can trust you. Empathic concern builds rapport quickly if it is sincere and genuine.

Imagine you are at a networking event your firm is hosting and you notice somebody isolated and alone, looking distinctly uncomfortable. Going over and talking to that person shows empathic concern and compassion. You chose to care. Empathy is the precursor to rapport and often the start of a relationship. The *limbic system* has a long memory.

Scientists at the Human Neuroimaging Lab in Virginia have found, using computational brain imaging devices like MRIs, that reciprocity expressed by one person builds trust in the other person during a conversation. This is because *mirror neurons*, those parts we saw in Chapter 1 that fire when we witness another person's suffering and give a scientific basis to empathy, are firing simultaneously when actions are copied.

I summarise this in my four mirrored boxes (Fig. 2.2).

Pause for thought
Think of a similar situation. Go through the Parallel Mind Social Intelligence framework. Ask yourself the following questions:

Social awareness
Did you notice the different personality traits of the people you were talking to? Were they introverted or extroverted for instance? Did they seem more interested in people or in tasks?

Social cognition
Were you aware of the power-play between different people of similar status compared to people of different status? Did you notice the subtle micro-expressions that signalled dominance or submissiveness?

Empathic concern
Did you show compassion and walk up to the lonely soul? If not, what held you back? Will you approach them next time?

Emotional resonance
Did you feel emotionally connected to any person you met? What made you feel connected? Did you notice your body language was mirroring theirs? Did you feel you could trust them? What did you do that would give them the confidence to trust you?

DISC Personality Profiling Tool

Your personality profile is a blueprint for your likely behaviour. It has an influence on what you say and do each day.

When you are consciously aware of how you are feeling, you can adjust your behaviour. As a result, when you meet others who have a different personality profile you can narrow this personality gap and so are more likely to have a positive outcome from your encounter, particularly when you have a

Social Awareness	Social Cognition
Empathic Concern	Emotional Resonance

Fig. 2.2 The Parallel Mind Social Intelligence Framework

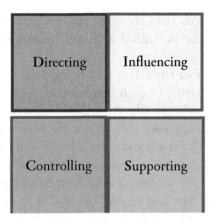

Fig. 2.3 DISC Personality Profiling Tool (adapted)

difficult situation to deal with. With your adjusted behaviour they still see the authentic you, only now you make more sense to them.

William Moulton Marston's DISC model dates back to 1928, yet it is a simple tool to quickly establish people's dominant personality traits. His Harvard-researched behaviour assessment tool remains one of the most widely used personality models in the world today. In my adapted **DISC** model, my labelling is as follows: **D** stands for Directing; **I** for Influencing; **S** for **S**upporting and **C** for **C**ontrolling (Fig. 2.3).

Ds have a strong need to achieve and are very direct. They are ambitious, competitive and like a challenge. They are often CEOs, partners in professional service firms or company directors. They are determined, strong-willed and tackle problems head-on. They want to control their environment. They lead by directing others.

Is are social and emotionally expressive. Friendly and outgoing, they get things done by using their social skills in groups. They are often entertainers, teachers or salespeople. They lead by influencing others through their natural enthusiasm.

Ss are steady, stable and patient. They take a predictable, measured approach to life. They tend to be accommodating and undemanding. They are very persistent and task-focused. They are sincere, honest and loyal to the people they support. They are typically nurses, office managers or call centre operatives. They lead by supporting others.

Cs are conscientious and focused on achieving the best quality results. They like structure, facts and detail. They are not really interested in people. They are systematic when focusing on the task in hand and are searching for accuracy and excellence. They are often lawyers, accountants and scientists. They have a need to be in control and lead by making sure people follow their rules.

You can put a number from 1 to 4 (1 being your most dominant trait, 4 your least dominant trait), in each quadrant of the above **DISC** model to get your personality styles profile. Armed with this knowledge, you will be better equipped to change your style to suit the person you are with and the situation you are in. This is a key skill for a leader and a coach.

It should be noted that we are a combination of all four of the main driving personality traits. We all have a dominant behaviour trait followed by a less strong secondary type and so on. The skill is to be aware of your driving personality traits and be able to modify your behaviours to close the gap when you are with others who have different personality traits.

So, if you are a strong "I" then you need to tone down your overfriendly, overenthusiastic style in favour of a more considered, business-focussed approach when pitching to a "D". The CEO wants to decide quickly, so just answer the questions!

If you have a high "C" element in your make-up, then consider whether your focus on tasks more than on people may mean others see dealing with you as just another task. That may not generate the best results: perhaps people may not go out of their way to help you if you do not seem to care much about them. Is dealing with you just a job?

The flip side is that your higher level of concern for people's well-being may be perceived as a weakness. Choosing to care may give the impression that you lack focus on getting things done, so are seen as ineffective as a leader.

Emotionally resonant leaders combine emotional and social intelligence to connect with others more effectively. Emotionally resonant leaders show compassion and improve the emotional health and well-being of their followers; they create hope and confidence, and their infectious enthusiasm carries people along. They give the person they are listening to their full undivided attention as if they were the only person in the world. When someone feels deeply heard, it gives them permission to be themselves. They feel liberated and can be at their creative best.

If this seems to be stretching too far into "soft" areas, note what was covered in Chapter 1, that humans are built upon an emotional, *limbic* brain.

In his book, *A Way of Being* Carl Rogers, the American psychologist and founding father of the humanistic approach to psychotherapy, sums this up as follows: "When a person realises he has been deeply heard, [their] eyes moisten. I think in some real sense [they are] weeping for joy. It is as though

[they] were saying, *Thank God, someone heard me. Someone knows what it's like to be me*".[5]

Cultural Intelligence

The definition of culture is: "the collective mental programming which distinguishes one group of people from another".[6] This collective programming influences patterns of thinking which is reflected in the meaning people attach to various aspects of life and which become crystallised in the institutions of society. And this collective programming can be seen by non-natives (if they notice), in the everyday behaviours of the indigenous population.

White cannot exist without black. Contrast is required to make things visible. Our own culture only becomes visible when it is contrasted against other cultures. We are blissfully unaware of our behaviours, like fish swimming in a tank totally oblivious to what is on the other side of the glass. We don't know who invented the ocean, but we know it wasn't a fish! We absorb our native culture.

Cultural messages are often subtle and usually totally pervasive. When we see people behaving differently from us, we instinctively feel something is wrong. We become judgemental. So, is there another way? Acceptance is another way, which brings us back to the fact that people are all human beings but are conditioned to see similar situations differently. And acceptance starts with awareness. We must see the gap before we can mind the gap! From awareness comes action. We can choose our behaviours. We can narrow the gap and at the same time keep our authenticity. The most important thing is to have a good heart, to have good intentions, to be respectful to people from other cultures.

Our shared humanity should unite us. We all have the same problems, but we deal with them in different ways. There is no right way, only a different way. Let's celebrate our differences and learn from them.

There is always a danger of stereotyping—consciously and unconsciously. The starting point to dealing with this dilemma is to understand that our primitive brains are wired to see a difference as potentially dangerous and unfortunately that can be transferred to colour of skin or different dress styles. Unconscious bias is part of being human. When we were living in

---

[5]Rogers, C. R. (1980). *A way of being*. Boston, MA: Houghton Miffin.
[6]Hofstede, Geert. (1991). *Cultures and Organizations: Software of the Mind*. London: McGraw-Hill. https://www.bbvaopenmind.com/wp-content/uploads/static/4libro/en/Nationalcultures.pdf.

caves, we needed to decide quickly whether someone was going to hunt with us or steal our food. This tribalism is still pervasive today. If you want to see it in action just go to a sports match! Identity is important to us. We want to belong to our special group. Who we are and what binds us together socially matters to us. Labelling helps us to map the world to find a safe path. As a leader, you need to go beyond the stereotypes, towards trying to understand what is driving cultural behaviours—the shared values and collective unconsciousness.

Developing Cultural Intelligence

In the increasingly interconnected world we live and work in, the importance of understanding cultural norms cannot be overstated. The starting point for culturally intelligent behaviours is noticing and observing. This builds the awareness and knowledge that leads to better understanding and insights. You are then able to be more sensitive and adjust your body language. You can look for the non-verbal feedback and adjust your communication style and tone. If you have the right intentions your cultural mistakes will be tolerated.

To avoid prejudiced statements and stereotypes, anthropologists and sociologists developed a quantitative method of comparing cultural values. They provide a yardstick, indicating whether the mainstream of people in one culture feels or behaves in a certain manner, whether most people in one culture are closer to this or that end of the spectrum, whether they are poles apart or close together. It is about averages and some individuals may diverge from their own cultural mainstream and be nearer the mainstream of another culture.

Before values can be measured, you need to identify and define "yardsticks". The basic approach is that human nature is essentially the same everywhere, but different cultures have developed their own responses to the human condition. These responses have been influenced by the unique history and geography of each culture. The cultural dimensions defined by the Dutch intercultural researchers Hofstede and Trompenaars are widely used as a common basis for intercultural comparisons and understanding.

There are five Cultural dimensions according to Hofstede, namely:

Power Distance (Hierarchical or Egalitarian)
Power distance is either large or small. In a culture, like France, where the power distance is large, there is a distinct hierarchy and a lot of bureaucracy. This means it is difficult to get access to the top people. There are many

layers you need to get past first. People in France generally accept this. In America, where there is a small power distance, it is easy to talk to the boss, you just walk into his office or home!

Individualism or Collectivism (I or We)
In collectivist societies, like China, there is a groupthink mentality. We before me. People do not exist as individuals only as part of their group.
Identity is based in their social system. If they are shamed individually, their whole group loses face. They say in Japan, another highly collectivist culture, "the nail that sticks out gets hammered down". In the UK, which is highly individualistic, people want to stand out and get noticed. Identity is based in the individual. The Beatles, four talented young musicians from Liverpool, wanted to be different, not the same. Just like the unique voices that made the distinctive sound of the Beach Boys on the other side of the Atlantic in America, the most individualistic culture in the world.

Femininity or Masculinity (F or M)
In feminine cultures, like the Netherlands and Sweden, people tend to be more caring than in more masculine cultures like the USA. People get hired and fired in America without first receiving the support they would get in Northern Europe. In feminine societies, you work to live. In masculine societies, you live to work. In Japan, the second most masculine culture in the world after Serbia, you won't find many women in management positions. In Sweden, there are more women CEOs than men CEOs. In Scandinavian countries, being a house husband is socially acceptable and normal.

Uncertainty Avoidance (Stability or Change)
Uncertainty avoidance is weak or strong and is a measure of how tolerant people are of ambiguity. In cultures, like Germany, where uncertainty avoidance is strong, there is a need for rules and regulations. Everything is spelt out in writing for people, so they know what they must do. The rules are the rules. In cultures where uncertainty avoidance is weak, like the USA, people take more risks. If there isn't a law to stop you doing something then just do it! Where there is strong uncertainty avoidance, there is generally higher anxiety and stress. There is an intolerance of deviant behaviour. Rules come before relationships.

Short-Term or Long-Term Orientation
In long-term cultures, like China, the focus is on the future. With a civilisation over 5000 years old, what is another year or two to sign a deal. For the Americans, this is difficult! They want to get the deal done and get on the plane. This is a short-term orientation. Big Corporations in America publish

their results every quarter! An American President has to be elected every 4 years with a maximum of two terms in office if re-elected. The General Secretary of the Communist Party of China and President of the People's Republic of China, Chairman of the central Military Commission, has been given all three jobs for life, with the title "Core" Leader.

My Parallel Mind Culture Circle (Fig. 2.4) adds a sixth dimension of Direct or Coded Communication. This is a by-product of a high or low context culture. In a high context culture, like China, the communication is indirect, or coded, and depends on the social context and the relative power of the parties involved. In a low context culture, like Germany, people communicate verbally and usually directly. It is clear from what they say, what they want you to do.

My Parallel Mind Culture Circle for India also includes the cultural dimension from Trompenaars of relationships before rules or rules before relationships.

In my circle, the strong cultural orientations are denoted by green dots away from the centre. For example, India is a predominantly masculine culture, so the green dot is near the edge of the circle.

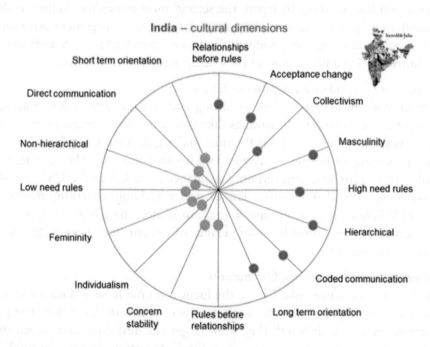

Fig. 2.4 The Parallel Mind Culture Circle

But no culture is one hundred per cent at one end of the cultural continuum, so India has some feminine characteristics which are signified by the orange dot being quite close to the centre of the circle.

Exercise

Draw a culture circle of your own country. Ask your colleagues of different nationalities you are collaborating with to do the same.
What do the differences between the cultural orientations reveal?
Discuss with your colleagues what can be done to narrow the gaps.

The understanding of the neuroscience of your brain at work is a fundamental driver for using the Culture Circle and DISC tools. The ideas put forward in my book will allow you to have a greater awareness of the other person's picture of reality.

For a more detailed analysis of working across cultures, I highly recommend you refer to *When Cultures Collide* by Richard D. Lewis.

The Power of Others

Oscar Wilde once remarked that, "most people are other people. Their thoughts are someone else's opinions, their lives a mimicry, their passions a quotation". We are not our thoughts!

Our need to co-operate with others, to survive in our social groups, means we are constantly being influenced by the power of others, either consciously or unconsciously. Our unconscious emotional brain, the *limbic system* covered in Chapter 1, is wired to pick up on the emotional cues contained in the micro-body language of the people we talk to in the multitude of conversations we have daily. In his book, *The Power of Others*, Michael Bond comments: "Our behaviour is influenced far more by others than we'd like to imagine. It is fear of social exclusion that binds us together. Don't stand out screams your reptilian brain at you, it's dangerous".

We are not who we think we are. Our experience of ourselves is misleading. The voice in the head is a mere supporting actor. Unaware of our unconscious mind, it coats things with an emotional significance, a stream of sensations, impulses, judgements and desires. These signals shape our interpretation of the world and guide us like a spiritual GPS as we chart our courses. And the power of others is constantly influencing our thoughts without us knowing. We may believe we are in charge but most of the time we are being steered by others. We are the victims of fashions and fads and social networks like Facebook. We are social through and through. Humans love groups. We construct an inner dialogue of us and them, good and bad, right and wrong, agree and disagree. Living in, and identifying with groups, makes evolutionary sense. Our tribal tendencies are part of our physiology, helped by the hormone *oxytocin*, which boosts people's love for their in-group. Social isolation is a dangerous place for human beings. The people in our lives affect every aspect of our behaviour in ways that we are often not consciously aware of.

The sudden and tragic death of Princess Diana on the 11th of August 1997 caused a public outpouring of shared emotions never seen before in the UK. It was if we had lost a close friend or relative ourselves. Emotional hysteria, driven by grief, swept the country.

In Egypt at the beginning of the Arab Spring, on 11 February 2011 in Tahrir Square, there was a public outpouring of joy caused by the news that President Mubarak had relinquished power.

Emotional contagion is just as pervasive in business life. Michael Bond refers to a study by Professor Peter Totterdell from the University of Sheffield into the ebb and flow of relationships among colleagues in a cricket team: "It turned out that each player's happiness at any one time was strongly linked to that of his teammates, regardless of whether or not things were going in their favour". As Michael Bond puts it, "It was if they were all plugged into a giant hubble-bubble, inhaling the collective mood like smoke".[7]

Peer pressure and groupthink dominate our working lives and where we all think alike, no one thinks very much. But we have the power to resist our copycat herding instinct. The *anterior cingulate cortex* helps us choose to use a more slow and mindful decision-making process. We just need to make sure that the *amygdala*, the centre of our emotional brain, doesn't hijack us.

Pause for thought

In what ways do the people around you shape your thinking and behaviour?

---

[7]Bond, M. H. (2015). *The power of others: Peer pressure, groupthink, and how the people around us shape everything we do*. London: Oneworld.

The Power of You

Power is the possession of control or authority over others and the course of events. When people have power over you, or you perceive they have, you can feel they are judging you. It is safer to be subservient than to be challenging. Even in groups of equal status, there is a tendency towards group think, the pressure to conform to group norms. Avoiding dissent may feel safe, but it can be very dangerous as seen in the aircraft disasters mentioned in Chapter 1. It can cause bad cognitive decisions and poor moral judgements. As seen with the doomed flights, polarisation happens when like-minded people only hear arguments that support their thinking and become blind to the obvious need to do something else, like to focus on the automatic pilot warning signal rather than the failed landing wheels warning light. Group think and polarisation help us understand the behaviours that can cause the failure of financial institutions, like Barings in the UK and Lehman Brothers in the USA. The lesson here is to take the controls and exert the power of you.

To find your authentic voice, as will be explored in depth in Chapter 3, you need to discover the power of you by consciously thinking about your thinking. Only by engaging your conscious mind will you be able to unleash your full potential. To be the change you seek, to fulfil your destiny and leave your legacy.

But will you take control? Will you make your thoughts your own? Will you unlock the frozen thoughts in your unconscious brain? Will you listen to your internal feelings, "the man within", as Adam Smith wrote in 1759, "the impartial and well-informed spectator" (refer also Chapter 1). Will you use your unconscious brain (*limbic system*) and conscious mind (*cortex*) together as one parallel mind? Will you ride your elephant? Will you stop trying to impress others and follow your true north compass where it leads you?

Steve Jobs knew who he was and what he wanted, and so did everyone around him. He didn't let dogma, the thoughts of others, stop him delivering his vision for a better world. He stayed, in his words, "hungry and foolish" in the pursuit of his dreams.

Is it time for you to step out? Is it time to release the power of you? Is it time for you to hatch, as a leader and as a coach?

Organisational Culture

The personality of the organisation is frozen in the unconscious minds of its people's embedded values and stories. The big challenge as a leader is to consciously cultivate the personality of the organisation.

Leaders should create the space to discuss values. Who we are, what we do, how we do it. Purpose is important. Ideally organisational values and personal values should be aligned.

I interviewed Des Hudson, formerly CEO of The Law Society, for this book and asked him, what would be the one thing he would do differently if he could have his time again. He told me he would be bolder. He felt that despite making significant progress he let the power of others control his destiny more than he would have liked. Organisational culture is powerful and resistant to change.

Pause for thought

Take a few minutes to think of your social groups within your organisation. Who is in the constellation of power?
What is your relationship to these power brokers? How could you have more influence?
What conversations will you have to improve your position?

In Summary

Many people are unaware of who they are and how their behaviours are read by others. In the immortal words of Robert Burns, Scotland's national poet, "Oh wad some power the giftie gie us; To see oursel's as others see us!"

Consider what you disclose to others, what you hide from others, and what others see but you are blind to. Coaching helps uncover the unknown Johari window, those things that are unknown to self and unknown to others.

You have habitual responses and behaviours, but unless you have stopped to look, you are likely to be unaware of these. Our lives are a mass of habits, but you can choose to change them.

Emotions are an expression of our needs. If you label your emotions, it helps your conscious mind deal with them. Four key aspects of emotional intelligence are self-awareness, self-management, social awareness and relationship management.

Empathy gives people the power to express themselves without fear, without feeling judged and found wanting. To be influential, you have to be good at empathic listening.

All individuals have dominant personality traits. Each trait can be beneficial and also detrimental to your success as a leader.

Cultural intelligence requires understanding how people view the world in terms of levels of hierarchy or egalitarianism, individualism or collectivism, care for others, tolerance of ambiguity, and focus on the short or long term.

Neuo Leadership Intelligence helps you lead with the brain in mind. It is important to understand the neuroscience behind what motivates people's behaviours and how they make decisions.

Organisational culture reflects how organisations do things and in some ways acts like an immune system preventing conflicting behaviours.

Beware the power of others. Take control. You have power within yourself. The power of you.

Those who dance are considered mad by those who cannot hear the music. Dance to your own tune.

Pause for Reflection

Reflect on the Johari Window. What are you hiding? What could you reveal?
   Think about the DISC model. How do you see yourself? Who are you?
   How do your colleagues see you?
   Looking in your mirror, what do you see as your key strengths?
   What do you see as your main opportunities to grow?

3

Finding Your Authentic Voice

Introduction

In Chapter 1 I took you on a journey to explore the mind, in Chapter 2 I asked you to look in the mirror to see yourself, and now in this chapter I turn to how you can find and speak with your true voice.

Here in this chapter I want to engage with you to help you find your authentic voice as a person, as a coach and as a leader.

Here I give you a space to think about your key beliefs and the values that drive your behaviour? What is your personality type? How well do you understand yourself and how congruent are you as a coach leader?

Here in my last chapter of Theme III, I ask you to reflect on how trusted and trustworthy you are. How approachable you are. What drives you? What is your purpose?

The principles discussed in this chapter are illuminated with real-life stories I researched for my book.

Finding Your Authentic Voice as a Person

I start with a true story of Fred, a mail carrier from Denver, Colorado in the USA, as told by Mark Sanborn in his powerful book, *The Fred Factor*.

Fred is no ordinary postman. He is a mail carrier who passionately loves his job and genuinely cares about the people he serves. Because of that, he is constantly going the extra mile handling the mail and sometimes watching

© The Author(s) 2019
N. Marson, *Leading by Coaching*, https://doi.org/10.1007/978-3-319-76378-1_3

over the houses of the people on his route, treating everyone he meets as a friend. While others might see delivering mail as monotonous drudgery, Fred sees an opportunity to make a difference in the lives of others.

Fred teaches us that if you put passion into your work and life, you can turn the ordinary into the extraordinary. "Whatever you are, be a good one"—attributed to Abraham Lincoln.

His book identifies four Fred Principles:

1. Are you making a difference?
2. Everything is built on relationships;
3. You must continually create value for others, and doing so doesn't have to cost a penny; and
4. You can reinvent yourself regularly; you can rejuvenate your working life.

How can you become a Fred? First, you can choose to be a Fred! Just choose to make a difference every day. Practise acts of kindness every day. Habits, as we have seen from Chapter 1, come from repetition.

Let me share how I experienced a Fred recently.

It was a dark and wet winter's Friday evening in London. I was cold and tired and looking forward to the weekend. The faster I could get home the better. I couldn't face the rush hour Underground crush, so I decided to treat myself to a taxi. All I could see around me was a plethora of taxis, but without any glowing yellow "hail me" lights. There was, however, a quick solution in my pocket. I got out my shiny new smartphone. Already I had downloaded a sea of apps. I scrolled impatiently until the taxi logo stared at me. A lift to the station was only a few clicks away. But something stopped my fingers. I was getting wetter and colder, but I didn't click the online taxi service. Why was this? Emotion was driving my decision. I would rather wait for a black cab with a cheery driver than use a company I was ambivalent about. Twenty minutes later as the black cab approached the station entrance, my driver said with a beaming smile "Thanks Guv and good luck with your football team tomorrow". He made me feel good.

As a business coach, I started to think on the train about the leadership lessons from my black cab experience. My first thought was that when you buy a product, it is the experience that counts. When you buy a taxi service, there is more to it than getting from A to B: it is how you arrive that matters. As Martin Luther King puts it, "if you are called to be a street sweeper, sweep the streets as Michelangelo painted or Beethoven composed music, or Shakespeare wrote poetry".[1] Do it wonderfully well. Fred was a postman and a good one because he wanted to make a difference to the community he served.

I call this the **art** of leadership: have the right **a**ttitude, that builds the right **r**elationships, that creates the right levels of **t**rust. And trust is the issue. As a leader, you lead at the speed of trust.

Employees treat customers as well as they are treated by their employers. Employees who trust their leaders and are proud of the company they are working for have a better attitude towards customers. They will smile more if they feel their bosses are listening to them and respecting their views. They will moan less if they feel their bosses are authentic and are treating them and others fairly.

If a taxi firm does not treat its drivers, like five-star drivers it is unlikely that customers will get a five-star service. The employees are custodians of the reputation of the company they work for and the CEO is the chief custodian. The best brands are loved by their loyal followers. Emotion trumps logic. Values translate into sustainable businesses.

This is about attitude. As John Maxwell observes about attitude, "it is a thing which draws people to us or repels them".[2] So does the leader of a firm make its people proud? Sadly, not always.

Time for an express course in employee relationships:

Listen, really listen to everyone;
Praise people and genuinely appreciate their contribution;
Start sentences with "Our".

Why does something so obvious and easy not happen? How do you as a leader overcome the *limbic* insecurities and destructive emotions that cause harm to your reputation, and the reputation of your company? You do this by becoming more aware, by training your mind. You should be present in the moment and fully conscious of what you are saying and doing. Mindful leadership is about being in control of your mind rather than your mind controlling you. If your thinking mind is in charge of your primitive emotional brain, you can deal effectively with whatever comes your way. Be the rider in charge of the elephant.

---

[1]https://www.youtube.com/watch?v=NlV_ODrEL0k.
[2]Rao, M. S. (2011, January 11). Book Review "Attitude" Authored By John C. Maxwell. Retrieved from http://profmsr.blogspot.com/2011/01/book-review-attitude-authored-by-john-c.html.

In a crowded marketplace, reputation makes you stand out. How the public, your customers and employees feel about your organisation will determine their loyalty to your brand. People choose with emotion and justify with logic.

Coca-Cola is one of the most recognisable and valuable brands in the world. They talk more about the lifestyle experience than the great taste. In McDonald's "*they're lovin' it*", the challenge for future business is how to add emotional value to the transaction.

To come back to my black cab experience: putting a smile on the face of your drivers so that they put a smile on the face of their passengers.

It's the little acts of kindness that build trust, those things that can too easily be seen as non-essentials that build relationships. Success comes from choosing to care and going the extra mile. And the road along the extra mile is travelled less frequently.

Understanding Beliefs and Values

When you understand yourself better, you will understand better, what drives you, what matters to you and how you feel the world ought to be. This is the concept of Self. Before you can find your authentic voice as a person, you need to find your authentic self first.

Pause for thought

Think of an event in your life that helped define who you are.
What guiding principle did that experience teach you?

Beliefs, values and behaviours are interrelated. In one view, variously attributed:

Your beliefs become your thoughts.
Your thoughts become your words.
Your words become your actions.
Your actions become your habits.
Your habits become your values.
Your values become your destiny.

If leadership is not about titles and positions, but about one life influencing another, what drives your leadership?

Beliefs are the assumptions we make from our life experiences that we hold to be true, whether or not they are. We generalise these past experiences and assume they will also apply in the future when making decisions. The Arab Spring was about a collective belief in the human right of freedom and autonomy.

As a leader, you need to have strong beliefs about what you hold to be right. You need to believe in yourself and what you are trying to do if you want your followers to believe in you as a leader. You are the **i** in belief.

Reflecting on interviews with Ronald and Nancy Reagan for CBS News, reporter Mike Wallace wrote: "When asked to name the last American leader he had a good deal of faith in, Mr. Reagan cited Franklin D. Roosevelt". "He took his case to the people", Mr. Reagan said. "The greatest leader is not necessarily the one who does the greatest things. He is the one that gets the people to do the greatest things". Looking back at the interview, Mrs. Reagan said that her husband lived up to his own definition. "He got them to believe in themselves once again", she said. "He got them to think about the whole country differently. Ronnie was always so optimistic. The glass was always half full. And he made people feel that way".[3]

Our values are a conscious operating guide in the sense that they drive our motivation. Values define what is important to us and what we aspire to. Our values stem from our beliefs and drive our behaviours.

Your personal values define who you are and reflect your needs. They can change as you change: for example, becoming a parent can change your values. Values drive your decision-making, your actions and your behaviours, and influence how you relate to your loved ones, your family, friends and your work colleagues.

Pause for thought

What are your top three personal values?
What personal value would you defend even at the cost of losing your job?
What corporate value would attract you towards a different job?
Think of a time when you have felt most proud, happy or fulfilled.
What made you feel that way?

Moral values are a code of conduct adapted by a culture, like the Ten Commandments from the Old Testament or the Universal Law of

---

[3]McDermott, T. (2004, June 6). Ronald Reagan Remembered. Retrieved from https://www.cbsnews.com/news/ronald-reagan-remembered/.

Buddhists. These values are widely admired within the group. In Medieval times, the Seven Christian Virtues held sway: Humility, Kindness, Temperance, Chastity, Patience, Charity and Diligence. In modern times, virtuous leaders define their role by serving others.

Serving others brings us to humility, an interesting concept given the size of egos visible in some leaders. It means you are not so blinded by your own brilliance that you are closed to the brilliance of others. Being modest means showing you respect the ideas and input of others, even when you are still the guiding light. Jim Collins, who wrote the ground-breaking book on sustainable organisations, *Good to Great*, writes that the highest-level leaders ("Level 5") show a paradoxical combination of "intense professional will and personal humility". They channel their ego needs away from themselves and into the larger good of building a great organisation. It doesn't mean that Level 5 leaders have no ego or self-interest, indeed they are incredibly ambitious, but their ambition is first and foremost for the organisation and not themselves. They are driven to produce sustained results for the organisation. Level 5 leaders don't talk about themselves; they talk about the contributions of others to the success of the organisation.

This requires courage: courage to trust yourself as a leader, courage to lead your followers to the top of their chosen mountains and courage to lead them beyond their boundaries. And courage is contagious.

In 2007 I had the privilege of talking to Leicester Tigers Academy about leadership. So how could a middle-aged consultant, whose athletic pinnacle was making the school's second rugby team, connect with a group of teenage sporting superstars?

I needed to get them engaged from the start. I decided to set them the task of choosing their leader. They could then explain their decision-making process and why they chose the person to be their captain. We talked about the personal qualities the person needed on and off the field and the behaviours they would expect from their leader. We then talked about the World Cup-winning England rugby team and how Sir Clive Woodward led them to victory. Winning for him was made possible by having the courage to follow your dreams and believing you can succeed. After the event, the academy manager told me the players had chosen the person that he had in his own mind as most suitable to be captain. They chose the person whose authentic voice best articulated their values and aspirations. A person who they believed had the courage and determination to lead them to achieve their sporting dreams.

Pause for thought

Who as a leader do you admire and why?

Organisations have values too. In Honda, they emphasise three things: making a difference today, doing the right thing and making time for each other. These are underpinned by a belief in respect for the individual and in making business and their products, a joyous experience.[4]

Organisational values should be part of your differentiation strategy, and they should give you a competitive advantage and energise people to join together.

If your personal values are not aligned with your organisational values, or indeed the way the organisation behaves negates values it publicly espouses, this will cause inner tension and stress. Your own ethical code will guide you when deciding what is right and what is wrong. It will help you resolve moral issues and be a true north compass for your behaviours.

Pause for thought

What are the values and beliefs of your organisation? Does it live them? Are they aligned to your personal values?
Are your values and beliefs conflicting with those of your organisation?
Can coaching reconcile conflicts between personal and corporate values?

Finding and Building Your Strengths

Exercise

Your child has just received their exam results. As expected she got an A in Politics, a B in philosophy, but only a D in History.
How would you start a conversation with her about her results?

Society has a fixation with what is wrong and bad instead of what is right and good. Health services have a focus on treating you when you are ill, not on how you can stay well. Our emotional brains, run by the *limbic system*,

---

[4]https://www.hondamanufacturing.co.uk/ethics-values/.

are running the show. How many training courses have you attended that focussed on developing the things you can be truly great at?

In the exercise above, did you start the conversation with the D in History or did you start by celebrating the A and B? Which might be most motivating for the child?

Playing to your strengths is a positive philosophy for growth and development. If you multiply the strengths of your talented people, then your organisation will be stronger. To excel in your chosen field, and to find lasting satisfaction in doing so, build your life around your strengths. Correcting your weaknesses will not make you excel but refining and focussing on your strengths will. Discover your strengths now and exploit them for your good and the good of others.

You have been given gifts to use them. As Marianne Williamson wrote in her book, *A Return to Love: Reflections on the Course of Miracles*, "Our deepest fear is not that we are inadequate, our deepest fear is that we are powerful beyond measure. It is our light, not our darkness, that most frightens us. We ask ourselves: Who am I to be brilliant, gorgeous, talented, and fabulous? Actually, who are you not to be? You are a child of God. Your playing small doesn't serve the world".[5]

Pause for thought

What are your top three strengths?
1.
2.
3.

One tool you can use to get a better understanding of your strengths is Don Clifton's strengthsfinder, based on research by Gallup. This looks at your natural patterns for thinking, feeling and behaving, with 34 resulting themes and five most dominant strengths. The power of strengthsfinder lies in the fact that it provides a common language to articulate the differences between people's strengths. There is a commonality of language. To master yourself you need to master the language to describe yourself. You need to be able to describe what you are and what you are not. And as a coach you need to master language so that you can master conversations.

---

[5]Mandela, N. (1994, May 9). Inaugural Address. Speech presented at Presidential Inauguration in South Africa, Cape Town. Retrieved from http://www.uh.edu/~hwagan/pnl/mandela.pdf.

While the previous chapter looked at personality traits via the DISC tool, we can also consider personality types. There is some blurring of the distinction between traits and types, or whether types are collections of traits, but in essence, traits tend to have more of a quantitative value while types have categories that are more qualitatively distinct.[6] Psychometric types can give you a broader indication of whether someone might suit a particular role. We can all develop skills in things we are less good at, but we are likely to perform best if we are true to type. These tests can also help you understand team dynamics, and why people with very different profiles might find the way colleagues approach tasks deeply frustrating.

For an alternative perspective on areas of strength, the Myers Briggs Type Indicator (MBTI) is well respected by Human Resources specialists, although its scientific rigour has been questioned by Merve Emre, an Associate Professor of English at Oxford University, in her 2018 book, *What's Your Type?* The MBTI instrument was developed by Isabel Myers and her mother Katharine Briggs as an application of Carl Jung's theory of psychological types. The theory suggests that we have opposite ways of gaining energy (Extraversion or Introversion), gathering or becoming aware of information (Sensing or Intuition), deciding or coming to a conclusion about that information (Thinking or Feeling) and dealing with the world around us (Judging or Perceiving). They propose 16 different types. For example, some people may be naturally stronger at analysing large amounts of data, while others are better at keeping harmony within a team; some may be frank and decisive, others may particularly want to understand what motivates people.

Finding Purpose

Many people do not take the time to work out what they really want in life, and what will make them fulfilled. It takes effort to consider if you are making a difference and whether that is the difference you really want to make. Finding your purpose in life will help you find your authentic voice.

Here are some examples of how two people in the film industry think about how they make a difference.

Walt Disney is credited with saying that he didn't make movies to make money, rather he made money to make movies. The Oscar winning Pixar

---

[6]Quenk, N. L. (1993). Personality Types or Personality Traits: What Difference Does It Make? *Bulletin of Psychological Type, 16*(2), 9–13. Retrieved from https://pdfs.semanticscholar.org/1867/e9e20c94ac37 d69ee3ee7f0cc2c2b38e91cc.pdf.

Director, Brad Bird, had a similar business ethos: "I want my films to make money, but money is just fuel for the rocket. What I really want to do is to go somewhere. I don't want to just collect more fuel".[7]

Other leaders have similarly been driven by purpose which gave them a distinctive and authentic voice.

Steve Jobs said in his 2005 Stanford University address: "Your time is limited, so don't waste it living someone else's life. Don't be trapped by dogma – which is living with the results of other people's thinking. Don't let the noise of other's opinions drown out your own inner voice. And most important, have the courage to follow your heart and intuition. They somehow already know what you truly want to become. Everything else is secondary".[8] He is sharing two powerful messages: take risks to pursue your dreams and see opportunities when you have setbacks. "Stay hungry. Stay foolish".

Richard Branson has also made a difference to his customers' lives. He advocates, in his book *The Virgin Way*, that "you should follow your dreams and just do it; do what you love; make a positive difference and do some good; believe in your ideas and be the best; have fun and look after your team; don't give up; listen; keep setting new challenges; delegate and spend more time with your family". He has an authentic voice and is able to clearly articulate his purpose. He is driven by his personal values and beliefs.

The straightest route to happiness is to find a purpose, a lifelong purpose that keeps you going through thick and thin. Einstein thought that you could only be happy if you attached yourself to a life purpose rather than people or possessions.

What is your purpose? What difference do you want to make to the world and to people who you have contact with? As American actress, comedian and producer Lily Tomlin is credited with saying, "I always wanted to be somebody, but now I realise I should have been more specific". Ask yourself: Why do I exist? What contribution do I want to make? The answers to these simple but profound questions will design your leadership footprint and leave your leadership legacy.

Finding a clear purpose, and being able to articulate it, will help you have more impactful conversations because it makes you more grounded, more

---

[7]Hayagreeva Rao, R. S. (2008, April). *Innovation lessons from Pixar: An interview with Oscar-winning director Brad Bird*. Retrieved from McKinsey Quarterly: https://www.mckinsey.com/business-functions/strategy-and-corporate-finance/our-insights/innovation-lessons-from-pixar-an-interview-with-oscar-winning-director-brad-bird.

[8]Huffington Post. (2011, May 10th). *Steve Jobs' 2005 Stanford Commencement Address: 'Your Time Is Limited, So Don't Waste It Living Someone Else's Life'*. Retrieved from Huffington Post: https://www.huffingtonpost.com/2011/10/05/steve-jobs-stanford-commencement-address_n_997301.html.

able to understand and appreciate other people's points of view. This is a vital quality for a coach. Self-exploration—the articulation of who I am—is the foundation stone of coaching.

Abraham Maslow, the late American psychologist, proposed a widely referred to "Hierarchy of Needs". While this is not based on significant empirical data, the source of its durability is because conceptually it is a thought-provoking framework. He believed that our most important personal need is to find meaning in our life by growing and learning, expressing our creativity and enthusiastically committing ourselves to a purpose. This philosophy is at the heart of Gestalt coaching which I turn to in Chapter 4. Self-actualisation is at the top of the hierarchy of needs and is the hardest to achieve for a lot of people. It happens when we can use our gifts to achieve a higher purpose. Let me take you down the hierarchy of needs pyramid. Below Self-actualisation at the top of the pyramid is Self-esteem.

Self-esteem is how we see ourselves in the world and the value we believe we bring. It shapes everything we do.

Love/belonging is a strong emotional driver for our species. We are social animals and we survive/thrive in our social groups.

Safety needs include avoiding or mitigating threats from the environment and other human beings.

Physiological needs sit at the bottom of the pyramid and includes water, food and shelter. These needs have to be satisfied before other needs surface.

Maslow's Hierarchy of Needs top three levels is useful as a framework for you the leader coach to ensure your people connect with their group, feel that the culture is psychologically safe, feel respected and feel that their job is worthwhile.

Self-Mastery

Self-mastery is self-knowledge. Inner knowledge of self. Self-discipline. Self-mastery is about resisting self-orientation and focussing your attentions on the needs of others. Your technical skills are not enough. You need people skills. You need to have personal influence. Your power comes from within you. Use your personal power, not your position, because as Napoleon Bonaparte remarked, "a throne is only a bench covered in velvet".

What defines you as a leader and as a coach is your emotional, social and cultural awareness. Leading and coaching with your brain in mind. Your inner leadership channelling your emotions into positive thinking. Thought is yourself in action.

Fig. 3.1 The Parallel Mind 7Ps Model

To master your enemies as Sun Tzu wisely observed in *The Art of War*, you must first master yourself: "If you know the enemy and know yourself, you need not fear the result of a hundred battles".

The Parallel Mind 7Ps Model (Fig. 3.1) will help you think around how you are satisfying your top three levels in the Hierarchy of Needs. Your purpose and how it drives your passion, helps you make the difference you want to make.

Thinking deeply about each of the 7Ps will help you find your authentic voice as a person, as a leader and as a coach. It will help you show you where you can shine most brightly.

How you are perceived is the culmination of all the 7Ps and is your personal brand. This is why self-awareness and reflection are so important for you to be the best leader you can be. It is why feedback is so critical to understanding the difference between your intentions and the impacts your communication has on others. Who will you ask to hold up the mirror? The important thing with your journey is to begin it. "Until one is committed, there is hesitancy, the chance to draw back, always ineffectiveness. Concerning all acts of initiative (and creation), there is one elementary truth, the ignorance of which kills countless ideas and splendid plans: that the moment one definitely commits oneself, then providence moves too. All sorts of things occur to help one that would never otherwise have occurred. A whole stream

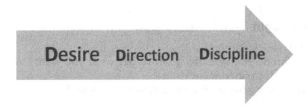

Fig. 3.2 The Parallel Mind 3Ds Model

of events issues from the decision, raising in one's favour all manner of unforeseen incidents and meetings and material assistance, which no man could have dreamt would have come his way… Whatever you can do or dream you can, begin it. Boldness has genius, power and magic in it!"[9] So start it now!

The Parallel Mind 3Ds for Success Framework is a simple model that may help you focus on what you want and help you get it (Fig. 3.2).

Desire is the most important of the three Ds. Without desire, you won't have the discipline to achieve your dreams. Desire is knowing what you want and wanting it greatly.

Direction: If you don't have a clear direction, you will end up somewhere, but it is unlikely to be where you would most want to be. A map can help. Your **map** is **m**astering your technical skills, having **a**utonomy, that is, freedom of action and having a clear **p**urpose. Direction is making sure you are on track to get what you desire.

Discipline: What will you sacrifice to achieve your dreams? What obstacles will you overcome? It is not how many times you fall down that matters, it is how many times you pick yourself up. How you deal with setbacks defines you.

For example, you are an associate in a professional services firm with a burning Desire to become a partner and that Direction does not seem to be possible at your firm. Are you prepared to give up what you like at your current firm and join another firm in order to become a partner. Will you be Disciplined in seeing through that change? Finding and staying true to the authentic you, takes courage and commitment.

To achieve your dreams, master yourself and lead from the inside out.

Self-mastery and inner leadership are prerequisites for finding and using your authentic voice.

---

[9]This quotation by W. H. Murray, the Scottish mountaineer, is from an extremely loose translation of Goethe's *Faust*, Goethe's *Faust* lines 214–230, made by John Anster in 1835 and is widely misattributed to Johann Wolfgang von Goethe.

Finding Your Authentic Voice as a Coach

Being authentic means being who you truly are, being fully comfortable in your skin. Being authentic is also about being non-judgemental and forgiving of yourself and of others.

Being an authentic coach is about bringing all of yourself to your coaching sessions. That requires not holding back, but having courage, knowing your strengths and weaknesses (which the previous section will have helped you with) and being positive: being true to yourself so you can allow those you are working with to be true to themselves.

Coaching is, in essence, a conversation with a purpose. If you want to be impactful, you must have a clear purpose that is shared by your client and that moves your organisation forward in its desired direction. Without purpose, passion is pointless. Coaching has to have a point to it. There must be a clear goal. Something to strive for that would be difficult to achieve alone.

You must find your authentic voice before you can help others find theirs. You have to be more of yourself to help people you coach to be more of themselves.

I found my authentic voice on the Advanced Level International Coach Federation Executive Coaching Programme in 2007. This is the feedback from my final dissertation: *Who I am as a Coach*

"A clear pass. Your essay was a real pleasure to read. What comes across most is that the courage at the heart of your model has been captured in the essay throughout, not least in adopting the style of writing from the heart. Further, your essay comes from a real place of knowing: knowing that coaching is an expression of humanity; knowing that personal mastery is a pre-requisite of a great coach; and knowing that you are enough. This knowledge—or wisdom—comes from your journey to find your authentic self. And it seems very much that you have. We look forward to hearing of your progress as you continue to put your learning into practice by increasing your percentage of coaching clients".

What I realised is that the most important thing about my coaching is to be myself. Who I am is enough in itself. As a coach, you listen to people and witness them. You give them a safe space to hear themselves.

Witnessing someone is to be with them, truly present with them, so they feel they are not alone. They feel someone is there for them trying to understand them.

The following true stories illustrate dramatically the power of just being there for someone, when they feel at their most vulnerable, and witnessing their pain as a fellow human being. You don't have to become their friend, but you should be committed to care about their well-being.

That is why coaching works. Because it is based on being human, being vulnerable and showing compassion.

On the East Coast of America, the Manhattan Suicide Prevention Hotline wasn't working. People were jumping off the Brooklyn Bridge with alarming regularity. So, what were the eager, well-trained New York City volunteers doing that was so wrong? After all, they were giving their desperate clients every reason to live. Today, thankfully, far fewer people are plunging to their death in the icy cold waters of the East River, a tributary of the Hudson River. So, what are the volunteers doing differently? It turns out their clients just wanted to be listened to, to feel that someone cared. Now the volunteers are trained to listen for the first ten minutes of the call, as a minimum. By just listening without interrupting, their clients can listen to themselves, to their own story. Their story is the common human bond. Empathy builds rapport which helps establish a trusting relationship. They don't want reasons why they shouldn't jump, rather they want to reassess what drove them to consider jumping in the first place.

On the West Coast of America, the Los Angeles Suicide Hotline also illustrates graphically how choosing to care about a fellow human being, by witnessing them and sharing their pain, saves lives.

Los Angeles Suicide Prevention Hotline

It was on 26 October 2015, 11 p.m., Nick Holt, a volunteer at the Didi Hirsch Suicide Prevention Hotline in Los Angeles sat by the phone in his glass cubicle. He was well-trained and confident but when your job is to save lives at the other end of the line, you can never be overconfident. You never know who is going to call, or who is truly on the line. What follows is Nick's account of that fateful October night. The emphasis in bold is mine.

I waited nervously for the first caller. After a few minutes, that seemed much longer,

the phone jumped into life. I picked it up nervously. A young man started to talk quickly,

his breathing quickening as he spoke.

He wasn't making much sense. When people call a suicide prevention hot-line, they often don't know how to start the conversation. How do you tell someone you want to kill yourself? Johnny was no different.

"My name is Nick, so what is going on Johnny?" I asked tentatively. "Everything is against me". Johnny replied hopelessly. He sounded distraught. "Are you thinking of suicide?" I asked. "Yes" He said. "And how are you thinking of killing yourself?" I asked nervously. "I'm going to jump in front of a train" he said.

I took a deep breath. I was shocked. Usually the answer is, "I don't know". "And where are you now?" I asked. "I'm lying down on the train tracks" came the reply. My stomach churned. My throat tightened. My foot began shaking, and I closed my eyes. I felt a bead of sweat run down the side of my face. Johnny's life was in the balance and he had no one to talk to except me.

I tuned into his voice, his cadence. I listened to his breathing, the sense of anxiety and dread building. **The absence of sound or talking could be just as important as filling the silence.** *But I had to find something I could use to connect. "How long have you been hurting Johnny?" I asked. "I'm done, nobody cares". Johnny replied. "You sound exhausted". I observed. Johnny was silent. In the distance, I thought I heard the piercing sound of a train's whistle. My heart rate quickened.*

"I wonder if there is a part of you that wants to live?" I asked. "I'm not sure I want to die". Johnny said. "That train sounds like it's getting closer" I said. "Yep, it's coming right at me". "Are you going to let it hit you?" I asked. The train whistle grew louder. Suddenly, Johnny took a deep breath and exhaled quickly.

"I think I want to live tonight". He said. I heard the cacophony of a train passing by, the whoosh of air in the receiver of the phone. The train had passed by inches away. My body shook with relief.[10]

Nick's story tells us that we all suffer but many of us suffer alone, and sharing, feeling connected to another person makes us feel alive. It builds our self-esteem. Loneliness is the subjective feeling of having inadequate social connections. Our brains, as we learned in Chapter 1, are social and need to feel connected to their social group. Opportunities to connect on a human level at work are scarce, indeed half of CEOs report feeling lonely in their

---

[10]Holt, N. (2016, October 26th). *How working for a suicide prevention hotline made me rethink pain and empathy.* Retrieved from Vox: https://www.vox.com/2015/10/26/9601710/suicide-prevention-hotline.

roles, many suffering from depression. As the 1990s billboard advertisements promoting *The Economist* magazine wittily put it, *It's lonely at the top, but at least there is something to read.*[11]

And a coach often acts as a confidant. Someone authentic and trusted to talk to.

Leaders are unlikely to encounter such bleak scenarios in conversations with their staff, and if they do, should turn to their HR department to direct people to professional help. But the stories illustrate the key message about the importance of connecting with others.

The point of telling these poignant stories is that people need to feel witnessed for their lives to make sense. And this is what coaches do, they witness their client's pain, so they feel heard and understood. Listening deeply allows their client to hear their own voice.

Coaching can be cathartic—only if the coach is authentic and is present with the client; only if the coach can hold long silences for the reality of the client's situation to emerge; only if the coach can suspend beliefs and be non-judgemental; and only if the coach can have unconditional regard for the client.

Coaches must be masters of themselves and masters of conversation to be masters of coaching. The right attitude is everything. "Attitude is a librarian of our past, a custodian of our present and a prophet of our future". John Maxwell.

Wendy Levinson, a medical researcher in the USA, found surgeons who had never been sued, spent more than three minutes longer with each patient than those who had been sued. They were more likely to engage in active listening, saying things like "Tell me more about that". There was no difference in the amount or quality of information they gave their patients. The difference was entirely in how they talked to their patients.[12] They had a more caring attitude.

Loneliness causes stress and chronic stress can hijack your brain's *prefrontal cortex*, which governs decision-making, planning, emotional regulation, analysis and abstract thinking. We live in the most technologically connected age in the history of civilisation. But despite Facebook, and other

[11]The Economist. (2008, September 16th). *Sympathy for the boss.* Retrieved from The Economist: https://www.economist.com/business/2008/09/16/sympathy-for-the-boss.
[12]Boodman, S. G. (1997, February 25th). *Silent Doctors More Likely to Be Sued.* Retrieved from The Washington Post: https://www.washingtonpost.com/gdpr-consent/?destination=%2farchive%2flifestyle%2fwellness%2f1997%2f02%2f25%2fsilent-doctors-more-likely-to-be-sued%2fa271caf1-5a0a-48ff-8c26-c7-19fcb8d91c%2f%253futm_term%253d.87b8103c6ce1%3f&utm_term=.dccc01d26aa3.

social platforms, 40% of adults in America report feeling lonely[13] and the number of people who report having a close confidant in their lives has been declining. Loneliness is an epidemic at home and at work.

The following organisational change story demonstrates how witnessing each other can build morale in a business.

Rabobank in the Netherlands sought to address plummeting morale, after the LIBOR interest rate scandal that hit many banks, by starting meetings asking three questions:

> how are you feeling?
>   is there something distracting you from being fully present at this meeting?
>   what is your intention for this meeting?[14]

People came to meetings to connect and learn, not to make their point or score points. Social interaction was more important than getting a reaction. A culture of dialogue, based on empathic listening, was emerging where people felt they belonged, they felt a shared sense of purpose. This culture of safety, where people could express their concerns freely, created a much more joined-up and productive bank. Engaging people's emotions boosts motivation and collaboration.

Google's research to find out what was different in their most effective teams discovered the main difference was psychological safety.[15] When people feel psychologically safe at work, they feel able to show themselves without fear of negative consequences to self-image, status or career. Feeling safe at work is dependent on four things: supervisor relations (which has a dramatic impact on psychological safety); co-worker relations; being fully engaged; and having meaningful work.

Individuals have a primary psychological motivation to seek meaning in their work. According to Gallup's 2017 research of over two million workers, the best performing firms manage to achieve 70% of their people being engaged compared with an abysmal global average of 13% engaged. Engagement means harnessing and fulfilling the human spirit at work. By

---

[13]Entis, L. (2016, June 22nd). Chronic Loneliness Is a Modern-Day Epidemic. Retrieved from Fortune: http://fortune.com/2016/06/22/loneliness-is-a-modern-day-epidemic/.

[14]Sadoulet, L. (2016, June 22nd). *Three Questions to a More Enlightened Business*. Retrieved from INSEAD Knowledge: https://knowledge.insead.edu/operations/three-questions-to-a-more-enlightened-business-4824#do2ctr6ZPBJg1wUV.99.

[15]Rozovsky, J. (2015, November 17). *The five keys to a successful Google team*. Retrieved from re:Work: https://rework.withgoogle.com/blog/five-keys-to-a-successful-google-team/.

contrast, the Gallup World Poll sadly reported that many people hate their work and especially their boss.[16]

According to Gallup, if leaders want to prioritise one action, it should be to equip their managers to become coaches. Organisations like Google, who have a systematic approach to using coaching as a personal development tool at all levels, improve organisational performance and are likely to have a more sustainable business. Better conversations lead to better outcomes.

Conversations build trust, develop talent and drive change. Conversations are the engine of change and trust is the fuel.

Employees want a coach, not a boss. Unlike telling people what to do, coaching builds self-reliance and engagement; the most powerful conversations are the ones that are personally meaningful. Everyday coaching conversations (covered in Chapter 6) focussed on development and growth are very motivating. It is no surprise that Google's most important managerial competency is coaching skill. Employees want a coach who trusts them and who they can trust. A coach who gives them psychological safety and who asks rather than tells. This is *Leading by Coaching* at the speed of trust, one conversation at a time.

Approachability

Coaching conversations should be everyday, anywhere conversations. Coaching conversations should be spontaneous as well as planned. This means leaders need to be approachable, to put aside their insecurities and vulnerabilities.

I asked my colleague Derek Benton to call on his considerable corporate experience of coaching and developing people to share his thoughts on being approachable as an authentic leader.[17]

> **"No surprises management"**
>
> My days in corporate life were brightened by the mantra of "No surprises management". It gave hope to the idea that almost anything could be said and discussed in the expectation that it was always better to be honest about the ups and downs of business life, to identify issues well in advance and to deal with

---

[16]Clifton, J. (2017, June 13th). *The World's Broken Workplace*. Retrieved from Gallup: http://news.gallup.com/opinion/chairman/212045/world-broken-workplace.aspx.

[17]Derek Benton is a Parallel Mind Consultant and former international Director of Martindale-Hubbell.

them in to your planning rather than to have an unexpected or undisclosed issue wreak havoc in an ever-darkening drama.

Note I say, "almost anything" could be said. What remained unsaid was largely a factor of the human condition, dependent on the trust and quality of relationships between individuals in the hierarchy of corporate life. And there lay the problem and the solution. Trust in a business relationship is built upon the quality of conversations between individuals and teams.

Surprise and delight and surprise and fright are two sides of the same coin

Dull as it may seem, to practise "No surprises management" you have to cover, encompass all potential surprises, good or bad. We all like nice surprises, but the conditions for those to arise are the same as the unwelcome surprise. Someone is holding back on some vital information, that if released would avoid unexpected tension and drama. In business, surprises mean you are not able to plan to manage the unforeseen, to either exploit it fully or mitigate it adequately. To encourage a "no surprises" culture that leads to quality conversations you have to be approachable, open to listening, both to the good and the bad that business life throws at you. Being approachable creates opportunities for learning by being truly open to non-judgemental listening.

An open door

"I have an open-door policy" is a favourite phrase of all who want to appear open and readily available to colleagues. But how often do colleagues, or indeed clients, take you up on the offer and to what end? Leaders in firms are successful people. Driven, decisive, courageous and dedicated are just some of the attributes that you would associate with good leaders in a complex organisation. But approachable? Most leaders would like to think so, but there are real obstacles to delivering on that promise.

Talking to power

As leaders take office and assume the power of their position, something happens. We talk about the aura and mantle of leadership. Those very words to describe the "condition" imply a physicality, almost a barrier around the leader that has to be overcome to get to the person within. Being approachable is to understand what it is like for an individual to make that approach, and the calculations made by them in expectation of the value, or threat, of that encounter with you. Being approachable means you need to understand what you need to offer of yourself, that will ensure an approach is welcomed and is a positive experience.

Senior leaders in professional services firms who coach and are involved in managing the career path of rising stars can be in shock and disbelief when that star decides to leave the organisation without any prior warning. Despite, in most cases, an extremely good working relationship, something had remained unsaid. This should set leaders thinking about the real costs of not being approachable for the conversations that really matter. The starting point is to choose to care about the welfare of a person first and then their performance as a colleague. People want to feel looked after by their leaders and need to feel psychologically safe.

Start to have better conversations

How can you have better, more impactful, conversations that lead to fewer surprises? Well, you can start with a reality check on your openness to listening to the good and the bad and thinking about your reaction and levels of empathy to the colleagues and clients engaged in conversations.

Ask yourself how many times in the last few months have I:

- had a colleague confide in me or confided in them?
- taken a colleague under my wing to lunch with no agenda?
- asked about their wellbeing and the balance of pressures?
- expressed an interest in their outside work activities?
- celebrated success?
- accepted failure with grace and a sense of learning?
- given informal feedback?
- asked for feedback?
- praised good work?
- shown gratitude for discretionary extra effort?
- introduced them to my key contacts?
- reflected on my communication and leadership styles?
- tried new approaches to being approachable?

Relationships that endure take time and the confidence to let them develop often builds one act at a time. So, think about the things that get in the way and the things that accelerate your approachability. Remember self-awareness is how you process your thinking about your thinking.

Barriers to approachability:

- inauthenticity
- professional mask
- lack of personal trust
- fear of losing formal authority
- perception of colleagues as competitors
- open door but shut mind

Addressing barriers:

- choosing to care
- showing empathy
- seeking first to understand
- humility
- deep listening
- straight talking

Pause for thought

Are you approachable? Do you have an open door? How authentic are you as a leader and a coach? What are the barriers for your people approaching you?

Finding Your Authentic Voice as a Leader

If one definition of a leader is somebody who people choose to follow, then why should anybody follow you? They may comply to protect their career, but why should they commit?

Pause for thought

Think of three reasons why anybody should follow you
1.
2.
3.

Know your strengths and play to them. Be who you are, not who you think other people want you to be. Be authentic at all times, and don't be afraid to show who you are when challenged. Defend your values and stand up for what you believe is right.

Is that an approach for how you might want to be in life?

There is no right way or wrong way to lead. Leadership style is a matter of personal choice and can change, depending on a number of factors.

The leadership style you choose depends on the situation you are in, the personalities involved, the context and the objectives you are trying to meet. Sometimes you need to be directing, sometimes supporting, sometimes delegating and, as much as possible, developing through coaching. You need to be a versatile leader.

My personal key principles of effective people leadership: rely on persuasion not power, delegate outcomes not actions, appreciate success and lessons from failure equally.

After Kenneth Lay, former Chief Executive of Enron, was convicted in 2006 of massive fraud and conspiracy charges, a whistle-blower made the following remark: "We want honest leaders who are decisive, creative, optimistic and even courageous. But often we don't even look for one of the most critical traits of a leader: humility".[18] A humble leader listens to others, values input from employees even if it is bad news. Humility is marked by an ability to admit mistakes.

---

[18]Yeshua Catholic International Leadership Institute. (2015, July 13th). *The Enron Lesson: Servant Leadership in the News*. Retrieved from Yeshua Leader: http://www.yeshualeader.com/Resources/News/articleType/ArticleView/articleId/2076/THE-ENRON-LESSON-SERVANT-LEADERSHIP-IN-THE-NEWS.

Kazuo Inamori, the 85-year-old former Chairman of Japan Airlines, makes the point that if one's attitude is negative, the results of life or work will also become negative. He notes that early in life, he developed a formula for life:

Life = Attitude × Effort × Ability. If attitude is even slightly negative then all the results become negative.[19]

Being driven by a strong guiding philosophy, he says, "creates a positive way of thinking: these positive thoughts are the seeds for beautiful flowers, and you must keep your thoughts pure by weeding the garden of your heart. Ask yourself what the right thing is to do as a human being?".

Businesses should be transparent and accountable to their stakeholders and open to public scrutiny and inspection. Businesses should be ethical, just because you can, doesn't mean you should.

Ethical leaders are designing the world they want, serving others through a common identity, creating meaning and belonging, seeing the whole as an interconnected system and leading mindfully. The ethical leaders are doing the right thing, not necessarily the easy thing.

As well as honesty, clearly lacking with Enron, other key elements of authenticity are integrity and sincerity. The word integrity is derived from the Latin word integritas meaning "wholeness". Integrity creates trust. Integrity is when your outside is a true reflection of your inside, when your actions are based on your values. You are being true to your personal guiding principles when you have no double standards. Integrity is about being true to others by not lying to yourself, by not letting your brain deceive itself.

Sincerity is saying what you mean and meaning what you say. Make your key beliefs and values explicit so you will be seen as authentic.

Authenticity reduces perceived personal risk, so it is the lifeblood of trust.

Authentic leaders are real people with a genuine personality whose behaviour is driven by their values and beliefs. They are open and transparent with clear, sincere intentions. You know where they stand, and you know where you stand with them. They are honest and have integrity, their outside reflects their inside. They are straight talkers but give feedback with sensitivity. Their followers are happy to give discretionary effort because they feel engaged, valued and appreciated.

---

[19]Inamori, K. (n.d.). *The Result of Life or Work = Attitude x Effort x Ability*. Retrieved from Official Website of Kazuo Inamori: https://global.kyocera.com/inamori/philosophy/philosophy03.html.

Inauthentic leaders are hiding behind their professional mask. Being all things to all people. Difficult to trust. You don't know what they are thinking and what their real motivations and intentions are, so you are always on your guard, always holding back. You do not respect inauthentic leaders because they lack integrity. You play the game, so they cannot criticise you, but you do the minimum you can get away with to stay off their radar. You do not feel engaged, valued or appreciated.

Pause for thought

Are you authentic as a leader? What makes you authentic?

Authenticity is the soul of a leader. Who you are should be who people follow. Who you are should be how you lead. Who you are matters. Being yourself matters. Self-awareness is the key to authenticity.

As T. S. Elliot put it in *Little Gidding*:

We shall not cease from exploration
And the end of all our exploring
Will be to arrive where we started
And know the place for the first time.[20]

Let us look at the attributes of an authentic leader with an example. The following interview is deliberately chosen from outside the business world. It provides a fresh perspective into the challenges you encounter as you develop and start to lead others. Everyone can be a leader by the standards they set and the example they give.

Everyday leadership can be observed everywhere, as I did when I first met Danny Martin washing the dishes at New Romney station café! Danny's story is important because it shows how his sense of self and self-awareness are important traits in developing an authentic *Leading by Coaching* style.

Interspersed with his story are my observations that highlight the points made in my book and the leadership lessons you can take away.

---

[20]Eliot, T. S. (1947). "Little Gidding." Four Quartets. Harcour: San Diego. http://www.columbia.edu/itc/history/winter/w3206/edit/tseliotlittlegidding.html.

My Leadership Journey

Danny Martin General Manager Romney, Hythe & Dymchurch Railway

This is Danny's unedited story as told to me.

My lifelong love affair with the RHDR started at the age of nine years old

As I stood with my dad on the bridge at New Romney station and witnessed the power of steam approach and disappear under me I was hooked. The magnificent engine, the smell of smoke, the sound of the whistle. This overpowering cocktail assaulted my senses. Two years later I signed up as a volunteer. It allowed me to escape my social isolation and overcome my shyness. Belonging felt good. Doing something for nothing also felt good. The railway was to become and define my life.

Observation: social isolation restricts people's development and contribution. We learn best in informal social groups where there is a shared interest, passion or, best of all, purpose. The brain is social.

Last train leaves the station

Then just when I was finding my social feet disaster struck. The railway was going to close in 1972. The money had run out. The last packed train had left the station, and with it my new world.

The station reopens

The local community was missing its railway. How could it be saved? Shares were offered to a consortium of enthusiasts. The railway reopened the following April. My father bought me 100 shares. I was now the part owner of my beloved railway. I continued as a volunteer. Life was good again.

Observation: people need to feel they belong, that they fit in with their group. People thrive in social groups and shared passion drives innovation. Commitment also comes with ownership: owners see things through different eyes than employees. Owners should remember this when they attempt to motivate employees.

Train to Loughborough

My train from Folkestone was taking me on a new journey beyond my cosseted world in Kent. I was embarking on my university education to study transport management and planning.

In the holidays, I returned to the RHDR to my first paid job on the railway at the age of 19.

Next stop Ramsgate Station

Having obtained a first-class degree, I joined the British Rail ("BR") graduate training programme in 1980.

Observation: achieving excellent results requires focusing. Focusing allows the brain to make more connections.

My first job was in charge of Ramsgate Station at the age of 22 and my first challenge was how to motivate 70 female cleaners who worked through the night to ensure the station was ready for the morning commuters. I soon realised that the most important factor for them was social interaction. So, I let them go home early to their families once they had finished their duties. I also empowered them to organise a cooking rota for a communal meal to keep them going through the night and have a good chat.

Observation: as well as being social the brain also likes autonomy, to be in control. If you give people both elements it is a powerful recipe for highly-motivated teams. Innovative organisations, such as Google, recognise this and empower their people to socialise and spark off each other. If you give people responsibility, they tend to take it.

I made sure that I knew all their names and used to get quite cross with myself if I occasionally forgot a name. This personal touch engendered a lot of loyalty. To this day I have always attached the most importance to making staff feel valued and appreciated, that they are part of a family of workers rather than employee numbers on a payroll.

Final British Rail stop Reading Station

My final role was in charge of Reading Station. With 1200 staff it was a bit more challenging to remember all their names, but I tried. The people that I had regular contact with were certainly easier to remember than the ones I bumped into occasionally on the platform. My people focus was still strong, but I was becoming a safety management specialist. After 20 years with BR I was looking to return to Kent and work more closely with people again.

Observation: identity is important to people. Calling me by my name reinforces my identity: you see me therefore I exist. It sends a signal that you care about me. You took the trouble to remember my name, so I will take the trouble to listen to you. This is the power of reciprocity.

Leading the world's smallest public railway

When John Snell, heritage railway pioneer, retired as managing director of RHDR in 1999 after 27 years I was asked to follow in his footsteps. It was a great honour and a daunting challenge. I spent the first five years learning how things were done.

A small group of staff were the stalwarts and the nucleus of the management powerhouse. But they were old school, used to giving orders, as their previous boss had done, and not expecting or wanting their authority to be challenged.

Gradually I changed the management culture, helped by retirements, to a more engaging, empowering and personal style. I practised and encouraged a coaching style of leading, sitting with employees and observing/coaching them on the job. Even when they did a perfect job it was good for them to get a "well done" from the boss to give some reinforcement of good practice and confirmation that they were doing a good job.

People matter: And when only 35 of the 135 RHDR railway staff are being paid it is vital that the volunteers feel listened to and their contributions are recognised. Their efforts are discretionary.

Observation: an autonomous style of leadership relies on fear to get results. This style limits the development of personal potential and stifles innovation. People tend to do their job without thinking and leave quickly at the end of their shift. Praise makes people grow. All motivation is intrinsic and self-directed. If you make people feel good about themselves, you get more co-operation and more energy.

Staff should also be accountable for their contribution, paid or not. Quality was the goal in everything on the railway and cost was also a critical factor. We needed a viable railway that was going to be our legacy. Our purpose in life was to preserve the unique and special steam experience for generations of 9-year olds and their parents.

Observation: the power of purpose and meaning in people's work, here preserving for the future, fuels their passion. Enthusiasm is infectious. It gets caught by the customers, as evidenced by the RHDR feedback on Tripadvisor.

Understanding money was an important part of an ongoing education programme. The triangle of focus was people, money and the railway. If you look after the first two, the last one looks after itself. I introduced an informal performance review system focusing on strengths and aspirations.

Observation: personal ownership of learning and development, with mentoring and coaching support, was the precursor to improving every aspect of the business. It produced 135 sets of eyes and ears all with the same goal of improving the RHDR customer experience. Engaging people is important and empowering and encouraging people to take initiatives to improve safety and service were critically important in developing this product and making the business more robust.

Fatality on the railway

The first of the two fatalities on the RHDR was a train driver at a level crossing. There followed a lot of emotional outpouring and overwhelming public support. The accident changed the style of management to make it more democratic.

Observation: fairness is important to the brain. Social standing in our group is important to our survival. People want to be consulted by their leader. They want to feel their voice is heard, their vote really counts, and so their social status is enhanced.

The power of emotions to bring about change should never be underestimated. The brain's limbic system has a strong memory and a huge impact on our unconscious feelings. This surfaces into our thinking brains and becomes a compelling change story that drives our actions. Shared grief binds people together, and emotional contagion is a powerful force for change.

The second fatality was also on a crossing but this one was different. This one was personal. The train driver who was killed was my wife Suzanne. This was the most difficult time of my life and I nearly left the railway. Suzanne was also my RHDR second in command. After much painful deliberation I chose to stay and make the RHDR even more safe and successful.

Observation: this demonstrates determination in the face of the worst adversity imaginable. Whatever our circumstances we always have choices.

We brought in more outside specialist volunteers to widen our vision and challenge our thinking. Over the last few years, the railway has gone from strength to strength. We carry over 180,000 passengers a year. We are financially independent and able to run our railway from the ticket receipts and commercial activities without any reliance on grants or gifts. We have a 30-year plan with cash in the bank for major station refurbishments.

Stepping down

I will always work on the RHDR but one day when I and others feel the time is right I will step down from my paid general manager role. Every business needs new ideas and fresh energy.

I believe my successor will need to have the following qualities: to care deeply about the railway; to care about the people that run the railway and to be strong, determined and resilient to make sure the railway continues to run for future generations.

My leadership legacy

I would like to be remembered as a leader "who cared about this railway and gave of their all".

The same words are on the gravestone of my wife Suzanne who gave her life for the railway.

Reflections on Danny's Leadership style:

Danny is a passionate man driven by a strong purpose and vision.

He is an authentic person. He engenders respect and support from his staff.

Danny cares about his people, he really cares. He is the epitome of a servant leader.

He is also an inspirational leader: he is the change he seeks.

Danny leads with moral authority. His followers choose to follow him. They believe he is a good person with a shared passion for the railway.

He leads by example. He becomes what he repeatedly does. Excellence is a habit. Habit rewires the brain: *what fires rewires.*

Danny also knows how to run a small business.

He understands how money works and the importance of cash. He is financially savvy.

His focus on people and money will ensure Danny leaves a strong RHDR legacy.

The next Managing Director has a hard act to follow.

The most impressive leaders are often invisible leaders and sometimes unsung heroes. My definition of a leader is somebody people choose to follow, rather than have to. The difference is brought to a sharp focus when you compare volunteers with paid employees. That is what is so impressive about Danny. His volunteers can walk away. Their effort is entirely discretionary. It needs a special type of leader who can motivate them to stay and put in the extra effort needed to keep things on track.

Pause for thought

What do you think are the attributes of a natural leader?

The Trusted Leader

The trusted leader behaves authentically, communicates with the listener in mind and engages emotionally (Fig. 3.3).

The word trust is derived from the Norse word traustr, meaning "strong".

Trust is like oxygen: vital to human flourishing and unnoticed until it goes missing. Relationships are based on trust. Trust is based on common values, understanding, reliability and shared boundaries about what is and isn't allowed. Boundaries define the space in which we operate. The greater the trust, the greater the space—the greater the opportunities to influence. Trust is a relationship based on listening conversations and behaviours.

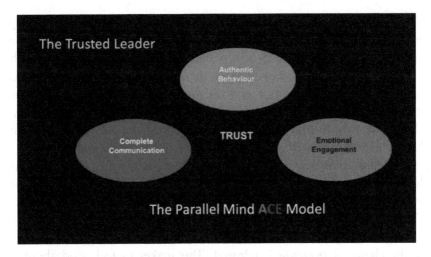

Fig. 3.3 The Parallel Mind ACE Model

Among the tribes of Northern Natal in South Africa, the most common greeting, equivalent to "hello" in English, is the expression: "Sawu bona". It literally means, "I see you". If you are a member of the tribe, you reply by saying: "Sikhona", "I am here". The order of the exchange is important: until you see me, I do not exist. It's as if, when you see me, you bring me into existence.

Trust is about predictability. People feel safer when their leader's behaviour is predictable. They know where they stand. They can then assess their situation and decide what to do in their own best interests. The brain craves certainty. It is wired to move towards reward and away from danger. Survival in the modern world depends on the ability to influence your peers in your social in-group. If you are working for an organisation where you don't trust your leaders, you will be less able to influence them because of a lack of intimacy. You are unlikely to have their ear. Your social brain will feel isolated and vulnerable, even threatened.

Trust involves taking a risk. Trust involves giving someone the benefit of the doubt. It is much easier to trust a person than an organisation. Trust in an organisation resides in its leader. The personality of the leader becomes the personality of the organisation. Trust is personal. Virgin *is* Richard Branson.

Christopher Columbus is credited with saying *You can never cross the ocean until you have the courage to lose sight of the shore.* But how *do* you know who to trust? People size you up in seconds, so first impressions matter. Harvard social psychologist Amy Cuddy says that people quickly answer two questions when they first meet you: Can I trust you? Can I respect you?[21] Psychologists refer to these dimensions as warmth and competence, respectively. Warmth or trustworthiness is the most important factor in how people evaluate you. When you share the values of your leader and believe them to be morally good as a person, you are more open to change, more accepting of risk, more collaborative, more innovative and more engaged.

From an evolutionary perspective, it is crucial to our survival to know whether a person deserves our trust. It was more important to figure out if your fellow man was going to kill you and steal your possessions than whether they could build a good fire. Strength only becomes a gift after trust is established.

When we trust someone, the chemical *oxytocin* is released, which makes us feel good. *Oxytocin* is a social lubricator. When leaders give us equal status, the chemical *serotonin* is released. This makes us feel good about ourselves and our leaders. These chemicals drive collaboration. They replace fear with reward. All progress is based on trust. Trust your gut feeling. As the Chinese proverb says, "if you suspect a man, don't employ him. If you employ him, don't suspect him".

Pause for thought

Why should anyone trust you as a leader?

How to build trust—your checklist, do you:
communicate openly and honestly
listen to your followers and value what they say
keep your promises and deliver on your commitments
put the interests of your followers first
take a real interest in your followers
disclose your real self—using your authentic voice
show your vulnerabilities, selectively

High levels of trust produce more engaging, impactful coaching conversations.

New neuroscientific research shows that in many ways our brains are hardwired to trust others. This aspect of our human nature is one reason

---

[21]Goudreau, J. (2016, January 16th). *A Harvard psychologist says people judge you based on 2 criteria when they first meet you.* Retrieved from Business Insider: https://www.businessinsider.com/harvard-psychologist-amy-cuddy-how-people-judge-you-2016-1?Fr=US&IR=T.

that having your trust betrayed can short-circuit your neurobiology and make it difficult to trust again.

In a new recent study, a team of brain researchers shed light on what motivates us to trust one another, especially during times of potential risk. In their August 2015 research study, "Computational Substrates of Social Value in Interpersonal Collaboration", reported in The Journal of Neuroscience,[22] participants were under the illusion that they were playing an economic investment game with three different players: a close friend, a stranger or a computerised slot machine. In reality, in every instance, the participants were actually playing against a computer with a simple algorithm that systematically reciprocated actions worthy of trust exactly 50% of the time. Based on perceptions of trust, the participants reported positive interactions with the "close friend" to be more rewarding than interactions with a stranger or slot machine. They were more likely to invest with the "close friend". This illustrates our innate human desire to connect with others and create close-knit bonds even if these ties are based on blind trust.

Brain imaging of the participants showed increased activity of the *ventral striatum* and *medial prefrontal cortex* was correlated with positive social value signals when participants made decisions based on a belief they were playing with a "good friend". Assumed authenticity was the deciding factor in perceiving who to trust first.

The *ventral striatum* is considered a key pathway in human reward processing and positive emotions. There is a correlation between enjoying positive emotions and sustained activation of the *ventral striatum*.

The *medial prefrontal cortex* is associated with how we perceive another person's mental state and monitoring what's happening outside our current focus of attention. The *medial prefrontal cortex* also plays a role in decision-making as well as retrieving and consolidating memories. Together, these brain regions provide additional evidence that participants felt a greater social reward when they believed their good friend had reciprocated co-operation during the game. Interestingly, feelings of trust occurred despite the reality of the situation. Even though reciprocity occurred half the time under every circumstance, participants consistently trusted the "good friend" more than the other imaginary players throughout the game.

---

[22]Fareri, D. S., Chang, L. J., & Delgado, M. R. (2015). Computational Substrates of Social Value in Interpersonal Collaboration. *Journal of Neuroscience, 35*(21), 8170–8180. https://doi.org/10.1523/JNEUROSCI.4775-14.2015. Retrieved from: http://www.jneurosci.org/content/35/21/8170.

This new study illustrates the mechanisms underlying the social value and importance of trust. Having faith in one another is in the best interest of both the individual and the collective, especially in times of risk and uncertainty. However, this experiment suggests that our instinct to trust can override logic. Collaboration and trust are essential for building healthy and strong interpersonal relationships. Ultimately, the social connectivity created by pro-social behaviour and wholehearted, trusting relationships fortifies our well-being at the deepest level.

Trust Across Cultures

It's funny how we're all different and yet all the same. Principles, you will recall, are universal but practices are not, nor are values: they are situationally specific. Every culture experiences principles in unique ways. We see the same thing but from a different place. As the saying goes, one smile has thousand meanings. So how can we build trust in a cross-cultural workplace?

In Chapter 2, I considered cultural intelligence, and the cultural preferences which distinguish one group from another. I examined how these behavioural preferences are seen through the dimensions of culture (power distance, individualism, femininity, tolerance of uncertainty, time orientation and the directness of communication). I also considered emotional intelligence, the capacity to discern your own emotions and the emotions of others which built on my examination, in Chapter 1 of how the emotional brain works.

Now I join these concepts together to look at how you can empathise with another culture. You can look for non-verbal communication cues to help you understand and engage at an emotional level. When you choose empathy, diversity becomes a strength. When you choose trust, commitment is created. When you choose to listen, to observe without judging, a connection is created. Trust is the vital ingredient in the performance of virtual teams in global organisations.

Your goal as an international leader must be to facilitate real and lasting connections with your multicultural teams. To illustrate how you can approach this difficult task, I will use China as an example based on my personal experience working in Hong Kong at the start of the Year of the Dragon (2000).

To create success and reputation in a relationship-based culture, like China, will require a sophisticated and sincere route map which plots both the rational process and the emotional landscape of business exchange. Trust is built slowly, one cup of tea at a time.

The deeper emotions and values which power the process of business relationships are vitally important to understand. In fact, in China, as in many cultures, if emotions, values and relationship signals do not fit, the business process will undoubtedly abort or implode. Using your authentic voice and being sincere in your intentions are critical factors in building the deep trust required for successful and sustained business relationships.

My approach to creating meaningful levels of connectivity across cultures is based on a fusion of the disciplines of emotional intelligence and cultural intelligence. It requires an analytical approach and a clearly defined methodology.

There are three steps which relate to each other in a dynamic rather than linear fashion.

1. Examine your own relating style, and your emotional framework.

You need to be aware of your own attitudes to trust, to relationship-building, collaboration and teamwork and how you evaluate the health of your relationships.

2. Look at how culturally loaded is your approach to relationships.

What attitudes, protocols, beliefs, values and behaviours have you internalised from unconscious cultural programming? What do you believe to be important in dealings with others? How "hard coded" are the effects of this on your behaviour and communications and where do you need to give most attention?

3. Bring to conscious awareness the communication style you are unconsciously deploying.

Do you communicate to maximise access to your thinking? Do you adjust for second language users of English? Do you use language which builds empathy through formulating common goals and similarities of intention? Is your communication culturally neutral so that it can build trust and business friendship? Or might it be perceived as culturally loaded suggesting judgement, leading to suspicion and mistrust?

The process of undertaking this analysis provides you with guidance for how to connect with people and understand their approach to business and protocols. The Chinese measure success by the stage the relationship has reached, not the business deal.

The next stage is for you to identify the destination. What works for the culture you are trying to relate to and why? Above all, who are they as people? What are their preferences, motivators and tastes? Who are their heroes? Understanding your own style, appreciating how your own culture influences you and then consciously reflecting that in how you communicate with others, will help people you are working with from another culture to understand your intentions and build trust.

You can apply this approach to any culture, whether you are clients, business partners, suppliers or employers. The above relationship route map will provide clear assistance in understanding the emotional, cultural and work style profiles of those you seek to build successful relationships with.

In seeking to build better connectivity with other cultures, your goals are the same as with any business relationship.

Establish trust

Build relationships from the inside out so that they are real, culturally meaningful and enduring

Find common values and shared objectives and experiences

Mark the phases of the relationship development

Celebrate success and create longevity in the relationship

Create, communicate and maintain respect in ways that span cultural differences.

The Chinese call trust as "thinking with the heart". It combines attention, logic and emotion. In China, trust is built at different levels in the hierarchy.

My brain friendly approach to building trust across cultures, combining emotional, social and cultural intelligences, will make the task of winning hearts and minds (which is what is really going on in intercultural dialogue) rich and enjoyable. It also makes good business sense.

Exercise

Choose a business partner you are collaborating with from another national culture and ask yourself the following questions:
How do you make them feel? Do they want to work with you?
Are you tolerant of their behaviours?
Are you respectful of their history and culture?
Do you show understanding by listening with your heart?
Are you hiding another intention behind your smile?
Above all do you have a sincere desire to build a relationship of equals?

The Parallel Mind TRUST acronym spells out five words:

Tolerant
Respectful
Understanding
Sincere
Transparent.

We live in an age of constant soul searching about the meaning of national identity. Does a British citizen, born in India 30 years ago, support England or India at Lord's Cricket Ground? Does a person born in Edinburgh feel more British than Scottish? Does a New York Jew feel more American than Jewish? People experience their identities very differently.

How their sense of belonging has been forged is complex and often contradictory. Identities are not fixed because they are rooted mainly in people's relationships. Identity never comes in a tidy carefully wrapped parcel, so we should never make assumptions about people's sense of identity.

Think how much more successful you could be internationally if you embrace diversity, celebrate individual identity and welcome others as fellow humans.

Trusted Leaders' Behaviours

Trustworthiness has three essential characteristics namely competency, consistency and care. As was noted under humility, trusted leaders are more interested in helping others than looking good. They choose to care and their sincere desire to help others means they will go out of their way to deliver value. They make themselves accountable. They listen to others not to themselves. Trusted leaders trust others first, have courage, are open, communicate with their listeners in mind and have more engaged followers.

Leadership lessons in trust from the sea

The Atlantic Rally for Cruisers Race from the Canary Islands to St Lucia is a gruelling exercise in teamwork requiring 15 people living together for 9 days at 23 knots per hour. Skipper Rick Bomer of Steelcase says:
"it takes great courage to trust others in these circumstances. We are literally putting our lives in each other's hands".[23]
He offers a number of leadership lessons:
feed on the energy that stress creates
communicate what is needed, when it's needed. Not more, not less
be sensitive when feeding back
be mindful, do the right thing, not the easy thing
anticipate risk and the consequences of your response
be willing to lose sight of the shore
As Bomer put it:

---

[23]Bomer, R. (n.d.). *Leadership at Sea: Lessons from the Atlantic Rally for Cruisers*. Retrieved from Steelcase: https://www.steelcase.com/research/articles/topics/leadership-culture/leadership-sea/.

> "Only when we are willing to lose sight of our established habits, instincts, and social conventions can we finally trust each other and truly, deeply connect as human beings".

If you want to check whether a leader's behaviour is trustworthy, ask yourself: Is it honest and truthful? Is it fair to all concerned? Will it build goodwill and better friendship? Will it be beneficial to the whole community affected?

If you want to find out how trustworthy you are as a leader, then complete the Trusted Leader checklist.

Exercise—The Trusted Leader Checklist

Are you honest with yourself about your strengths and weaknesses? ☐

Are you prepared to show your vulnerabilities? ☐

Are you aware of your emotional mood in the moment? ☐

Do you pick up the emotional state of others when you are with them? ☐

Are you aware of your behaviours and their impact on others? ☐

Do you listen deeply beyond the words to their emotional messages? ☐

Do you feedback regularly and praise people for their contributions? ☐

Do you demonstrate empathic concern to your people? ☐

Are you compassionate when your followers are in a personal crisis? ☐

Do you do the right thing when it is far easier to do the popular thing? ☐

For every box you ticked honestly you scored 10% towards being a trusted leader. If you ticked all the ten boxes you are 100% trusted as a leader!

If you want a reality check however, ask the people who work closely with you to complete the checklist. Remember their perception is your reality. Mind that gap!

Trustworthiness defines leadership, it is the essence of leadership. Trusted leaders are trusted because they are driven by their values, they care, they have a sense of purpose, they are authentic. Trusted leaders are **O**pen, **R**eliable, **C**ongruent and **A**ccepting.

Openness— honest intentions and willingness to listen to others
Reliability— keeping your commitments
Congruence— your actions aligned with your feelings and thoughts
Acceptance— being non-judgemental

Trusted leaders transform their organisations at the speed of trust.

Charles H. Green, co-author of the "The Trusted Advisor", suggests the formula for building trust is:

Trust = (Credibility × Reliability × Intimacy/Self-Orientation.

Modern society is a paradox of freedom. On the one hand, it is characterised by freedom, and on the other, it is characterised by insecurity. Everything is becoming liquid, and when that happens it can flow away and leave us empty and feeling unfulfilled. Trusted leaders should provide a solid sense of themselves and their place in a changing world, for them and for their followers. Coaching conversations help people to connect the dots, to find new ways of adding value to their group in an increasingly fluid world. We need to find new ways to increase our social well-being through stable relationships based on trust. Trust allows us to have freedom and security, while accepting a periodic need to redefine our relationships and shared values. On the one hand, there is ambition, on the other, our shared vulnerability: together these bind us as human beings and provide a common narrative. What narrative do you want your followers to have?

In Summary

Attitude matters. The right attitude builds the right relationships that create the right level of trust.

Beliefs are assumptions from our life experiences that we hold to be true, whether or not they are. Values reflect what we hold to be important.

Play to your strengths. Your gifts define you.

Find your purpose. The difference you want to make in the world will give you energy and perseverance.

You have to find your own authentic voice before you can help others find theirs.

Create a psychologically safe place for your followers.

Relationships are built on trust. You lead and coach, one conversation at a time, at the speed of trust.

Successfully working across cultures requires you to understand how your own culture affects your behaviour and so how you might consciously moderate your communication. Remember the acronym Tolerance, Respect, Understanding, Sincerity and Transparency.

Pause for Reflection

In your next business meeting ask yourself the following questions:

am I aware of my emotions?
am I aware of others' emotions?
am I aware of different communication styles?
am I speaking with my authentic voice?
am I listening deeply?
am I engaging emotionally?

Theme II

Looking Out—*Coaching*

Overview

Theme II answers the question, *how can I use the knowledge about how my brain works and how I work gained in **Theme I** to help me work better with others?*

Theme II provides a framework and the basic tools for coaching conversations with tomorrow's business leaders. Coaching conversations are dissected scientifically to illuminate the interaction of the players on the coaching stage.

Conversations matter in business. The purpose of leaders is to make sense to their followers, so that they can engage in a shared vision by defining and polishing their personal goals. Ultimately successful delivery of strategy requires a meeting of minds and the energy for collaborative action.

The more quality conversations, the less opportunities the brain has for making its own assumptions. The brain is systemic, meaning making, always looking for patterns based on purpose. Coaching helps people find where they can bring all their talents to achieving the goals of the organisation.

The Parallel Mind THINK DO Coaching Model is based on Gestalt, a systemic approach in the pursuit of wholeness through creative growth.

Theme II explains the fundamental scientific principles of why coaching works. And how to make coaching conversations work for you, using your whole mind. Fundamentally a coaching conversation is one in which you listen to someone, so they can hear themselves. People just want to feel witnessed and understood. They want to be coached by someone who they trust enough to confide in, and who cares about their welfare and growth.

The instrument of coaching is the coach and their most powerful tool is SILENCE. Deep listening, witnessing another human being, helps them understand their story, think about their thinking and find ways of moving on.

In a time-poor world, quality coaching conversations drive the most efficient use of human capital.

My Coaching Journey

My book is written to guide you on your path to becoming a leadership coach. You don't have to declare yourself as a coach in order to have coaching conversations. There are many different expressions of coaching, a full spectrum of coaching activities, from formal coaching sessions to informal everyday coaching conversations. *Leading by Coaching* is a leadership style. You can, however, decide to become a leadership coach. Being a coach as well as a leader. Making coach a separate part of your identity.

There may be a multitude of reasons you might want to become a leadership coach in your own right. The starting point will probably be that you enjoy coaching! You may like to help people develop, especially talented people. You may want tomorrow's leaders to be your legacy. You may want to leave your organisation as a more sustainable business, able to adapt better with a new breed of leaders. More than any other activity coaching can, in whatever form, have a powerful impact on change in any organisation.

All good coaching conversations start with a sincere desire to help a fellow human being on their journey. The greatest impact of coaching is when your sole focus is on improving the working lives of others through coaching conversations.

It is important to understand that my book, *Leading by Coaching*, is not designed as a self-help manual. There is no substitute for professional coach training (see the Parallel Mind Leadership Coaching offering at the end of this book), and formal coaching activities should always be supervised by a qualified coach supervisor. This chapter specifically, and the book generally, will not replace the actual experience of coaching, however will give you a good picture of what is involved and a framework for your *Leading by Coaching* conversations. I repeat the themes and principles of my book throughout the text to help you reinforce your learning and place them in your context.

If you are new to coaching, it will give you a space to think about who you are as a coach and give you some ideas for your coaching. If you are an experienced coach, my book will give you a chance to reinforce what you already know and provide you with some new learning insights. I want to provoke your thinking—lead you to fresh perspectives and new opportunities to grow.

Wherever you are on your coaching journey I hope *Leading by Coaching* inspires you to develop your unique coach signature presence and expand your coaching footprint.

My book, unlike so many other books on leadership and coaching, strings together a multitude of threads into a "theory of everything" so you can see the complete picture without having to read a plethora of books and journals, as I have done over the years. *Leading by Coaching* is your guide to inspire you to think about, reflect on and experiment with your endless coaching possibilities, *looking in, looking out, and looking beyond.* I hope it will be your personal companion on your *Leading by Coaching* journey to help the future leaders in your care find their authentic voice through purposeful, meaningful and insightful conversations.

Before you start reading Theme II, I want to share with you my story as a coach and some stories from my coaching.

My Coach Story

Trainer

The starting point of my business education journey began in my marketing director role in Standard Chartered Bank. My responsibilities included sales training in new products and call centre management. I enjoyed helping my colleagues learn and develop their skills, and the feedback reflected my enthusiasm. It became clear to me that my vocation lay beyond the shackles of my office-bound desk to the wider world of helping people learn, develop and grow. When the opportunity arose, I decided to change career direction and enrolled on a full-time **P**ost **G**raduate **C**ertificate in **E**ducation and training at the University of Wales, Cardiff.

Teacher

I loved my time as a mature student on the teaching course. My business experience quickly attracted younger students to ask for my counsel and I unwittingly became a role model. I loved being a learner. I quickly realised that learning was about change, and we all deal with change differently. We all learn differently, so a teaching by coaching style, that targets individual's different learning needs, is the most effective way to teach. The affective learning domain, concerned with attitudes, emotions and feelings, is where the deepest, most internalised and, therefore, most permanent learning, takes place. As a teacher, you have to hold up a mirror to your learners, so that your teaching reflects their moods and body language.

I enjoyed teaching at my local colleges in Newport and Bristol. Later in my career, my teaching qualifications and experience helped me get a lecturing post at the University of Munich, teaching intercultural communication skills to over 200 international undergraduates. There is an overlap between teaching and coaching. They both rely on listening and facilitation skills to create a reflective learning experience. They both need the stillness of silence to create the space for thinking.

Coach

My big breakthrough as a coach started on an industrial estate outside Cardiff in 1999. I met a young lady at the reception of a company that was servicing the wheelchair for my son Christopher who told me her father, who was the Managing Director of Black Isle Consultants, was looking for someone like me to train up as a communication skills consultant. The next thing I knew I was in Hong Kong, in the year of the Dragon, being trained by John Miers, the Chairman of the British company, in the receiver-driven communication skills that he had learnt from his previous business partner, Lee Bowman Junior. Lee coached Bill Clinton in the same skills and his father Lee Bowman coached Ronald Reagan, the so-called, "great communicator".

Two years later, I set up my own training and coaching company for business leaders, The Parallel Mind Ltd, now focusing on training leaders in coaching skills based on the principles and ideas set out in this book.

My Coaching Stories

Over the last decade, I have had the privilege of coaching many different people in many different businesses. I want to share my personal insights from the many coaching conversations I have enjoyed. I want you to know the power that even informal conversations have to change people's thinking and take a different path. In these conversations, looking back, the following three truths emerged to me about the power of coaching conversations through the instrument of the coach, to change people's lives.

My Coaching Truths

My First Truth: The Power of Listening

My first truth is that people need someone who they can trust to listen deeply and witness who they are. The simple act of listening to someone helps them hear themselves. It helps them validate who they are and the difference they want to make. It helps them to clarify their thinking, to clear their path, and see more clearly the way ahead. I remember many informal conversations, over a coffee or a beer, with senior associates of international law firms about their frustration at not becoming a partner fast enough. They felt stuck and powerless to change their situation.

Over a period of many months and many conversations, their truth started to emerge. These witnessing conversations helped them to become unstuck and move on. They said that their conversations with me seemed often cathartic and healing. Some of them became partners in their firms. Some of them became partners in other firms. Some of them went in-house. All of them moved on. All of them moved on professionally and personally. All of them moved towards themselves.

My Second Truth: The Power of Belief

Belief is everything. If you believe you can, you probably will. But no person is an island. We need other people to believe in us before we can believe in ourselves. The brain, as we have seen, is social, and we often need social recognition and proof to believe our own story. Confidence to have the courage of our own convictions.

I remember a lawyer coming to me at the end of a two-day "develop your business" course looking distressed. Within a few minutes of our private conversation, she burst into tears. She was totally frustrated with her partner who she felt was blocking her progress in the firm. She was thinking of setting up a boutique law firm but could not find the courage to just do it. I told her that I believed she could do it and by making a decision to leave her firm she would free up her mind and move on. Within six months of our conversation, she was the proud owner of her own firm and has not looked back since. She sent me an invitation card to the official launch of her new office and on it was the following message, "Dear Nick, thanks again for giving me the courage to follow my own path!"

My Third Truth: The Power of Your Authentic Voice

I have formally coached a number of CEOs and have been struck by their sense of isolation and even loneliness. Our conversations, it seemed, helped them feel less isolated, less alone. Having a neutral confidant helped share their pain and anxieties. Having someone to talk to, which understood business but was outside their business, was a great comfort to them and a valuable sounding board. I found that a common concern they had was they did not know how to show their authentic self when talking in public. So, in many cases, my coaching objective was to help them find their authentic voice and use it powerfully. Coaching helped them to better understand their strengths and to acknowledge their weaknesses. They realised that they did not need to be superhuman to be credible leaders. What their followers wanted was a real person they could believe in.

I remember coaching a CEO of an international insurance company who was technically very strong but struggled to find their leader inside. Over six coaching sessions, his inner leader emerged. It was wonderful to see. He realised that who he was, is enough in itself. He did not need to prove himself he just needed to be himself.

We are all on a journey to find ourselves. To find our personal truth. To find and use the power of our authentic voice to make the difference, we want and can make.

Find your authentic voice and use its power to help others find theirs, *Leading by Coaching one conversation at a time.*

4

Person-Centred Coaching

Here is Edward Bear, coming downstairs now, bump, bump, bump, on the back of his head, behind Christopher Robin. It is, as far as he knows, the only way of coming downstairs, but sometimes he feels that there really is another way, if only he could stop bumping for a moment and think of it. *Winnie the Pooh* -A A Milne

Introduction

Now you have looked in, to understand yourself better, you can look out to understand how you can have better, more effective coaching conversations that nurture and develop future leaders.

In this chapter I guide you through the process of person-centred, mindful coaching. This follows Carl Rogers' view that change occurs when you become the person you are, not when you try to be the person you are not.

I introduce Gestalt, as the person-centred coaching concept. A Gestalt coach's underlying intention is to raise the client's awareness in the present moment, because more awareness means more choices: indeed, in that way, the Gestalt coach is more of an awareness agent than a change agent. Accepting yourself as you are, paradoxically, allows you to change.

My Parallel Mind THINK DO Coaching system, uniquely combines neuroscience with Gestalt principles. I outline the importance of being actively present, listening deeply and holding the space for the real issues to emerge. The power of the pause is to give the client the silence to think about their thinking.

© The Author(s) 2019
N. Marson, *Leading by Coaching*, https://doi.org/10.1007/978-3-319-76378-1_4

The chapter explains the science behind Gestalt coaching, the power of presence in the silences.

This chapter includes some Gestalt coaching awareness exercises and experiments you can try.

My Gestalt Coaching Learning Experience

My moment of truth arrived in the second year of my Gestalt Coaching learning experience.

We were watching the course leader being coached by a fellow learner. Suddenly he became energised and shouted out, *I've got it! Who I am is enough in itself.* This was my "Aha" moment of insight when the course started to make sense to me.

I had been missing the point for the past year. It is not about being a better coach than my co-learners. It is enough to be me as a coach, to bring all of myself to my coaching, to be authentically me and truly present with my client. Gestalt Coaching, the penny dropped, is about being authentic and sincere as a coach not about "doing" coaching. Being with the client, not coaching them. Going on a journey with them with no predetermined destination. Just letting things emerge and being more aware of the possibilities. Being in a *dance* with my client.

At the end of the second year of this coaching programme we had to write a dissertation on our unique coaching model and coaching style. Ten thousand words is a lot of writing, and the first step is the most difficult one on a journey of ten thousand words! I sat at my desk and reflected on my learning experience and the day my co-learner had altered my state of consciousness and given me this wonderful insight. I started to write. "Who I am is enough in itself". "I want to improve myself, but I don't have to prove myself". I watched my hand write. Ten thousand words flew onto the page. I was in a flow.

My coaching has been in a flow ever since. I no longer focus on myself and my performance. I focus on what is emerging in my *dance* with my clients. My job, as a coach is to listen to my clients, so they can hear themselves. Person-centred coaching is about putting the emphasis on developing people as opposed to directing them. It is about leading people by coaching them, *one conversation at a time.* It is about treating someone as a person first, and an employee second. It is about helping people develop and grow. It is about developing tomorrow's leaders.

Gestalt Coaching System

The Gestalt coaching system attracted me because it is based on the fundamental principles of human thought and behaviour and provides an easy to follow and practical framework for coaching people through change. It is about changing by not changing. Becoming who you are and not trying to be who you are not.

Gestalt coaching has its roots in Gestalt therapy and the social sciences. We know coaching works but by combining, as I do for the first time, Gestalt coaching with Neuroscience, the scientific study of how the brain works, we now know **why** it works. The science of coaching is in the silences. The brain is a prediction making machine. That is why silence is uncomfortable. The brain wants to fill the gaps based on its own assumptions to make meaning of a situation, so it can predict the future. The brain is an autonomous system for making order out of chaos. And no two brains are the same, they make predictions based on their own unique experiences. That is why people are so unpredictable. They don't always do what they should do. Or what you want them to do. Their emotional brain can override your logical brain.

Silence forces clear thinking. Silence gives the brain the processing time to think back into past experiences—to bear witness to what happened before—to see what information can be used to predict likely outcomes and, therefore, select safe actions in response to the situation.

Why Is Gestalt Coaching Relevant to You?

Gestalt coaching is relevant today because Gestalt concepts and ideas are supported by Neuroscientific research into understanding how the brain works. This duality of Gestalt and Neuroscience has driven my thinking for this book and underpins the Parallel Mind THINK DO Coaching Framework.

Through practical application, Gestalt has developed a rich language to describe human thought, ideas and behaviours that assist communication of coaching principles. When overlaid with insights from Neuroscience, the basic Gestalt principles become even more powerful.

Origins of Gestalt

In the late nineteenth century, a number of philosophers, writers and therapists became interested in ideas of relatedness, how different versions of something can be recognised as part of the same underlying form. In 1890, Austrian philosopher Christian von Ehrenfels wrote an article *On Gestalt Qualities*[1] bringing together ideas and proposing that the whole was something other than the sum of the parts. "Is a melody a mere sum of elements, or something novel … distinguishable from the sum of elements?" It is not that the whole is greater than the sum of its parts; it is that the resulting whole is something other than a combination of the parts.

Around that time, Sigmund Freud's "talking cure" invented the language of therapy. Freud invited his patients to say what was on their minds, to "free associate", to find their own words. Unlike other medical practitioners of the time he would not tell: he would first listen and then listen some more. By allowing space, he hoped to free his patients from the traumas buried deep in their unconscious brains. Freud's aim was to enable the individual to face their conflicts rather than repress them. He believed that through talking freely their difficult conflicts could be resolved, and their symptoms would dissolve. Freud's big idea was that patients could, through their own speech, discover what was troubling them and so heal themselves. This was the birth of psychoanalytic practice, the practice of listening, observing, feeling and reflecting.

The therapist, and equally the coach, observe how words are used, the way they are said and the body language in the spaces between. They monitor energy levels in themselves and in their patients or clients.

Words, like music's tempo of, melody, chords and notes, form a structure. A structure is personal and unique. Words conceal and reveal trapped feelings frozen in the unconscious brain. Words unify mind and body. Words tell a human story. Words liberate the human soul. And the coach tunes in and translates the clients' words to help them understand their multi-layered inner world.

Gestalt therapy as such was founded by Fritz and Laura Perls in the 1950s, with a particular emphasis on restoring self-awareness. "Get out of your mind and come to your senses!"—Fritz Perls. Among other sources, they were heavily influenced by the humanistic movement of Carl Rogers, who is also considered as one of the founding figures of coaching. Rogers' Person-Centred Approach in his own words "moved away from the idea that the therapist was the expert and towards a theory that trusted the innate tendency (known as the actualising tendency) of human beings to find

---

[1]*Christian von Ehrenfels.* (2015, May 2018). Retrieved from Stanford Encyclopedia of Philosophy: https://plato.stanford.edu/entries/ehrenfels/#GesQua.

fulfilment of their personal potential. An important part of this theory is that… the fulfilment of personal potential includes sociability, the need to be with other human beings and a desire to know and be known by other people. It also includes being open to experience, being trusting and trustworthy, being curious about the world, being creative and compassionate".[2]

Chapter 3 introduced the idea of purpose and meaning and Maslow's Hierarchy of Needs, which placed self-actualisation at the top of the pyramid of human needs. Rogers added the need for openness and self-disclosure, for being listened to, and for acceptance. All these propositions have influenced the development of Gestalt coaching.

Gestalt coaching, like Gestalt therapy where it comes from, tries to understand our ability to have meaningful perceptions from the chaotic world we live in. Viktor Frankl's seminal work, *Man's Search for Meaning*, which was based on his experience as a prisoner of war, is also at the heart of Gestalt existentialism. We always have choices however dire our circumstances. We can always choose how we experience a situation and find some meaning as Frankl did. The healthy mind is the one that finds meaning from purpose.

Gestalt Coaching

Gestalt coaching works with the natural resistance to the inevitable change that comes out of the complexity of human experience. Gestalt coaching is systems based and recognises that the brain is constantly searching for patterns to make sense of its constantly evolving environment. Gestalt coaching is fundamentally about increasing awareness through observation, dialogue and creative experimentation/adaptation.

The Figure in the Ground

We are the whole and we are the part. And the whole is bigger than the parts. Systems are self-organising, and there is a natural order. We only make sense as part of the system. Coherence helps us see our place in the system as a whole. And being whole gives us purpose and a sense of belonging. It's our relatedness to the collective whole that makes us human. Coherence is the weave of learning.

---

[2]The Person Centred Association. (n.d.). *What is the Person-Centred Approach?* Retrieved from The Person Centred Association: https://www.bapca.org.uk/about/what-is-it.html.

The brain is systems based. We need the big picture to see the connection. Context is essential. If we can find our place in the system, we will find our purpose and become whole again. "The whole exists through continually manifesting in the parts, and the parts exist as embodiments of the whole, the one brings the many out of itself"—Goethe.

The issues that rise to the top of our consciousness become the focus of our *Attention*. We need to resolve what is on our mind to *Withdraw* and get back in sync with our world, see the bigger picture. In Gestalt that burning issue is called a *Figure*. The context that the issue is raising itself in, is called the *Ground* (Fig. 4.1).

We cannot deal with the figure (the issue) without understanding its relationship to the ground (the context). What does the client perceive first, the figure (the issue) in the foreground or the ground (the context) in the background? We need to change the configuration—the issue and the context are inextricably linked. The *Figure* must be in the *Ground*.

For example, the words printed on this page are the figure, and the pages are the ground. This is often used in optical illusions, for example, where the eye may be uncertain whether it sees the black silhouette of two faces facing each other or whether it sees a white vase in front of a black background.

In the second picture above, is there a white circle in front of a black square, or is there a black square with a hole through it?

I remember a partner in a law firm talking about how he lost a star associate without any warning. This was the issue my client wanted to resolve,

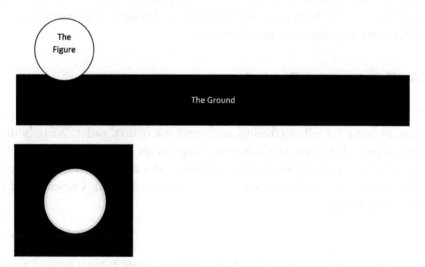

Fig. 4.1 Gestalt Figure in the Ground

the *Figure* that was in the forefront of his mind. The context, the *Ground*, it transpired was my client's leadership style, which made him difficult to approach for informal chats. The associate didn't feel able to tell my client he was unhappy in his role. By seeing the issue in its wider context, the *Figure* in the *Ground*, my client was able to adjust his leadership style and make it more informal and became more approachable. His associates were less afraid to talk about issues that were on their mind so that they could be nipped in the bud before it was too late. This was an important piece of learning for my client he told me. He had completed his Gestalt and moved on.

Fundamentally, Gestalt is about our relationships within the social system we operate. Paradoxically, we change by not changing but by accepting. The coach helps the client stay with their "stuckness", until coherence emerges. Resistance blocks change and resolution. To move on, we must accept who we are and adapt to our new situation.

The Paradoxical Theory of Change

The only constant in life is change itself. We are constantly adapting to fulfil our changing needs. The paradox is that we change, not by changing to be something other than who we are, but by adapting to the changed conditions and being more of who we are.

When we experience significant, and sometimes even traumatic change, our self-esteem often drops dramatically. We are first in a state of shock and disbelief. We are fighting denial. We pretend that the change hasn't really happened, or it will go away. Self-doubt kicks in. We start blaming ourselves instead of reconciling views from the people close to us. Finally, comes acceptance that the change is here to stay, and we need to adapt ourselves and move on. At this point, our self-esteem is getting back near to the level it was before the change hit us. We are now in the experimentation phase where we are trying to find a way to fit into the changed system, to complete the circle and be whole again. As part of this process of finding closure, completing a Gestalt, and moving on, we search for new meaning by finding renewed purpose. We can then integrate ourselves into the new or changed system and be healthy again. This simplified change process is called, *the Gestalt Coaching Unit of Work*, as developed by the Gestalt Institute of Cleveland. The coach starts and completes a coaching gestalt in three steps, a *Unit of Work*. The process can be seen in the model below and provides a simple marker for the coach (Fig. 4.2).

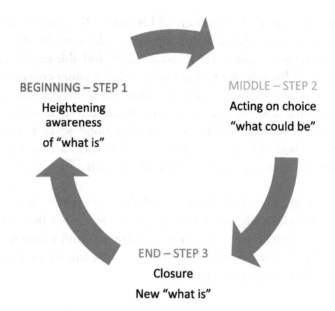

BEGINNING – STEP 1
Heightening
awareness
of "what is"

MIDDLE – STEP 2
Acting on choice
"what could be"

END – STEP 3
Closure
New "what is"

Fig. 4.2 Gestalt Coaching Unit of Work

Central Principle of Gestalt

We have a need to constantly adapt to our social system to find the natural order to achieve "wholeness". We need to see freshly, from the heart, from the whole. The heart has its own neural network linked to the brain. *The heart sees what is invisible to the eye.* Antoine de Saint-Exupery *Le Petit Prince* (1943).

When we see from the whole a larger context emerges. Purpose, meaning and a sense of belonging comes from the whole. Change comes by not changing but by finding our place in the whole.

Gestalt is defined in the Times English Dictionary (2000 Limited Edition) as: "a structure, configuration, or pattern made up of perceptions so integrated as to constitute a functional whole whose properties are not derivable from the sum of its parts". It is derived from the German word *gestalt* which, literally translated means "shape", "form" or "pattern".

The central principle of gestalt psychology is that the mind forms a global whole with self-organising tendencies. Following this systems orientation principle, we tend to order our experience in a manner that is regular, orderly, symmetrical and simple.

When our mind forms a percept or Gestalt from complex interactions, the whole has a reality of its own, independent of the parts. Rather than the

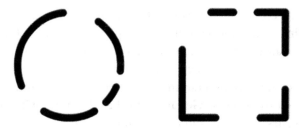

Fig. 4.3   Gestalt Law of Closure

mistranslation that the whole is "greater" than the sum of the parts it is that the whole is "other" than the sum of the parts, which is a different concept entirely. The whole has an independent existence. We see a joined-up circle or square even though there are broken lines. When we look at Georges Seurat's *Sunday Afternoon on the Island of the Grande Jette* we do not see his tiny pointillism brush strokes, dots of complimentary colours, we see the impression of a picture. From a distance our brain sees the bigger picture not the smaller dots. We see a picture on our tv screen not the dots that make it up. The dots are combined optically on the retina to create an illusion of a picture. Our brains are meaning-making machines.

In the incomplete shapes, our brains have a strong need to see the shapes. To join up the dots to see the whole. This is the Gestalt Law of Closure (Fig. 4.3).

The Gestalt Law of Closure

Human perception or awareness is based on the whole picture not the sum of the parts. We remember peoples' faces not their features. Can you remember the colour of the eyes of your friends or colleagues? Maybe not, but you would recognise their faces even at a distance. This is the **Gestalt** or the whole picture, the recognisable image, or figure, retained by the brain.

This is the Gestalt Law of Closure. The mind understands external stimuli as a whole, rather than the sum of the parts. The mind demands that each component be considered as part of a system of dynamic relationships. The brain is always looking for connections and meaning from the changing environment it is operating in.

Humans will naturally move towards *closure* of each perceived figure: the process of perception compels them to "fill the gaps". When you have this sentence, your brain will have automatically inserted the word *read* before *this sentence* to complete the gap and make sense of it and meaning from it. Your brain's *auto pilot* completes the picture for you. Our perception becomes our reality. That is why I need someone else to copy check my writing in this book. I see what I expect to see, not what is there!

The human brain is programmed to compensate to find closure whenever it can, to form a "good Gestalt". Our healthy mind will naturally move towards wholeness, stability and equilibrium.

Our mind can become unhealthy when figures are unfinished. For example, when we have an unhealthy, low trust relationship with a colleague who we need to get on with. This incomplete figure is unfinished business that needs to be closed to stop it interfering with the formation of new figures.

Unfinished business makes us restless and stuck. The coach helps their client deal with unfinished situations through a creative adaptation process in search of closure and wholeness.

I remember another coaching session where my client was frustrated by a partner in an office in another country who was blocking access to a mutual client. My client wanted to cross sell but needed to be introduced by the partner that had the influence in this country. The insight that came out of the coaching session was that it was really an inter-cultural communication issue rather than a personal relationship one. My client realised he needed to be less direct in approaching the partner and more sensitive to the fear that the other partner had of letting go. We worked out a culturally sensitive approach for the partner which resulted in a meeting with the client. This allowed the figure to be completed and closed so my client could move on and form a new figure. Finding closure energises us and drives change.

Gestalt Centred Coaching

Gestalt coaching is centred on the present because that is the only time that actually exists, and it is the only point at which you can make a difference: therefore, you hold your client in the present space, so they can stop avoiding an issue and truly engage with whatever is holding them back. That is why Gestalt is more concerned with "being" than "doing"—or more accurately it is a very different type of "doing".

Who we are is how we coach. That is the gift we bring. The gift of ourselves. The gift of our humanity. The gift of our light. And it takes courage to shine because as Nelson Mandela observed, *it is our light that most frightens us.* Your job as a coach is to listen to your clients so they can hear themselves. To focus on what is emerging in the *dance* with your client as they think about their thinking. To hold the space for your client to put their pieces together and become whole again.

All the techniques in the world cannot prepare you for the unique and wonderful human creation in front of your eyes. You coach with your soul from your heart and not from your head. The heart sees more than the eyes can ever see. You coach at the speed of trust and one conversation at a time.

Out of the space held by the Gestalt coach insights emerge and truths surface for the client. The coach experiments with the client to help them find new meaning and purpose. Ultimately, they find closure through adapting to fit into their new context. They have completed their Gestalt and can move on to their next Gestalt, or issue, they are confronted with.

You change by not changing: you change by accepting yourself and adapting to meet new challenges in a turning world.

Gestalt coaching works with natural resistance rather than fighting or attacking it.

As leader and coach, you help others to become more aware by observing how words are used, the way they are said, the body language in the spaces between, and note what seems to be unsaid so you can reflect this back to them.

This person-centred approach to coaching is about putting the emphasis on developing and empowering people as opposed to telling them what to do and directing them.

Gestalt, on the one hand, therefore, is simple and elegant, and on the other hand, it is complex and multi-faceted. Above all Gestalt coaching, in the hands of skilled practitioners, is a powerful instrument for learning.

Gestalt coaching in practice

Mike was a young high flyer in the finance department of an international accountancy firm.

Mike hated being coached. He couldn't see the point of it. His previous coaches didn't understand who he was, or his world and didn't have the answers to his problems. His HR department, however, thought Mike needed a coach to fulfil his potential and they approached me.

I remember Mike striding into the corporate meeting room. He looked confident. I was feeling less certain. I had been told that Mike didn't want a coach, yet he had agreed to meet me.

"How are you?" I asked. "Good". Mike replied. "I am here to listen to your story" I said. This is a very unusual statement to receive. There followed a long silence. Then, for the next hour, Mike just poured out his heart. I just listened to Mike telling me about his journey so far. He started quickly and filled the narrative with his many success milestones.

I listened. I witnessed him. After a while Mike's positive energy seemed to be dissipating. He started talking about his fears and vulnerabilities, his frustrations and challenges. He seemed overwhelmed by his success to date. I shared his pain in the silences. Mike was human rather than superhuman after all.

I, on the other hand, started to be aware of my own physicality becoming more confident in how I could help him. I could feel a deep natural empathic concern for his well-being. I remembered when I was a manager at his age feeling isolated. There was no one to share my journey with, no one to mentor or coach me. I could sense there was a bond forming between us.

Mike was now talking about the issues that were on his mind. We were present in the here and now and his figure was emerging from the ground.

I resisted the urge to give him the solutions he craved. I held the space for him to fill. I understood the value of staying with the uncertainty and seeing what emerged.

The time flowed quickly. Mike signalled that our meeting was drawing to a close.

I asked him how he had felt about our discussion. He seemed energised. I felt a strong sense that having someone listen to his story had been cathartic for Mike.

"So, would you like me to be your coach", I said confidently. "Yes", he said confidently.

This was the start of a partnership that would last for two years and which formally came to a natural conclusion when Mike was appointed Finance Director in the firm. He is now the COO and a Partner.

The above experience I had of Gestalt coaching in practice shows the power of silence: just being there for your client.

Neuroscience Coaching Model

My integration of Gestalt and Neuroscientific research is a powerful platform for coaching. The human brain is a labyrinth. Humans make associations, one thought following another in an endless parade, never seeing the whole design, restless to find the centre and navigate a way out. The Gestalt trained coach leads the client to find a clear path through their mind-maze. Meaningful coaching conversations provide the red thread that help the client connect the dots that make up their story. And stories create comfort because they have a beginning and an end. The client finds a way out of the labyrinth. The figure is safely in the ground. Time to move on.

I repeat the brain is a meaning-making organism. It continuously scans the environment or *ground* to "join the dots" in order to solve the issue or *figure*. As a coach, you are helping your client understand their new reality and make some meaning from it, find closure and move on.

Essentially, the brain navigates the flow of change it experiences by constructing a series of Gestalts, continuously reconciling the figure in the ground and finding equilibrium. It is a self-organising system, finding a natural order and finding coherence. When we find our place in the system we are whole, our mind is calm again.

Thought is a system. It is an unbroken field of mutually informing thoughts based on the integration of body, brain and mind, and driven by emotion. Thought has a participating nature. It is inclusive of feelings, in the form of latent emotional experiences. The individual is a mixture of the collective movement of values, meanings and intentions. Thought and knowledge are primarily collective phenomena. The "flow of meaning" between people is more fundamental than any individuals' particular thoughts. Each of us is a blend of the distinctive and the common, the unique and the shared. Implicate order comes out of wholeness. My thought and your thought are part of the same system. The brain seeks social relationships to make sense of the world. We operate in an emergent non-linear system. This system is constantly changing and self-organising. The social brain is collective.

To be an effective Gestalt coach, it is important to be aware of the constant stream of your subconscious thoughts. Without alertness and cognitive thought in your conscious mind you cannot make sense of what is going on for you and your client.

You can engage your unconscious mind and conscious mind in parallel and benefit from the power of parallel processing, the power of your parallel mind. I call this **N**euro **L**eadership **I**ntelligence.

NLI is your ability to lead yourself and others intelligently with your brain in mind as covered in Theme I, Chapter 2.

Power of Focus and Attention

Dealing with your emotions saps your energy. You can control the impulsive thoughts of your primitive and powerful unconscious "elephant brain", the *basal ganglia*, but you require a lot of energy from your conscious brain, the *prefrontal cortex*, to be "the rider". *Volition*—willpower has a price. If you want *Veto Power*, you need a lot of discipline to exert authority over your emotions. This is the power of focus and attention. Attention is a matter of will. As we saw earlier when the enormous elephant wants to stomp off into the jungle it takes a lot of will power for the little rider sitting on top to direct the animal to take a different path!

When you focus, the *neurons* in your brain fire. When you do something repeatedly your brain rewires itself and creates new neural pathways and forms new habits.

The Quiet Stage

We need a *Quiet Stage*, according to David Rock in his book, "Quiet Leadership" (2009), to focus our attention. Our mind is like a stage with new characters coming and going. When a new character is on the stage they are in the spotlight of our attention. The stage is the *ground* or context and the character is the *figure* or issue. They are inextricably linked. One cannot exist without the other. When our conscious thought has illuminated the issue on our mind we get some insights that help us resolve the issue and move on until another character appears on our mind's stage.

Sometimes we are too close to the characters and need to be directed so we can see the connection with the other characters on the stage. The director, or coach, helps us see the connection and, therefore, the meaning as the play emerges. To take another analogy, we cannot see the shape of the cloud when we are flying through it!

The Parallel Mind Coaching System

I have developed my Parallel Mind Coaching System to allow you to coach in a brain friendly way. Out of my coaching sessions has emerged a deeper understanding of how people think. My system integrates Gestalt and Neuroscientific principles to bring awareness, focus and action. My coaching experiences and results convinced me that Gestalt theory works in practice, but I was curious to find out why it works. This book is the result of my quest to answer the why. Studying the research findings of neuroscientists into how the brain works gave me the answer to the why and is the bedrock of my coaching and the basis of the Parallel Mind Coaching System.

This is the coaching system that I have developed. It is based on Gestalt principles and linked to Neuroscience. This is a three-part integrated system comprising of:

Part One: The Parallel Mind **THINK DO** Coaching Model
Part Two: The Parallel Mind Feeling Seeing Changing Coaching Process
Part Three: The Parallel Mind **Coaching Conversation** Framework

The Parallel Mind **THINK DO** Model

See Fig. 4.4.

The Parallel Mind Feeling Seeing Changing Coaching Process

In simple terms, a coaching session consists of three stages. **Feeling** the tension of the unknown and the unsaid. **Sensing** what is going on. Holding the space for the client to think about their thinking and for insights to emerge. The coach holds the space for the client, so by staying in their stuckness, the client starts Seeing their sensing, finding new meaning, and harnessing their energy to start **Changing**. Connecting the dots to find wholeness and move on. Finding closure. Completing the Gestalt. Dots of colour take a picture, like in a Seurat neo-impressionist painting, but only the picture tells the story. This is the process of transcendence. Thinking about my thoughts; feeling my feelings; sensing my senses; seeing my seeing (Fig. 4.5).

Transcendence alters our state of consciousness. Our thoughts become us. Consciousness is beyond thinking to knowing.

Our search for wholeness starts in our stuckness. We are stuck in our story, frozen in our unconscious brain. We need antifreeze to create new brain narratives. Narratives are relevant to our changing world. Attention is

THINK

Thinking about thinking raising conscious awareness
Holding the space being here now and seeing what merges

Imagining what could be and gaining insights

Networking adapting to the wider system by connecting the dots
Knowing taking the learning to form new mental maps

DO

Deciding what to do to reframe things to complete the Gestalt
Optimising following through the decision using all available resources

Fig. 4.4 The Parallel Mind **THINK DO** Model

Fig. 4.5 The Parallel Mind Feeling Seeing Changing Coaching Process

the antifreeze that is consciously defrosting our stuckness. Our thinking is guided by the questions we ask ourselves.

"I cannot teach anybody anything. I can only make them think". Socrates

The Parallel Mind Coaching Conversation Framework

Puts the **THINK DO** **Coaching** Model into action in a coaching conversation (Fig. 4.6).

The coach holds the space for the client to think about their thinking. In the silences of the *dance* insights emerge and the client begins to see their seeing.

This new learning is facilitated by the coach through listening deeply and bringing into presence what is being sensed and realised by the client. The client sees and feels change. Then the client decides to act and discusses with the coach options for following through in the optimal way. The critical skill of the Gestalt coach is to hold the space for the silences. To use and harness the power of the pause. The longer the pause, the more time the client has to reflect on what has been said. They hear themselves in the silence the coach gives them after they speak. You coach by listening to your client so that they can hear their own thoughts. By holding the pause, the coach allows

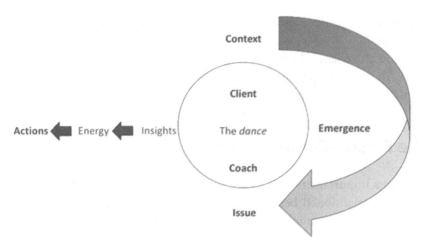

Fig. 4.6   The Parallel Mind Coaching Conversation Framework

the client to adjust, modify, and add context to their thoughts. To literally think about their thinking. To pay attention. Attention harnesses and directs the energy to make connections. This self-directed choice is the power of focus. Attention creates new mind maps. Maps of the client's world that make more sense to them. Maps that make them whole again.

This Framework is a visual representation of how I have integrated Gestalt coaching with Neuroscience.

Coaching with the Brain in Mind

Your brain functions by regulating the flow of energy and information to steer you away from danger or towards reward. It operates on a simple binary system—towards or away. People tend to have a habitual preference, either moving towards things they want, or focussing more on moving away from things they don't want. Increased awareness of this flow can help you direct your brain towards what you choose to focus on. You become the *rider* and the *elephant* is your servant. You become mindful.

When you coach bear in mind, the client's brain is always on high alert scanning for threats. Today, in a work environment, those threats are more likely to be psychological challenges to the ego than physical dangers to life. So, you need to recognise those danger responses to avoid an *Amygdala* attack in the emotional seat of their brain as described by Daniel Goleman in, Emotional Intelligence (1995). You should focus your attention on solutions rather than problems. You should help your clients label their emotions.

Say to the client: "I am noticing your fear when talking about this situation". You need to pay attention to your own threat responses. Be aware of your body sensations in the moment.

The Person-Centred Coach

The most important tool in Gestalt coaching is the coach. His or her quality lies, as mentioned before, much more in "being" than in doing, in the music not the instrument. Action results from holding attention rather than overt pressure for action. Paradoxically this apparent "inaction" in Gestalt Coaching often improves performance more than "performance" coaching because it helps people move towards themselves to find their true purpose and natural passion.

A Gestalt Coach's underlying intention, and the essence of Gestalt Coaching, is to raise the client's awareness in the present moment. More awareness means more choices. The Gestalt Coach is an awareness agent rather than a change agent.

Coaching is a conversational catalyst for accelerated learning and change.

And coaching is a series of conversations with a purpose.

> **Pause for thought**
> Ask yourself what conversations do you need to have with the people you lead?
> What has stopped you having them? Take a few minutes to reflect.

What were the main reasons you came up with? What stopped you? Maybe, one reason was fear. Fear of the unknown. How will people react to a conversation about a difficult situation? Or to some unexpected, unwanted or even unwelcome feedback? What about your relationship with this person? How could this be affected? When will you have this conversation? Where? In the office? Whose office? Outside the office? Formally or informally? How will you start the conversation? How will you facilitate good outcomes?

These are all questions that can be addressed by coaching. Coaching conversational techniques can be used in the workplace for resolving issues and developing people. Good coaching provides powerful listening and productive questioning that leads to greater clarity in everyday work issues. Coaching allows the unsaid to be said and is cathartic both at an individual and at an organisational level. It makes people feel valued by their leaders for who they are, not just respected for what they do.

A Gestalt Coach can go deeper more quickly. It is, however, important to recognise the situations where experienced coaches add value. Confidentially and independence are essential. Coaching is often used in the most relationship sensitive situations, so trust is assumed. You coach at the speed of trust.

Attending so closely to what is happening in the moment makes Gestalt Coaching transformational. The Gestalt Coach needs to be intuitive and self-aware. The coach is an instrument attuned to his or her own and the client's body, energy, thoughts and feelings. The Gestalt Coach has an "embodied presence"—that is alive to being here and now. The Gestalt Coach is really present with their client—tuning into their emotional band width, helping them understand their world, helping them accept themselves as they are and deal with what is there and to move on.

The coach picks up and feeds back what is going on in the here and now of the coaching session through the physicality of breathing, posture, expressions, gestures and voice. Bodily sensations, emotional experiences and intellectualising form an unbroken wave of thought. Thought is fractal and whole. It is a mix of concrete and abstract, individual and collective, logical thought and emotional impact on thought. You are your thoughts. You are what you think. Inside your brain is the story of you.

Gestalt coaching is rooted in the present unlike other coaching styles which are rooted in the past or in the future. This awareness of the present is the focus of attention and the starting point for experimentation.

Gestalt coaching is about the way people experience things. It is about an increasing awareness of who you are and what you want. It is about your relationship with others in your world. Fundamentally, Gestalt is about acknowledging that change is an ever-flowing river, and we need to adapt to our changing world, find closure and move on. Paradoxically, you change by not changing: you change by being. The more you try to change the more resistance you encounter. "The curious paradox is that when I accept myself just as I am, then I can change"—Carl Rogers.

The Gestalt coach holds the space for new insights to emerge through a creative process, helping the client find new ways to be relevant. The Gestalt coach is fundamentally curious, helping the client deepen their awareness, always inquiring but never judgmental. Gestalt Coaching is holistic and synergistic. It embraces complexity and resists reductionism.

The Gestalt coach helps the client deal with dilemmas, conflict and uncertainty, learning to let go and let be, learning to be more of themselves. Essentially, Gestalt coaching is about human experience. It is about finding meaning and purpose. A search for wholeness. Personal identity and vision are central to our being. Personal beliefs and values drive our thinking.

Gestalt coaching is an open and fluid process; it is a compass rather than a road map. It is a journey into the unknown of the "fertile void" (John Leary Joyce, 2015), holding the space in which realisation and responses can grow. The Gestalt Coach encourages productive thinking that helps the client solve a problem with insight. This firing of the brain *synapses* or connectors helps the brain rewire when it is reinforced. This dynamic learning process produces new neural paths in the brain and opens the gateway to new behaviours. In this way, the Gestalt Coaching process is often life changing.

Gestalt Coaching Process

The process of Gestalt coaching is essentially about the flow of energy over time. Energy drives awareness as experienced by the coach and the client in a figurative "dance". The challenge is to stick to the not knowing and to hold the space for the figure to emerge. The aim of the coach is to discover how the client makes meaning of their situation, to help them accept their situation, make choices and take responsibility for decisions.

The coach is a researcher and a detective. A detective like Colombo rather than Sherlock Holmes. Colombo soaks up information like a sponge until the pieces form a pattern in his mind, whereas Sherlock Holmes focusses on the fine details.

Gestalt Coaching is thus not an "outcome-based" approach. The only goal is awareness and from this all will flow.

The paradox is that, by not focussing on outcomes, better outcomes can be achieved.

Dealing with Resistance and Change as a Gestalt Coach

You change by not changing. You change by experiencing the nature of the resistance until you understand it and accept it. It requires becoming aware, then challenging your assumptions and experimenting in a creative process to find closure and move on.

Thus, change is a continuous learning experience throughout life. Coaching accelerates this learning process. If you do not learn, reframe and internalise, then you will become stuck. The coach, by asking "How are you experiencing that now", can observe and feedback emotional leakage that helps the client to understand their resistance and deal with it.

The driving principle of Gestalt is that there is a continuous flow of experience. This flow is interrupted by changes to our environment and our relationships within it. To move on we need to be aware of the stages we must go through in order to deal with the issue. We need to increase our zone of awareness.

We are in a continuous cycle of attention, contact and withdrawal. This is the rhythm of life itself. We need to access our emotions, feelings and thoughts as they occur, deepening and heightening our awareness. We need to understand the true meaning of our everyday existence in the here-and-now of our experience. We need to integrate ourselves into the "whole" to find our true purpose.

The Gestalt coach is a *transmitter of life*, allowing the client to translate experience into meaning and purpose.

Resistance Is Normal

Resistance is normal and is part of a heathy functioning. We survive by constantly adjusting the balance between dealing with the opposing forces of wants and habits. Resistance, or an interruption of the cycle of experience, occurs as a defence mechanism to real or perceived fears. Resistance causes trouble when it is unconscious and leaves unfinished business.

This incomplete Gestalt causes a lack of equilibrium and instability and reduced ability to deal with fresh challenges. Paradoxically, the person must stay with the resistance before change can take place.

Gestalt Coaching in Practice

The Gestalt coach uses experiments to raise awareness in the client and gain insight.

One coaching technique borrowed from Gestalt therapy, to deal with resistance uses two chairs to physically separate out the players in an inter personal conflict, either between the client and another person or between the client and another part of themselves with which they are in conflict.

"Changing Chairs" Experiment

The coach invites the client to talk about a conflict situation from their own perspective.

The coach observes the body language that the client leaks emotionally when talking about the conflict.

The coach invites the client to feedback what they were experiencing in their bodies when talking.

The coach feeds back what they observed.

A discussion then takes place about what was observed by the coach, and felt by the client, what was similar and what was different.

The coach then invites the client to "change chairs" and talk about the same conflict situation but from the perspective of the other person or part of themselves.

Again, the coach observes the body language displayed this time.

The coach then asks the client how it felt when they talked as the other person or part of themselves.

Again, the coach feeds back what they observed.

A discussion then takes place about what was observed by the coach and felt by the client that was different.

Finally, an honest and open discussion takes place about the insights the client gained from the experiment and the options there are to resolve this conflict, complete the Gestalt and move on.

The experiment is a tool used by the coach to create awareness and insights in the physical experience of the client.

The paradox in this experiment is, that you have to experience uncertainty to make it real and deal with it.

By helping your client deal with ambiguity by experiencing it head on you can increase their comfort zone.

Pause for thought

What opportunities can you see to use the "Changing Chairs" Experiment?

"The Empty Chair" Experiment

Another experiment that can give your client greater awareness—and the opportunity to change that comes with it—is "The Empty Chair". This dialogue with the other person, imagining them to be sitting in front of you in the empty chair, allows you to tell them how you feel about their specific behaviour and general attitude. This opportunity to voice your opinion in the here and now is a powerful instrument of self-awareness. The coach by witnessing and accepting their emotional outpouring is validating the client's internal experience and now it is out in the open it can be explored. This heightened self-awareness from externalising the internal debate provides an opportunity for resolving the conflict. The coach facilitates an integration of thoughts and feelings to help the client find closure.

Pause for thought

What opportunities can you see to use the "The Empty Chair" Experiment?

What Does This Mean for a Coach?

Coaching is a conversation and an exchange. The coach starts by asking questions to open an expression of views, opinions, facts, beliefs and values. Elsewhere we will discuss the importance of confidence and trust in the coach/client relationship, but although it's a given, that relationship has to start somewhere. Clients may come with concerns about confidentiality, power constellations and hierarchy within the organisation. To move on and achieve a successful coaching experience for the client, it is important to explain that resistance is considered part of the process. You will want to ask your client about their assumptions, to surface their concerns, to challenge them to look at things from the perspective of others inside and outside their organisation. You want your client to be looking out at the bigger picture.

When we talk about Gestalt—*that is to integrate ourselves into the "whole"*—we talk about the big picture, to understand how we fit into it the whole, how we can get new perspectives that allow us to be creative, to look at things differently to find our place again in the turning world. Life is a constant flow of change that we need to be aware of and adapt to. We are the whole <u>and</u> we are all the parts. The whole is bigger than the parts and something different to a simple addition of the parts. Parts self-organise to make a natural whole. Awareness creates different wholes. By facing and resolving resistance and achieving closure you become more whole. Being whole gives us purpose and a sense of belonging. It's our relatedness to the collective whole that makes us human.

Life is complex and simple at the same time. Complexity and simplicity are part of the same system. Things may be complex because of too much detail, or complex because there are many ways in which parts may fit together. But our brains try to make everything simple, to take mental shortcuts. Evolution has endowed the human brain with all kinds of mental shortcuts that make life manageable.

But sometimes we need to make our brains do some critical thinking to resolve an issue to find a creative way to interpret it and move on. Gestalt coaching can help our brains to join the dots between disparate information to create simple stories that explain our complex world and give us meaning and purpose.

According to Peter Senge, in his classic book, "The Fifth Discipline", real leverage comes from taking a systems approach. The brain is systemic as is the organisation. The collective organisation is in effect a mirror of the individual brains of its members.

Pause for thought

Think of your organisation as a collective brain, a mirror of the brain.
What characteristics of the brain are driving the behaviours of the people in your organisation?
Is the emotional brain or the logical brain running the show?
How can you use your brain to influence the behaviour of the collective brain?

The Learning Challenge

We learn through social experiences. Our emotions impact on our learning as we saw in Chapter 1. A non-threatening environment allows the *limbic system*, at the centre of our emotional brain, to stay calm and let our thinking *cortex* operate without being emotionally hijacked by the *amygdala*, the brain's fight or flight response mechanism. On the other hand, a positive emotional feeling of joy, when we have an *Aha* moment of insight, can greatly enhance our learning experience as the feel-good hormone *dopamine* quickly kicks in. Even the feeling of negative emotions, experienced in a coaching session when talking about a difficult situation or relationship, can be a source of learning and a catalyst for finding closure to move on. The client is encouraged to reflect on their experience and adjust accordingly. They can then integrate their learning into planning for the next experience. This single-loop process is a continuous feedback wheel of experiencing, reflecting, adjusting, integrating, planning and experiencing again. Coaching goes beyond this simple model to create double-loop learning by challenging the fundamental beliefs about how the clients see themselves fitting into their world.

Real Learning

Facilitation of insight is real learning, not the delivery of content. People quickly forget what they have learned. Learning only sticks when the ideas are connected to a network. Activating the network will give you the whole map, and you need the map to see the connection.

The brain is a connection making machine. Learning is about making meaningful connections. Ideas come from insights and fit into the learners mental maps, their picture of the world. Linking ideas together builds a clearly defined central thread, a coherent weave. New mental maps develop. Constant focus reinforces ideas and rewires the brain: we learn through experience.

Importance of Insight

Having powerful insights changes the brain and releases *dopamine* pleasure molecules and little hits of *oxytocin*, the reward chemical of the brain. This happens in the *anterior cingulate cortex*, the brain region for detecting novelty. When we have an insight, the brain oscillates in the *gamma* band—the fastest brain frequency waves—at forty times a second. Insight is central to long-term change, but each person needs to have their own insight and not just listen to their leader's insight. To encourage thinking, leaders need to ask questions with the word "think" in them. *What do you think about what I have just said?* Attention drives change and is the active ingredient for changing the brain. A leader's job is to help others to think better for themselves.

The flow of experience can be translated into my simplified Gestalt Coaching Process below, loosely based on The Gestalt Coaching Unit of Work (developed by the Gestalt Institute of Cleveland)

MOBILISATION *thinking and talking about possibilities*

Awareness of the figure increases, as it becomes sharper. Interest in it starts to grow. Motivation increases. Mobilisation begins.

CHOICE *deciding what to do*

Energy is released generating the power of making choices. Before a final choice is made an exploration of the possibilities and their likely consequences must be made. Greater awareness of what is going on will lead to a more effective choice. Intuition as well as logic, thinking fast, thinking slow, helps the decision-making process.

ACTION *preparing and starting to do something*

Creative adaptation and experimentation helps overcome obstacles to clear the way for action.

CONTACT *doing it*

The concentrated focus of attention allows the best quality contact and most lived experience.

Contact describes the point at which the boundaries between the person and their environment meet.

CLOSURE *letting go of it and feeing relief and joy*

This is the point at which satisfaction is attained. The figure disappears into the ground. Satisfaction does not have to be absolute. With satisfaction comes the point of reflection and review.

WITHDRAWL *reflecting and learning from the experience*

Represents the act of extracting meaning and learning from the experience. It is an extremely important stage as it creates a readiness for a new figure to form from a state of letting go.

Pause for thought

Think of a time when you had something on your mind and you felt in a flow of thought and solved your dilemma.

What Is Reality?

Human experience relies on awareness of what is available to our conscious minds. Awareness is based on our perception of reality. The world we see around us is not the real world itself but merely an internal representation of that world, a guided hallucination based on sensory stimulation.

When we are riding a bicycle only another person can see us pedalling our bicycle. Our brain has to scan the surroundings and put an image of us on our bike cycling along into that landscape. So, our image of ourselves cycling is a construction by our brain. The world is in our head. Conscious experience is a mechanism of the brain. Shapes, colours and movements are all made real by our brain. The brain makes sense of its environment by conceptualising, abstracting and visualising. We are living in a virtual reality experience made to appear real by our conscious brain. And importantly this conscious experience is sugar-coated, or sour-coated, depending on the emotions we experience deep inside us.

Awareness and Gestalt Coaching

The Gestalt-orientated coach must be aware of what is going on in the here and now. The key skill of the Gestalt coach is heightened awareness. This a skill deep within you but gets dulled as you get older. You need to rediscover it, nurture and practice it. I invite you to try the following exercise.

> Sit by an open window either in your office or at home at a time you are less likely to be disturbed. Switch off your computer and mobile phone. What can you see and sense?
> the smell of fresh air?
> the sound of voices from outside?
> the colour of some flowers?

This simple exercise will heighten your awareness and develop your Gestalt coaching ability.

A checklist for yourself could include being aware of:

Your own breathing, your physical position, and the extent to which you are centred in yourself
Thoughts that appear in your mind
Feelings, for example anxiety, uncertainty, curiosity, excitement
Looking and listening non-judgmentally, simply observing
Internalising experiences so you can empathise with your client
Personalising the rhythm with which you interact, the speed with which you speak, the level of energy
Your personal needs, e.g. time out to reflect and gather yourself.
A checklist of how you relate to your client could include:

Level of eye contact
Signalling attention to your client's hand movements
Using rich language and using their words
Sharing energy, sensations and impressions
Acknowledging and accepting
Keeping focus on what is happening here and now
Say what you are thinking, volunteer a suggestion only if the client is completely stuck and you have first asked permission.

Here is another awareness exercise

This exercise is to do with being aware of "other" in relation to "self" and experiencing them as a system fully in the present.

Ask your colleague to talk to you about a client situation that you are not perpersonally involved in.

Notice: their voice, loudness, pitch and tone, their non-verbal communication signals, their body posture and movements.

Respond: Starting sentences with "I hear you say …" "I hear the frustration in your voice"; "I hear the anger in your tone"; I hear the excitement in your pitch".

Include your observation of their presence with "I see you … smile, tighten your lips, cross your arms, sit back in your chair, lean forwards, look down etc".

Now include yourself "I feel your pain; I feel your nervousness; I feel your tension; I feel your joy".

Now include your imagination "I imagine you must be feeling like a canoeist without a paddle, a hostage to the whims of the fast-flowing river".

Now include your opinion "I think you may be on taking the wrong course" "In my experience…"

Ask how they are feeling about moving on.

Somatic Cognitive Coaching

The bedrock of Gestalt Coaching principles is based on Ontology, the study of being. Being with the client and establishing a flow of awareness, the Gestalt coach is in touch with their own body and the body of the client. What is the body and all its processes, "Somatic", telling them about what is emerging? How is this bodily feedback shaping thinking and knowing, "Cognitive"?

This *bodywork* experience is about paying attention to, and acting on, the vast amount of information from our own and others' bodies. This information combined with our thoughts and perceptions, informs us how we are dynamically interacting with our client. The Gestalt coach, as a facilitator, will notice and feedback observations of bodily patterns, language and verbal expressions to ground our client in their reality.

Somatic cognitive coaching is thus a tool to create awareness from what is happening in the moment. Somatic cognitive coaching significantly enriches the coaching experience to enhance our effectiveness to help create powerful, sustainable changes for our client through awareness. Somatic cognitive coaching works externally to support deeper changes internally.

You will recall how I pointed out that emotions—especially negative ones—are recorded by the unconscious part of the brain. Our body and our client's body often cling onto old thought patterns, frequently outside our conscious awareness. We carry this past with us, in our minds and our beliefs, and physically reflect it in the tension and imbalance in our body.

This is why, reading our clients real communication through their body language, and feeding back our observations, can create a powerful awareness of the frozen emotions inhibiting their development and growth. We can then, therefore, help our clients enhance their resilience and manage their stress better, leading to an improvement in their well-being and effectiveness.

Somatic Cognitive Coaching in Action—The "Dance of Hands"

Our clients hands are often in motion as they are talking, framing, shaping, supporting or disagreeing with the spoken word, normally out of the client's awareness. This deep, highly visible (to us) link between the external and the internal is a powerful information and intervention source.

The principles of somatic cognitive coaching are: being present; being centred; being comfortable; being silent; being aware; being attentive; being non-directive; being creative and being courageous.

Coaching, using bodywork, requires extreme skill and concentration and is a tool that needs to be practiced regularly to be effective.

Using bodywork in coaching requires the permission of the client. It requires intimacy, the coach needs to immerse themselves in the emotional world of the client.

> What lies behind us and lies before us are small matters compared to what is within us. And when we bring what is within us out into the world, miracles happen—Henry David Thoreau

Developing a Strong Presence as a Coach

Developing a strong individual or "signature" presence as a coach (I refer you to Chapter 9), requires belief and confidence in yourself. This allows the authentic communication that builds trust. And you can only coach at the speed of trust. Good examples of famous leaders who have or had a strong "signature" presence include, Michele and Barack Obama, Bill Clinton, The Dalai Lama, Martin Luther King, and Nelson Mandela. All share the common characteristics of a strong sense of purpose and a deep belief in human potential.

A strong signature presence, where you are authentically yourself, will help you: to set a positive mood; to be spontaneous; to show empathic concern; to engage emotionally; to reflect on how what is emerging makes you feel; to respond to emotions in others; to speak the truth; to stay true to yourself; to deal with what is there; to give full control to the client; to stay in the moment; to be comfortable with ambiguity; to face resistance, anger and impatience; to command attention when you need to challenge; to keep the equilibrium and above all to recognise your own limitations and be comfortable that you are only human.

> The most precious gift we can offer others is our presence—Thich Nhat Hanh, Zen Master Vietnamese Buddhist monk

The Complete Gestalt Coach

The professional Gestalt coach is authentic; gives self completely; has unconditional positive regard for clients; is fully present; has presence; shows empathic concern; creates positive tension; relies on intuition and gut feel; is aware of micro non-verbal feedback; sees with the heart; is able to follow the client's thought process; questions effectively; facilitates understanding; is not afraid to feedback and challenge; promotes action; is an instrument of the coaching and is part of the process, working within the system rather than imposing a model; works with what is there rather than what should be there; sees resistance as normal and healthy and works with it rather than against it; applies the latest neuroscience and social science research; knows the philosophical and psychological concepts informing their coaching; is up to date with the business world and leadership styles; listens deeply; expresses self; manages personal boundaries; focuses on outcomes; reflects on and develops their coaching; invests in developing themselves; knows and manages their coaching boundaries; and is supervised by a Gestalt supervisor coach.

Gestalt Coach Supervision Principles

Gestalt Coach Supervision is multidimensional. Effective supervision depends on understanding the world of the coach and the world of the client. The coach supervisor needs to understand how Gestalt Coaching works and the wider context of the coaching to be able to supervise the coach's work. The coach supervisor must understand the nature of the relationship between the coach and their client. The supervisor's role is to support the coach and be a tool for personal and professional development and growth. The supervisor should never be judgemental and always challenging. Like all coaching conversations, the level of honesty will depend on the level of trust—the core of the coach supervisor relationship.

Gestalt Coaching and the Power of Now

Gestalt coaching captures the power of now. It concerns itself about what is going on in the present. Gestalt coaching is a powerful and uplifting process based on awareness. It is concerned with constantly evolving and developing systems. Sensing what is emerging and being creative in experimenting, exploring and adapting to find a return to wholeness through emergent solutions. A deep split between biological self-actualisation and our social existence leads to inner conflicts. Gestalt coaching deals with uncertainty and unfinished situations and allows people to move on by understanding where they fit in. It facilitates a healthy mind and personal development and growth. Gestalt is an open and fluid process, dealing with the experience of being human.

Gestalt becomes a way of being. It becomes embedded in us. It is about being who you are. It is a catalyst for change by being more of yourself rather than striving to be someone other than yourself.

The Gestalt oriented coach is engaged in a continuous process of awareness and skills development—Gestalt is a compass not a road map.

Gestalt is a journey into the unknown that comes back to a place called home, that we recognise for the first time. We are constantly evolving in a search for our true authentic ourselves, constantly adapting in a turning world to find a place we can call our own.

Nature's music is never over; her silences are pauses, not conclusions—Mary Webb, English novelist

In Summary

Change occurs when you become who you are, not when you try to be who you are not.

Hold a quiet stage for your client to hear the other actors, the people who form the *ground*. They can then start to see the *issue* more clearly, remove the actors from the stage and move on to the next act.

Coaching is a conversational catalyst for accelerated learning and change: it is a series of conversations with a purpose. And the Gestalt coach is the instrument of coaching. You coach as you are.

The Gestalt coach is fully and actively present, so you are aware of both yourself and your client.

Resistance to change is normal and part of healthy functioning. Finding a common language, narrative and meaning helps relate issues with personal experience and provides the mutual understanding necessary for impactful coaching conversations.

The THINK DO Coaching Model involves: helping your client think; by holding a quiet space; helping them imagine what could be different; networking and connecting their ideas into a path ahead; knowing more about themselves; deciding to make the change; and optimising the results.

Somatic Cognitive Coaching is a tool for awareness that uses the vast amount of information from your own and others' physical bodies to sense what is emerging.

Until your client has found closure they will be unable to move on. And the essence of coaching is that it is a conversation that leads to closure.

Gestalt becomes part of who you are and how you coach.

Pause for Reflection

Does the Gestalt System fit in with your thinking?

Would you integrate a Gestalt approach into your coaching conversations?

5

Leadership Coaching

Introduction

This chapter asks what coaching is, why it works and when it may be an appropriate intervention I examine who should coach. I guide you in how to coach, with particular reference to Gestalt coaching and neuroscience, as covered in the previous chapters. The chapter looks at how you frame the coaching relationship and gives examples of questions that might help unpack different kinds of problem. In Chapter 4 I explained the Gestalt coaching process and concentrated more on the psychological aspect of how coaching helps someone become internally whole. In this chapter I illustrate the key coaching competencies and the important ethical principles a coach should follow.

The What, Who, Why, When, Where and How

The What

The first use of the term coaching, to mean an instructor or trainer, arose around 1830 at Oxford University as slang for a tutor who "carries" a student through an exam.

Coaching, thus, has been used to describe the process quite simply to transport people from where they are to where they want to go.

© The Author(s) 2019
N. Marson, *Leading by Coaching*, https://doi.org/10.1007/978-3-319-76378-1_5

Professional coaching uses a range of communication skills to help clients shift their perspectives and thereby discover different approaches to achieve their goals. Business coaches help their clients advance towards specific professional goals. Leadership coaching focusses on helping tomorrow's leaders develop and grow.

Coaching is not counselling or therapy. Coaching put simply is, about helping people help themselves. Or more precisely, coaching is a learning conversation that achieves agreed outcomes and a sustainable improvement in performance. In the context of leadership coaching, it unlocks latent leadership potential.

It is essentially a non-directive form of development focussing on improving skills. The emphasis is on performance at work providing people with feedback on their strengths and weaknesses. Coaching activities have both personal and organisational goals. It can be formal, with regular fixed sessions, or a series of informal but focussed everyday conversations. Leadership coaching develops leaders and leadership competencies.

Principles of Coaching

The driving principle of coaching is that the client, the coachee, is resourceful. The role of the coach is to access the client's resourcefulness. The coach treats the client as a whole person and presents themselves as a whole person. The client sets the agenda. The coach and client are equals. And the final principle is that coaching must be change and action orientated.

Ultimately all coaching should increase the clients' circle of awareness and social connectedness, thereby leading them to a healthier and a more conscious integration of their mind. We are social through and through and feeling connected makes us feel safer because we feel we fit into our social circle.

Business Coaching

Business coaches always work with individuals in an organisational context. They are paid by the organisation to develop the potential of people or to enhance their performance. Outcomes are likely to be results orientated. The dilemma for the coach is to focus on the needs of the coachee which may conflict with the interests of the client who is paying the coach.

Gestalt coaches put outcomes before results. The result is that the client returns to wholeness by increasing their awareness, resolving an issue or dilemma creatively and moving on. The client is always the person being coached, the coachee.

Non-business Coaching

Coaching is not counselling, but the boundaries are more blurred in life coaching. Life coaches help people deal with personal dilemmas or conflicts and move on in their private lives. Sports coaching focusses on performance and has a physical and psychological element. In recent years, coaches of professional sports people, like Professor Steve Peters working with the players of Liverpool Football Club, have used neuroscience research to help athletes perform better under pressure. Former Liverpool and England Captain Stephen Gerard says he is able to perform better on the pitch from understanding the brain at work.

Coaching in a Professional Services Firm

In a professional services firm, everyone is a leader, and no one is a leader. There is a reluctance to be seen to be leading or politicking. Leaders hide in a cloak of ambiguity. They lead by social influence and stealth. In an organisation characterised by individual autonomy, like a professional services firm, a leader has no formal power. Leadership is plural, as one law firm partner put it, "frankly nobody has to follow anybody". It is something that happens between people seeking to influence each other. There is a "leadership constellation", as described by Professor Laura Empson of CASS Business School, an inner circle of influencers who are leading the firm. The leaders leave no mark—the partners will say, "we have done it ourselves".

Leading by Coaching is very often an informal activity that embeds the firm culture and values in young partners. A growing number of firms offer one to one coaching as part of a new partner development programme. Being an effective leader requires the political skills of social awareness, influencing and networking. And these skills need to be delivered whilst behaving in a sincere and apolitical way at all times.

> The interesting thing in this role (of Senior Partner) is that you can't achieve anything except through other people ... You can only make things happen by essentially working with this group (of key influencers) who in turn influence the wider group (of key influencers) who in turn influence the wider group,

so power has a different meaning I think to power in other organisations.— Senior Partner aw Firm[1]

A more embedded coaching culture will, I believe, be needed to develop a new breed of partners that are better equipped to deal with an ever more complex world and more demanding clients.

> **Pause for thought**
>
> Does your organisation have a formal system for leader coach training?
>   Is a more formal system of coaching tomorrow's leaders needed?
>   Where are you in your professional development as a coach?

Coaching Talent

In the world's leading organisations, attracting, retaining and developing talent is a key imperative. Coaching these talented people on a day-to-day basis is a vital role of the leader. Today's talent will be tomorrow's leaders so this *Leading by Coaching* activity is crucial to the sustainability of the organisation. And coach them, don't tell them. As the late Steve Jobs wisely commented,

> It doesn't make sense to hire smart people and then tell them what to do, we hire smart people, so they can tell us what to do.

Coaching Clever People

Leading by Coaching clever people is tricky. They know better than you. Just let them get on with it.

The trick is to empower them and give them a safe environment rather than push them according to Rob Goffee and Gareth Jones of London Business School.[2]

Coaching should be seen as developmental, targeted at personal growth, full of opportunities to experiment and have fun. It should be conducted with a light touch. A series of everyday conversations that softly guides young talented future leaders rather than having full-blooded coaching sessions.

---

[1]Empson, L. (2014). *Reluctant leaders and autonomous followers: Leadership tactics in professional service firms*. London: Cass Business School.

[2]Goffee, R., & Jones, G. (2007, March). Leading Clever People. *Harvard Business Review*. Retrieved from https://hbr.org/2007/03/leading-clever-people.

Coaching Business Skills for Future Leaders

The business skills needed by a future leader can be grouped into four main areas of awareness:

1. Developing and applying the self
2. Understanding and relating to your clients
3. Collaborating with your colleagues and leading
4. Innovating in the business and delivering results.

Coaching helps greatly in consciously expanding the above areas of awareness by improving sensing, thinking and seeing skills. It can also give people a greater sense of purpose. The most powerfully motivating condition people experience at work is making progress at something that is personally meaningful. If your role involves leading others, the most important thing you can do each day is to help your team members experience progress through meaningful work.

Do you understand what drives each person? Do you help build connections between each person's work and the firm's mission and strategic objectives? Do you give your people a profound sense of purpose and direction?

Do you give timely and sensitive feedback? People want to know how they are doing to feel safe. Help each person learn and grow on an ongoing basis. Set them challenges to get them out of their comfort zone and go beyond. Regular developmental communication—having *coaching* conversations—is essential. Google found, in their research project Aristotle—its quest to build the perfect team—that psychological safety was the important requirement for team members. Coaching is the most important managerial competency that separates highly effective managers from average ones.[3]

> **Pause for thought**
> Do you have coaching conversations every day with your people?

---

[3]Duhigg, C. (2016, February 25th). *What Google Learned From Its Quest to Build the Perfect Team.* Retrieved from The New York Times Magazine: https://www.nytimes.com/2016/02/28/magazine/what-google-learned-from-its-quest-to-build-the-perfect-team.html.

Essence of Coaching

The essence of coaching is engaging another person to help them raise their awareness and, therefore, their ability to act. Coaching is science and art. The science is the neuroscience of how the brain works and the consequences to human behaviour (see Chapters 1 and 2). The art is pragmatic humanism. Intuition and emotional Intelligence are the key competencies of great coaching. Great coaches are deep listeners who make their clients feel fully heard and understood. You coach at the speed of trust. The key attribute of an effective coach is empathy. Empathy has the power to build rapport, generate trust and get commitment. It is the great enabler. It creates an emotional connection and bond at a deeply human level. It is the basis of all relationships.

Empathy activates the older parts of the brain beneath the *cortex*, the emotional centre of the brain—the *amygdala, hypothalamus* and the *hippocampus*—which allows us to experience feelings quickly. These areas, according to Antonio Damasco in his book *Emotion, Reason and the Human Brain*, arouse the same emotional states in us as others are experiencing. And this happens in the *mirror neurons* in our brain. This is how the brain experiences—"I feel your pain".

Cognitive Empathy

Sometimes empathy is unhelpful. We need a detached perspective. Cognitive empathy or perspective taking enables us to understand how someone else understands the problem at a rational level. To see their point of view without feeling their emotions.

Pause for thought

Are people born with empathy or is it something that can be learned? What do you think?

According to Amy Cuddy, of Harvard University, acting as if you are empathic can build ability to become better at it. If you act in a caring way—looking people in the eye and paying attention to their expressions—you can start to feel more engaged. Putting yourself physically into an empathic state can generate changed hormone levels consistent with that adopted state.

I believe compassionate empathy from the heart always beats cognitive empathy from the head because it taps into our collective experience into what it is to be human.

Change and Coaching

The world is changing faster than in any other period in history. Clients are changing faster? But do you know where your clients are going? And are you going with them? And most importantly are you helping your people to keep up by coaching them. Coaching accelerates learning. Coaching helps your people to adapt faster to change. You will remember from the previous chapter that in Gestalt coaching, the paradox is that you change by not changing. By being not doing. By being more of yourself not trying to be a different self.

How Helpful Is Navel Gazing?

We are living in a selfie world where the precious self is at the centre of our Universe. In this new social order, we are under more and more pressure to improve ourselves. To look better, to be seen to be more successful, especially on *facebook*, and to feel better about ourselves. But are we getting any happier? Is this constant social pressure causing young people especially to suffer with more anxiety and mental health issues? This daily struggle to improve ourselves is relentless.

Is there an alternative to this constant navel gazing? Svend Brinkmann, Professor of Psychology at Aalborg University in Denmark certainly thinks so. He invites us to throw away our self-improvement books, embrace negativity and "stand firm" against the wave of positivity. He is against the anti-social "success at any cost" mantra of guru Anthony Robbins, who has coached George W Bush. Following your dreams isn't for everyone. Some people want to wallow in the actual or perceived hopelessness of their situation. It makes them feel better. After all, things can only get better when expectations are at rock bottom.

Ancient stoics such as Seneca and Epictetus provide an antidote to today's self-help narrative. Rather than practising positive visualisation of "this is what I want", they advocated the opposite. Negative visualisation—imagining losing everything you have—makes you appreciate what you have and be less attached to it. As mentioned previously in Chapter 3, Albert Einstein observed, "you will be happier if you attach yourself to a life of purpose rather than people and possessions".

The concept of "defensive pessimism" can be an effective strategy to manage anxiety. Constantly thinking on the bright side doesn't work for everyone.

For some people, the glass will always be half empty and that is the lesson we should learn as coaches. A good dose of stoic reflection may be the right tonic for some. Navel gazing doesn't work for everyone.

The Brain and Coaching

You will recall your brief tour of the brain and the unravelling of some of its mysteries in Chapter 1. So, what has the brain got to do with coaching? Quite a lot as it turns out. Coaching takes place in people's heads. This means that a brain-based approach to coaching should underpin the coach's work. This scientific approach—pioneered by Jeffrey M. Schwartz, M.D. in *The Mind & The Brain* and translated into a digestible language by David Rock—feels more grounded for senior professionals than the traditional psychological approach which conjures up images of therapy and navel gazing.

They want something more tangible and evidence based. And HR professionals want an approach that is more systemic and measurable. They want a coaching system that speaks to the organisation in a language it understands so that coaching becomes a standard instrument for organisational transformation.

Gestalt methodology fits perfectly into this brain-based approach as they both are based on perception and awareness in the here and now.

Coaching with the brain in mind can help in many areas including: the understanding of the basic towards and away motivation and behaviour; how our choices change the functions of our brain; the power of attention and focus on our learning; the profound power of others on our thoughts and actions; why change is much harder than we imagine; how the "Aha" moment of insight can "fire and rewire" the brain; and finally understanding the importance of reflection and thinking about our thinking.

Neuroscience is the best explanation of how and why coaching works. It improves the coach's ability to coach and train other coaches. Getting people to change is a growing organisational imperative. Brain-based coaching helps people on their journey because it works and translates well into the hard-headed language of the Professional Service organisation.

It works equally well in FTSE 100 companies that are coming to terms with the digital age of disruption.

Paradox of Coaching

The wise Tao coach is teaching without telling. Allows without commanding. Cares without claiming. Hears through silence. Is empty, yet infinitely full. The enlightened coach finds the essential truth. The paradox of coaching is that you coach by not coaching. You coach by witnessing. You coach by being, not doing.

> To live life in accord with the Tao is to be in harmony with all others, with the environment and with one's self. It is to live in synchronicity with processes, and to be completely authentic, sincere, natural and innocent—Lao Tzu

The Who

In the workplace there is a good reason for everyone to be coached at some level, however it can be hard to implement if the habit is not imbedded at Board Level and down through the Senior Management. A rigorous coaching culture can be the competitive advantage if it is aligned to strategy and a balanced scorecard approach to performance management.

Training leaders to be coaches should be a core competency, but very often no formal training is given to leaders in this skill. The result is leaders shy away from this activity at worst and dabble with it at best. Talented people deserve better.

Who Delivers Coaching?

Coaching is delivered by internal coaches and external coaches. Internal coaches are either line managers or part-time coaches who are HR managers. External coaches are hired normally for developing leaders. They are often transformational. The choice of using an internal coach or hiring an external coach is a critical and difficult one.

If the choice is an internal coach, are they far enough removed from the individual's day-to-day work and reporting line? Trust and confidentiality are essential for a successful relationship. It is difficult to avoid conflict with their hierarchical relationship. There is a big difference between adopting a *Leading by Coaching* style and conducting a formal coaching programme.

One other major difference between internal and external coaches is that the latter have a wider perspective, looking in from the outside, independent of the organisation, free from any internal influences. External coaches are not blinded by groupthink and can be more challenging as they are outsiders.

Choosing a Coach

Before you choose a coach ask yourself the following questions:

Where do I need support?
Does the coach have the relevant professional experience?
What is his/her track record for successful outcomes?
Does the coach have a good understanding of my industry?
Am I clear on my coaching expectations?
Is there a good personal chemistry so critical for a successful outcome?

The Gestalt Coach

Gestalt coaching is relevant in our increasingly disruptive world because it is systems based. We are all part of a bigger system. Our actions have an impact on the system. Confrontation is the basis of all authentic relationships, and we are constantly adapting to maintain our unique personal significance. Being is a stream of change.

Gestalt coaching is an emergent process rooted to the present unlike other coaching styles which are rooted in the past or in the future. This awareness of the present is the focus of attention and the starting point of experimentation. Gestalt is about the way people experience things. It is about an increasing awareness of who you are and what you want. It is about your relationship with others in your world. It's our relatedness to the collective whole that makes us human.

Fundamentally, Gestalt is about acknowledging that change is an ever-flowing river, and we need to constantly adapt to find closure and move on. The Gestalt coach encourages productive thinking that helps the client solve a problem with insight.

The Why

Why Coaching?

There is no widely accepted theoretical framework that explains why we require coaching. What we do know, based on neuroscience research, is that our brains need coaching.

For people to change, their brains need to change. The brain is a social organ and looks for validation from other brains! People want to be assured by their coach before they can accept their own truths!

What are the Benefits of Coaching

Coaching:

improves performance and productivity;
develops talent;
creates deeper relationships;
encourages creativity and innovation;
reduces inertia to change;
motivates employees;
enhances leadership capability;
leads to better collaboration;

Why Coaching Works

Coaching helps by keeping people focussed on the change they seek, for themselves and others. Coaching is a safe place for thinking and experimenting with alternative scenarios. Insights from coaching help the brain develop new neural pathways that lead to changed behaviours with different outcomes. The brain requires autonomy and so self-directed learning through coaching is more brain friendly than being told to change.

Limits to Coaching

For coaching to be effective, a high level of personal trust and psychological safety is paramount. Internal coaching may not allow these optimum Coaching conditions because the coachee cannot rely on the complete confidentiality of their coach, who may have formal power over them. External coaches provide greater independence and the inherent safety that is required for coaching to work. Matching the right coach, with the right personal chemistry with the coachee, is also equally critical to the success of coaching interventions. Coaching by its very nature is built on personal trust.

The Brain Science of the Why

Coaching encourages a greater sense of purpose and a new focus for attention. And paying long enough attention changes the brain itself through the electrochemical signalling of *neurons*. This attention density describes our mental focus and concentration. The power of the brain, directed by coaching, lies in the focus. The questions you ask when coaching affect the quality of the connections the brain makes as it forms new mental maps in its bid to make sense of a changing world. Your *plastic* brain changes itself constantly in order to adapt to the new challenges it faces.

Developing a Coaching Culture

Coaching works best when it is owned from the top of the organisation, it is sponsored by the CEO, Board members and senior leaders, and its value is promoted throughout.

According to David Clutterbuck, coaching is "the predominant style of managing and working together where commitment to improving the organisation is embedded in a parallel commitment to improving people".

It is critical to coach talented people to help them develop their potential, contribute more to the organisation and prepare them for future leadership roles.

In the race to secure and retain the services of talented people, opportunities for personal growth can be the deciding factor.

Stakeholders in Coaching

A coaching contract has three sides: the coachee, the coach and the organisation.

The organisation may have multiple stakeholders or sponsors including the line manager and the Human Resources Department.

It is critically important to be clear in your mind that your client is the person you are coaching. When you make your client the focus of attention, then the interests of other stakeholders should be well served.

> **Pause for thought**
>
> How would you handle the following dilemma: You are in conflict with a stakeholder who you perceive is jeopardising the confidential nature of your coaching relationship?

Coaching is a Style of Leadership

Coaching is a style of leadership that can be used in situations where self-directed learning will accelerate individual growth and development.

Before coaching anyone, start by asking yourself, why would anyone want to be coached by you?

People follow people who they believe, believe in, what they believe in. They need to know why people they follow believe in what they believe in. Over 250,000 people came to hear Dr. Martin Luther King deliver his now famous, "I have a dream" speech, because they shared his dream of, "being free at last, finally we are free at last". They came for themselves not for him.

If Dr. King had said "I have a plan" instead of "I have a dream" the speech wouldn't have been powerful. The emotional brain is much more powerful than the logical brain. The why is more important than the how or the what. The why starts in the emotional centre of the brain, the *limbic system*. The how and the what are processed by the *neo cortex* thinking brain. We feel before we think. Purpose drives passion. Passion drives action. All motivation is self-motivation.

We need to believe in the messenger before we believe in their message. The Who and Why are inextricably linked. The messenger must be ethical in our eyes and share the same values before we will act on their message. We must believe in the coach before we will let them coach us.

Coaching Across Cultures

Traditional coaching operates within the confines of your cultural norms, values and belief systems. Coaching across cultures challenges your assumptions and propels you beyond these limitations. This provides a wonderful opportunity to create solutions by leveraging cultural differences.

Coaching with cultural sensitivity in a global professional services firm or FTSE 100 international company will optimise human potential and improve cross border collaboration.

I touched on cultural orientation when coaching across Culture in Chapters 3 and more deeply in Chapter 6.

Coaching Trends in Learning & Development

The Chartered Institute for Personnel and Development Learning and Development Coaching Trends Survey, published in 2015, found the following:

In-house methods are favoured over external practices
80% of organisations offer coaching and mentoring
Coaching talent is a top priority for 90% of organisations
Line managers are responsible for delivering coaching in 63% of cases
60% of organisations use external coaches to design coaching programmes
Leadership development is the main purpose of coaching in 20% of
    organisations.

The When

Coaching for Performance

Coaching is a conversation with a purpose that can take place anytime and anywhere. Improved performance comes from greater self-awareness and self-directed motivation to change, energised by insights from coaching conversations.

Coaching for Purpose—Gestalt

I chose Gestalt as the basis for my coaching because the approach felt in line with who I am and how I think. My experience of my ICF Advanced Level Gestalt-based business coaching programme profoundly changed me as a person and as a coach. It made me realise that I, my authentic self, was the instrument of my coaching and the catalyst for change in myself and in others. I realised that just being truly present with my client and witnessing them was enough for them to hear their own authentic voice and rediscover their purpose.

Gestalt coaching, as you learned in Chapter 4, is fundamentally concerned with finding purpose by moving towards yourself. This is achieved by the coach through increasing the self-awareness of the client. You change by being, not doing. The primary motivation of the human brain is to make meaning or sense from its operating environment.

An incomplete Gestalt is a lack of self-awareness. Helping my client create and adapt to get closure and complete their Gestalt is, for me, the heart of my coaching. It requires staying with my client in their stuckness, helping them understand what is happening and what choices they have to move on. The paradox, as mentioned before, is you change, as a leader and a coach, by not changing. You change by being. By accepting yourself; being happy with yourself; moving towards yourself. Celebrating your strengths and the unique contribution you make to your communities.

Coaching for Change

Coaching creates clarity and clarity drives change. If a pond is clouded with mud, there's nothing you can do to make the water clear. But when you allow the mud to settle, it will clear on its own, because clarity is the water's natural state. You change by not changing but by allowing your mind to settle into its natural state. The only constant in change is change itself. You can't stop the waves coming but you can ride the surf. And the coach can help you stay on your surf board by helping you deal with the big waves.

Change and the Brain

The brain hates change. It craves certainty. It wants to know the outcomes. It doesn't like surprises. The elephant's primitive brain will resist the rider's executive brain from taking a turn from the well-trodden path. The brain loves habits.

The brain makes change hard as we saw in Chapter 1. The brain-friendly coach can help the rider steer the elephant by knowing what motivates the elephant. The bigger the perceived risk, the bigger the perceived reward must be. The promise of pleasure must be bigger than the threat of pain. The brain operates on a binary system.

The Where

The Coaching Continuum

The type of leadership intervention will largely depend on the situation and the experience of the follower. The coaching continuum allows a full spectrum of intervention from push to pull. Coaching sits firmly at the pull end of the spectrum as it relies on self-directed learning. It is a management behaviour that lies at the opposite end of the spectrum to command and control.

Coaching has the power to optimise both performance and potential as opposed to training which should be seen as an important method to impart knowledge and improve specific skills. Training because it is typically a group activity, does not allow the optimum conditions for personal development and growth.

Is Coaching an Appropriate Intervention?

For coaching to work, the coach needs to have the right attitude, a sincere wish to help and an open mind. Good attitude is driven by a strong sense of purpose.

The coachee must be coachable, that means wanting to be coached and committed to completing the coaching. Are some people uncoachable? Maybe.

I once was asked to talk with someone who did not believe in coaching because she had had a bad experience with a coach. I ended up coaching her because she wanted someone to confide in rather than be coached. I happened to be the right person with the critically important right chemistry required to build the high levels of personal trust necessary for the coaching relationship to work.

There are some people, on the other hand, who don't want to let someone get too close to them. They don't want to disclose the real person behind the professional mask. Coaching will probably help them come out of their shadow, but they need to give themselves permission first to be coached and then give the coach permission to coach them.

Differences Between Mentoring and Coaching

Mentoring is an alternative to coaching where a senior colleague can give career guidance based on their experience. Generally speaking the main differences can be summarised in Fig. 5.1.

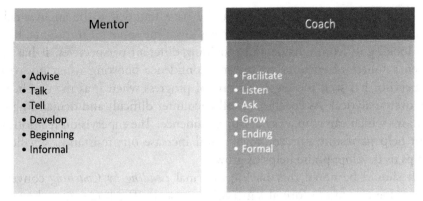

Mentor	Coach
• Advise	• Facilitate
• Talk	• Listen
• Tell	• Ask
• Develop	• Grow
• Beginning	• Ending
• Informal	• Formal

Fig. 5.1 The Parallel Mind Mentor and Coach Framework

Coaching is a facilitated discussion that focusses on specific goals. It is self-directed. Coaching is a conversation with a purpose. A space to learn, develop and grow. Coaching conversations are discussed in detail in the next chapter.

Coaching Supervision

Supervision can be defined as:

> The process by which a coach, with the help of a supervisor, can attend to understanding better both the client system and themselves as part of the client-coach system, and by so doing transform their work and develop their craft. (Hawkins and Smith 2006)

Fundamentally coaching supervision is a source of individual and organisational learning. Supervision provides a valuable chance for reflection on formal coaching practice. It forms an important part of the continuous professional development of the coach. It is an important part of the quality assurance needed by the client. A chance for the coach supervisor to pick up on critical issues like coaching boundary management and conflict resolution. Also, it provides an important source of organisational learning about the effectiveness of coaching and coaches. It is highly desirable and advisable that a Gestalt-trained coach is supervised by a supervisor who understands how a Gestalt coach operates.

Coaching supervision maximises the potential of coaching. I believe supervision can make a substantial difference to how we develop as coaches to support our clients. I have certainly benefited from supervision.

All my coaching is supervised, and I have found it to be an invaluable source of support and knowledge. It has given me some great insights, based on looking in from outside and providing different perspectives. It has also been a source of encouragement and confidence boosting when my coach supervisor has seen the bigger picture of progress when I, as the coach, can be over analytical. As coaches, we all encounter difficult and demanding situations which can chip away at our confidence. The supervision relationship can help us restore our confidence and increase our resistance. Challenge helps us develop; praise helps us grow.

It should be noted that having informal *Leading by Coaching* conversations doesn't require formal supervision as such. The leader may, however, confide in someone who has experience in coaching—perhaps in the HR function. You can also keep a coaching learning journal to record your reflections and capture insights on your coaching experiences. This is a valuable source of learning that can be referred to before coaching sessions.

Supervision plays a key role in the continuing professional development of both internal and external coaches. Supervision is a place to have deep conversations that change both the supervised and the supervisor. Supervision is a place to think creatively. Supervision is a place to walk together, a reflective space to be treasured.

Coaching supervision helps us as coaches to be more aware of what is going on inside us, so we can be more aware of our impact on our coachee. Supervision provides a lens to focus on our coaching and our coaching relationship. It provides new light and changed dynamics. Supervision creates a s u p e r - v i s i o n !

The Elements of Supervision are: formal, interpersonal, reflective and developmental

Supervision Structure:

Check-in
Agree session focus
Agree session outcomes
Discuss client coaching session
Personal issues arising from the coaching
Development needs as a coach
Concerns about coaching and coaching supervision
Learning from supervision session
Actions to be taken.

Supervision Good Practice

Supervision good practice has at its heart the focus on the coach and client relationship. The supervisor supports the coach by understanding the client-coach system and in so doing is able to improve the awareness of the coach so that the client has an element of quality control over the coaching received. Supervision manages ethical boundaries of the coaching by providing a place to have deep conversations about where the line is, for example, between coaching and counselling. Supervision provides the coach with valuable continuous professional development. Internal supervision is a source of organisational learning about coach development and coaching effectiveness. Confidentiality must, however, be respected and maintained. It is important that supervision takes place regularly so that the narrative is uninterrupted (Fig. 5.2).

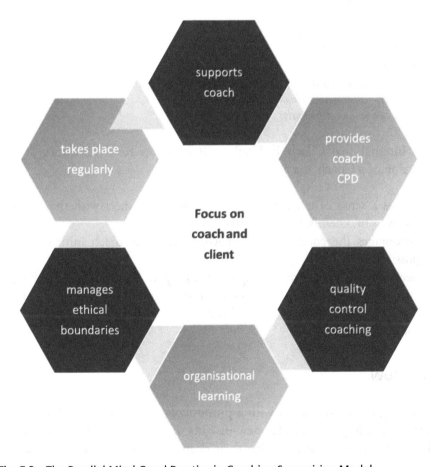

Fig. 5.2   The Parallel Mind Good Practice in Coaching Supervision Model

Who You Are, Is How You Supervise

Our state of being is the only real source of our ability to influence those around us. The success of any intervention depends on our inner emotional state. How we work is how we bring ourselves to our clients. It is our signature presence as a coach and as a supervisor. It is experienced by our clients, moment by moment through our energy and presence.

Who we are is the ground on which we stand. How we see ourselves.

What is important to us.

Our essence is in our scripts. The everyday conversations provide a common thread to our life's purpose. Who we are is what we do and say. Our work is the place where our intimate self meets the world.

Supervision Questions

How's the coaching going?
What is going well?
What is difficult?
How are you feeling in the difficult moments?
What are you learning about yourself as a coach?
What can you do differently?

The International Coach Federation (ICF) states Key Guidelines for the Selection of a Coach as a Supervisor:

- evokes a sense of trust and has the ability to connect with the coach in terms of fit, chemistry and compatibility
- encourages the coach to reach beyond what the coach initially feels is possible
- demonstrates equal partnership by being open, vulnerable and willing to take appropriate risks, for example, in providing feedback that may make one or both individuals uncomfortable, in the context of the supervisory role.

The How

Coaching is a conversation with a purpose. The coach is both observer and catalyst, holding the stage for new insights to emerge. The methods used by the Gestalt-trained coach, using their deep knowledge of the neuroscience of how the brain processes and regulates the transfer of information and energy, allow the client to understand what is driving their thinking; to practice the power of focus; to develop insights and to generate the motivation to act.

What works in coaching may, largely, be explained scientifically and through our innate understanding of what it is to be human.

Agreeing a Contract

Coaching is a contract, and it is essential that the terms of the contract are explicit. Both parties ought to have a full and frank discussion about what they want to gain from the coaching: the behaviours expected and the boundaries. There are also some vital ingredients of a coaching relationship that are implicit like trust, honesty and confidentiality. Above all both parties must have good intentions and be committed to complete the coaching process.

Opening the Coaching Session

> The beginning is the most important part of the work—Plato

The most important thing is to turn up. Be in the right positive frame of mind. Choose to care. Your coaching has the potential to change someone's life. Hold it carefully and with a light touch. Listen to the client's story and don't be afraid to tell your story, if it helps, in the learning space that is coaching.

Acknowledging the Client

People just want to be witnessed and understood. They want somebody to listen to their pain and show they care. They want somebody to talk to.

The CEOs I have coached felt quite lonely at the top of their organisations. They just wanted someone to listen to them, so they could hear themselves.

Coaching Skills

The coach needs many skills to be effective: staying centred, listening authentically, building rapport and trust, finding congruence, letting come and letting go, questioning effectively, using the clients' language, challenging, checking motivation, summarising and getting commitment to action.

Key Coaching Skills

Listening Authentically

As you saw earlier in my book in Chapter 3, in the Suicide Prevention Hotline stories, listening deeply to another person and witnessing them shows you care and builds trust.

Just being present is enough. Your presence as another human being who is compassionate gives people strength and opens them up to talk about their pain and deepest fears.

Essentially coaching is about being there for another person and sharing your humanity. To be human is to be vulnerable and to share our vulnerability gives people the confidence and energy to deal with their issues, complete their Gestalts and move on.

Questioning Effectively

> We cannot solve our problems with the same thinking we used when we created them—Albert Einstein

Asking the right questions, at the right time, and in the right way, is the tool coaches use to keep the client moving forward. Effective questions raise awareness, produce insights, encourage responsibility and commit people to action.

Different types of questions unlock different types of obstacles. Open questions like, what or how, get people thinking about obstacles and how they might overcome them. Asking why should be used with care as it can be felt as accusing, judging or criticising. *What was on your mind?* is less personal than, *why did you do that?* Closed questions require a *Yes* or *No* answer and, therefore, force people to make decisions and make step by step progress. Socratic reasoning can also be a useful here. Short questions are normally better than long ones because they get to the point quicker so that people can think more clearly about an answer. When questions require clarification or reframing, the essence of the question can be lost, and the direction of the intended conversation can be derailed.

Sample Questions

Clarity–

Where are you now?

Awareness–

What do you enjoy most about your work?
What do you enjoy least about your work?
What inspires you?
What matters most to you?

Aspiration–

Where do you want to be?
What opportunities do you see?
What do you want to achieve?
What do you feel you are really good at?

Capability–

What do you want to change?
What are your biggest challenges?
What can help you achieve your ambitions?
What would you like to be better at?

Confidence–

Where do you lack confidence?
Who can support you on your journey?
Where do you need support?
Why would they support you?

Challenging

The confident coach challenges when incongruence is detected in the client between the **words**, *what they say*; the **music**, *how they say the words*; and the **dance**, *how they look when they say the words*. This leakage allows the coach to probe to help them confront their truth, deal with it and move on. Coaching is ultimately a search for the truth.

Good questions can reframe a problem to find a solution from another place, from another point of view.

The Dynamics of Change

Staying in the client's stuckness, in silence, is the hardest thing a coach needs to do. There is a real discipline in holding back, in not offering solutions and advice, in not trying to be helpful. Just shutting up is a key skill! Letting the client think about their thinking and seeing what emerges is a beautiful thing. The client needs space to understand where they are in their **S**ystem and to see possible ways they can **T**ranscend and go beyond their self-imposed boundaries. The coach helps the client in **A**nalysing the situation and discusses the **R**elational positions between the issue and the context or, in Gestalt terms, the figure and the ground. These change dynamics can be represented in the simple Parallel Mind STAR Change dynamics model in Fig. 5.3.

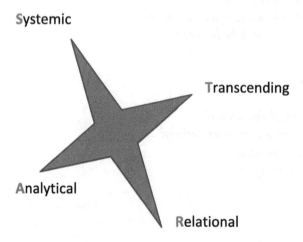

Fig. 5.3 The Parallel Mind STAR Change Dynamics Model

Preparing to Coach

> Learn your theories and techniques as well as you can and then be prepared to set them aside when you meet the miracle of the living soul in front of you—Carl Jung

Getting into the coaching zone before a coaching session is essentially about preparing yourself to turn up, be present and have presence. Coaching sessions should be full of energy, excitement and empathy. The paradox of coaching is that it is about "being" rather than "doing" but it is still a performance. A performance because it requires conscious awareness, emotional control and perspective taking. It requires the coach to take off their clothes, to be naked in front of the client, in the hope they will do the same, metaphorically speaking of course! Being a coach requires honesty and courage. Connecting emotionally builds the trust to give both parties the confidence to show their vulnerabilities. And being an actor and director on the coaching stage is a performance art. Your unique coach signature presence shines through.

Coaching Tools

The Parallel Mind **THINK DO** Coaching Model, I describe in Chapter 4, combines the latest research findings from neuroscience into the working of the brain with Gestalt coaching practice. My active model provides a simple framework for coaching with the brain in mind. From thinking to knowing to doing (At this point, it will be useful for you to refer back to Chapter 4 and review the **THINK DO** Coaching Model).

The Gestalt search for "wholeness" is facilitated by the coach, through understanding the power of silence to enable frozen thoughts from the unconscious brain to surface into the conscious brain. These moments of transcendence produce the insights and focus necessary to harness the energy that drives action and leads to finding wholeness.

The key skill of the Gestalt coach is to hold the space for the client to find their authentic voice. The coach by staying with their client's stuckness, letting go and letting come, produces a state of flow that creates closure through a creative, adaptive, and emergent process.

Coaching Competencies

The starting point is to refer you back to the Daniel Goleman Emotional Intelligence Competencies Framework and the Social Competencies I covered in Theme I where I also introduce Cultural Intelligence Competencies and Neuro Leadership Intelligence and Self-Mastery Competencies.

Daniel Goleman discusses E I competencies in *Working with Emotional Intelligence* (Bantam 1998). These competencies are the foundation stones of coaching.

The following guide is in three parts: Personal; Social and Cultural. It will help you reflect on your coaching competencies and flag up in your mind areas for self-development.

Personal Competencies

Self-awareness is about knowing yourself. Knowing the difference, you want to make. Knowing your beliefs and values. Knowing what drives and motivates you. Knowing your strengths and limitations.

Self-awareness is about knowing how you are feeling in the moment. Recognising your mood and how it is affecting others. Understanding and labelling the emotions, you are feeling and what is causing them.

Self-awareness is about being open to feedback. Always looking for opportunities to get new perspectives to learn and improve your performance and develop professionally. Always reflecting on experiences and making adjustments.

Self-awareness promotes self-confidence. Self-confidence is not taking yourself too seriously. Keeping things in perspective. Being self-confident but knowing that you don't know what you don't know. Sureness about one's self-worth and capabilities. Having authentic presence. Doing the right thing even when it is unpopular. Being decisive and surefooted in the face of adversity and ambiguity.

Self-management is about self-regulation and self-motivation.

Managing distressing and disruptive emotions by **self-regulation** is important for mental well-being and social mobility. Being able to stay calm and composed when under pressure is a critical skill for a leader and a coach. When being challenged as a coach, you need to think clearly and stay focussed, even though your emotional brain is feeling threatened and putting your body into a state of alert.

Emotionally intelligent leader coaches are **self-motivated** to be authentic; honest; ethical; principled; reliable and, therefore, trustworthy. They are conscientious; keep promises and meet commitments. They feel accountable for their performance and standards of behaviour. They uphold the values of their group. They are achievement-focussed and results-driven. They commit themselves to the purpose and goals of their organisation and the people they are coaching. They are persistent in achieving and helping others they coach achieve, their challenging goals. They are catalysts for change and are fluid in their responses to a rapidly changing environment. They model the change they seek. They hunt for new ideas from multiple sources to drive innovation. They are original thinkers. They are optimists, taking the initiative to seize opportunities and sometimes taking calculated risks. When they face setbacks head-on, they just keep going, without any discernible loss of enthusiasm. They see an opportunity to learn from every failure. They are agents of hope. The glass is always half full.

Social Competencies

Social awareness is the ability to read the social situation and the behaviours required to be socially acceptable. It consists of social cognition, empathic concern and emotional resonance.

Social cognition is about reading emotional currents from other peoples' non-verbal body language, so you can better understand how they are feeling.

People who show **empathic concern** sense others' feelings and take an active interest in their concerns. They are attentive to emotional cues and listen well. They show sensitivity and seek to help based on understanding others' perspectives, needs and feelings.

Emotional resonance occurs when you register the emotional cues in the other person's message and tune into their emotional frequency. They feel that you understand them at a human level. This creates a deep rapport which is the foundation for building trust.

Managing relationships is about balancing tasks with relationships, promoting a friendly, co-operative climate and leveraging diversity. Managing relationships is about sensing what others need in order to help them reach their aspirations and optimise their talents. Leaders with this competence acknowledge and reward peoples' strengths and appreciate their contributions. They offer useful feedback and identify peoples' needs for development. They give regular and timely coaching, and actively look for assignments that challenge and grow a person's skills.

Leaders nurture personal relationships by building and deepening personal trust. They manage relationships by accurately reading political situations in organisations and external realities. By accurately reading the key power relationships and detecting crucial social networks.

These social skills to effectively manage relationships include, listening deeply, influencing, persuading, communicating clearly, presenting convincingly, building consensus and dealing with conflict—with diplomacy and tact.

The Personal Competencies above are underpinned by a deep understanding of how your brain influences behaviour and expressed in my Neuro Leadership Intelligence framework in Chapter 2.

Cultural Competencies

As you have already read in Chapter 2, and will learn more later in Chapter 6, it is vitally important to understand the cultural orientation of other nationalities to make coaching context specific in global organisations.

Neuro Leadership Intelligence Competencies

Neuro Leadership Intelligence is about leading with the brain in mind. Also covered in Chapter 2. To be consciously competent as a coach you must have a deep understanding of how the brain and mind work together in parallel.

Self-Mastery is about knowing and playing to your strengths; being emotionally resilient and practising the mindful leader's way—the art of making the right decisions.

> Self-Mastery—"Analysing others is knowledge; knowing yourself is true wisdom. Mastering others is strength; mastering yourself is true power".—Lao Tzu

Your Coaching Shadow

You coach at the speed of trust. The more shadow the less trust, the more trust the less shadow. Bad coaches hold back, they do not want to be discovered, unmasked. And their clients hold back too.

Good coaches don't hold back, and this high level of disclosure encourages their clients to be honest and open. This creates more awareness and more options that lead to better outcomes.

Coaching Shadow

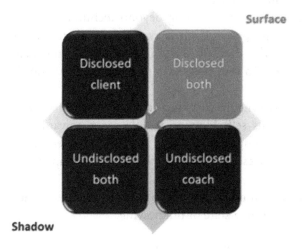

Fig. 5.4 The Parallel Mind Coaching Shadow Model

The Parallel Mind Coaching Shadow Model is based on the Johari Window Model in Chapter 2 (Fig. 5.4).

Leading by Coaching

Are you ready? Are you ready to lead your organisation by coaching talented individuals who have the potential to be the next breed of leaders? If you are ready just start. Start today! Start, by having a conversation with one of those talented individuals. Just check in with them. *How are they? How are they doing? What is on their mind?* And don't forget to praise them for what they do. Praise makes people grow. Just have an everyday coaching conversation. Frequent and casual conversations build trust and accelerate change. People change one conversation at a time. Organisations change one person at a time. *Leading by Coaching* for impactful change and one conversation at a time.

The Art of Masterful Coaching

The Paradox of Wisdom—"Knowing is beyond knowledge, experience transcends analysis, we need to be before we become"—Lao Tzu

The paradox of coaching is that you cannot become a great coach by wishing to become a great coach. You become a masterful coach by understanding you can never master coaching.

Masterful coaching is coaching beyond techniques. Helping people find a clear sense of purpose, which is essential for their success. Helping people understand who they are. Inspiring people to find their voice. To celebrate their talent. To find new ways to make relevant contributions to their networks.

Masterful coaching is coaching in the moment. Gaining insight from the pure conscious self. Helping people move towards themselves. Using the Gestalt coaching approach to increase awareness. More awareness means more choices. The chance for creative adaptation to a changing environment.

Masterful coaching is when the coach as an authentic catalyst for change. Learning comes from a state of unknowing.

> The supreme good is like water, which nourishes all things without trying to.—Lao Tzu

The Paradox of Coaching

Coaching is about knowing coaching techniques but never using them.

It is about having a powerful presence but being powerless in front of the client.

Coaching is about forming a relationship of intimacy without being intimate.

It is about being self-vigilant but at the same time noticing the smallest change in the micro-expressions of the client.

Coaching is about being in control of the coaching process but at the same time letting the client take control at any time.

Barriers to Coaching

There are many real and imaginary barriers to coaching. Insufficient trust is an intangible but a very real barrier. Coaching is like riding a tandem bicycle—duality is essential to keep going forward. And no two brains are the same. Coaching conversations are based on equality. Power must be equal. For coaching to work, coach and coachee must be authentic, open and honest. They should not hide behind their professional mask. They should disclose who they really are. Be authentic and fully transparent. Both parties ought to show have a sincere desire for the process to work and be committed to seeing it through and come to a natural conclusion. There has to be a safe psychological space to work in. Both parties should have the courage to seek and confront the truth. Being and staying present in the moment and letting things emerge creates insights and real learning. The focus should be on establishing clarity rather than digging for detail. Listening deeply with genuine empathy and witnessing the other person as another human being builds intimacy. And humility and compassion deepen bonds. Failure to pick up on non-verbal body cues can be a barrier to understanding what is really said. Cultural misunderstandings can also hinder progress. Above all the biggest barrier to coaching is not choosing to care.

Challenges to Coaching

In some cultures, national and organisational, coaching can be a sign of shameful failure. The assumption of weakness can be real in the mind of the coachee who may go to great lengths to hide their coaching sessions. Coaching can still be seen as remedial and a sign of needing help. Coaching can feel like losing control, resisting it can be an emotional pothole of the mind. Other coaching potholes include, fear of being found out, the self-sabotaging internal critical voice, the unconscious ego, fear of being judged, needing permission and unconscious bias. To be coached and to coach takes courage. The courage to overcome fear. Coaching is a journey into the unknown, and there is no turning back.

Team Coaching

Emotional support for Senior Management across a global business can be achieved by setting up, "mini-advisory boards", consisting of groups of six executives who have had leadership training together and had built mutual trust over the years. These mini boards offer mutual support and are good coaches for one another. They offer the business a source of diverse cultural and business perspectives that can be tapped into.

Developing a Coaching Culture

Coaching works best when it is embedded in the organisation and owned by the Board of Directors who are committed to improving human capacity.

The relevance and value of coaching is enhanced when it is promoted and sponsored by senior managers throughout the organisation. Spending money on coaching without first ensuring that the groundwork has been done is a fast track to failure. Make sure your training and development budget delivers what you need by first creating a culture that supports coaching.[4]

The Coaching Challenge for HR is to ensure that organisations are realising the potential contribution that coaching can make. This requires a strategic approach, moving from a human resource perspective to a human capital mindset.

The right coaching culture can give an organisation a strategic advantage in the war to attract and retain talented individuals, who can be developed into tomorrow's leaders—*Leading by Coaching*, one person at a time, *one conversation at a time.*

Ethical Coaching

This chapter concludes with my thoughts about ethical coaching. Ethics is about the moral value of human conduct and the rules and principles that ought to govern it. Ethical means to be in accordance with these principles of conduct that are considered correct behaviour. Ethical coaching, therefore, is the expected behaviour of the leader coach based on the principles laid out in the accepted coaching code of conduct. By way of example, I set out below our **Parallel Mind Coaching Principles** and our **Parallel Mind Code of Ethics for Coaching**.

Parallel Mind Coaching Principles

We are committed to your success
We put you first in everything we do
We always have total positive regard for you
We will always provide honest, timely feedback to you
We will always deliver feedback with sensitivity
We will only work with you if you are committed to change

---

[4]Clutterbuck, D., and Megginson, D. (2005). *Making coaching work: Creating a coaching culture.*

We are courageous and challenge, if we believe an intervention will help you move forward

We continually develop ourselves so that we can be the best we can for you.

Our coaching practice adheres to the International Coach Federation (ICF) Code of Ethics

We follow strict rules on confidentiality and establish coaching agreements to provide transparency with our clients and those being coached

Parallel Mind coaches are professionally qualified coaches

We are committed to CPD and coach supervision.

Parallel Mind Code of Ethics for Coaching

Mutual trust
Complete confidentiality
Total belief in the client
No organisation interference tolerated
Clear unambiguous coaching contract
Open to outcomes not to results
Guide client to his or her own solutions
Partnership approach
Ownership with the client
We know our limits as coaches and stick within them
We are clear that our client is always the person we are coaching
We use straightforward business communication using a business context
We always stay true to ourselves
We give impartial and sensitive feedback based on a learning focus
We reflect on our coaching and discuss with our coach supervisor
We ask our clients to keep a reflective diary
We seek feedback and use it to improve our performance as a coach
We value diversity and like to learn from seeing things from different perspectives
We believe that we can all be leaders by the example we set by our behaviour
We treat our clients as we would wish to be treated.

The International Coach Federation Code of Ethics for Coaching

The ICF Code of Ethics defines the code of ethics for coaching. The ICF code is designed to provide appropriate guidelines, accountability and enforceable standards of conduct for all ICF Members. It also provides a good check list for coaches to think about and decide on their ethical boundaries. Refer to www.icf.com for the full code.

The Future of Coaching

My thoughts on the future of coaching

It doesn't matter how many times you fall. What really matters is how many times you pick yourself up. Failure defines you. Failure helps you grow. And coaching helps you grow faster.

Elise Christie, the British speed skating world champion, returned from the Winter Olympics in South Korea in 2018 without a medal. Just an injured body and an injured pride. Only the memory of broken dreams. But she will be in Beijing in 2022 to try one more time for that elusive gold medal. Her coach will help her pick up the shattered pieces and get back training on the ice again. Her coach will help repair the emotional damage caused by the series of unfortunate events that struck her. The accidents, the injuries and disqualification that are now embedded in her emotional brain. Her coach will help Elise complete her Gestalt, become whole again, and move on—coaching her nervous system back to full health.

The world of business can be just as brutal. The margins between success and failure are just as small. The competition is just as great. It is difficult to pick yourself up when there is no one there to support you. No one there to sit with you; no one to listen to your story, no one to witness your pain. Everyone should have the chance to be listened to, so they can hear themselves selves. Everyone should have a coach to guide their light.

The future of coaching is that, everybody is a leader, and everyone is a coach. The future of coaching is that, it is an everyday conversation. Everyday conversations full of purpose, hope and optimism. Everyday conversations that are life fulfilling and life changing.

The future of coaching is the future of work. Successful organisations in the future will make work an enjoyable, fulfilling part of people's lives. People will come to work to learn, develop and grow. Learning organisations will have an embodied coaching culture promoted from the top by the Board who will also be coached.

Everyday coaching conversations will be the meta skill for passionate, committed leaders. Making a difference to the lives of others, *Leading by Coaching* to drive impactful change, *one conversation at a time.*

In Summary

Coaching is a self-directive form of development focussing on helping people develop and grow. It can significantly improve personal productivity and performance.

Coaching takes people beyond their self-imposed boundaries. It transforms people and strengthens organisations. Coaching is a catalyst for change whereby the coachee makes the difference.

Being a "perfect" coach is a lifelong journey that will end where you started—the imperfect human being you are. Paradoxically, it is our vulnerabilities that unlock our potential. The biggest gift you can bring as a leader and a coach is to help people accept themselves as they are and find their authentic voice.

You will learn as much about yourself as the people you coach learn about themselves. Self-mastery starts with self-awareness. I hope my book will help you think about what it means to be a coach, get you on the right track and speed you on your coaching journey.

In a business context there may be a conflict between the agenda of the individual and that of the organisation. More than that, if you are coaching someone who is junior to you there can be a dilemma between what you seek and the extent to which they feel safe to say what they really want. External coaches may be psychologically safer because they are independent, neutral and unbiased. Mentoring is different to coaching because it is ongoing and focusses on managing a career.

Coaching benefits all levels; however, it is difficult to embed unless it is endorsed by HR and at Board level.

Pause for Reflection

Do you want to make being a leadership coach an integral part of your identity?

What difference can being a leadership coach make to your leadership capability?

How will you improve your coaching skills and gain more experience of formal coaching?

6

Coaching Conversations

Introduction

In this chapter I look at how we, and our businesses, change one conversation at a time. The purpose of conversation is to frame the desired outcomes. Energised coaching conversations lead to action. And without action, there can be no progress. Quality coaching conversations are critical to the success of any business enterprise.

The key requirement for quality coaching conversations is trust. You coach at the speed of trust, one conversation at a time. You build trust by being authentic, by choosing to care, by listening deeply, by witnessing another human story and by holding a space for people to hear themselves.

Silence creates stillness in the mind to think. To think about your thinking. To think about where your thinking comes from.

Successful conversations require personal mastery by the coach. You control your quality conversations.

In this chapter I consider how you can build a true partnership that builds the necessary relationships for meaningful dialogue and collaboration. Conversations connect people together. Communication should be driven by the receiver, and the chapter updates the Aristotelian notion of Ethos, Logos and Pathos.

The chapter considers a wide variety of types of conversation, including an explanation of mindfulness and mindful conversations. It also looks at different kinds of difficult conversation and how to approach them in a brain-friendly way as covered in Chapter 1. I conclude by underlining the critical importance of understanding how communication styles vary in different cultures.

© The Author(s) 2019   **171**
N. Marson, *Leading by Coaching*, https://doi.org/10.1007/978-3-319-76378-1_6

Our lives are defined by our conversations: indeed, our conversations define our lives, both personally and professionally. "What truly matters in our lives is measured through conversation. Conversation is the most powerful source about where we stand". Peter Block. The word conversation stems from the Latin conversare *to turn constantly*. Conversation is the quick interchange through speech of information and ideas. Conversation is a constant flow of turning thoughts. It is where "in a turning world the dance is" to return to those immortal words of T. S. Eliot.

Our conversations enhance and validate who we are. Conversations provide opportunities for reinforcing our purpose and giving meaning to our relationships. Conversations provide opportunities for conferring new meaning. Refocussing our conversations enables us to see our lives in a new light. Our in-groups shape our thinking in powerful ways. Our identity is important to us. Who we are and where we come from is an important part of our story and shapes our lives.

We survive by collaborating and contributing to our in-group in work and play. Sometimes this inter-dependency causes tension that can only be resolved through conversation. Collaborative conversations redress the balance of power in relationships. People can feel valued for their contribution. Conversations highlight the value we bring and the values we share. We are at the same time, "like all others, like some others, and like no others" (Kluckhohn, Murray, and Schneider, Personality in Nature, Society, and Culture, 1953). Every one of us is unique and has a unique contribution to make.

People change one conversation at a time. Trust powers relationships and conversations full of care build trust. You lead at the speed of trust you engender.

Conversations with shared meaning and purpose create motivation to act and direct the flow of energy. Energy creates movement and movement creates change. Change creates progress. All progress comes from positive conversations.

Conversations are the vital delivery system for *Leading by Coaching*. We change one conversation at a time. Having thoughtful and mindful conversations helps us and others grow. Effective conversations increase engagement, motivation and productivity through individualised attention. Employees want to know that somebody cares about them and is listening to their concerns.

Coaching conversations help your business grow. More frequent, less formal and more effective conversations are your gateway to better performance.

Brain-Based Conversations

The Neuroscience of Conversations

In Chapter 1, you learned the brain is a simple binary prediction-making machine. Based on information from its sensory information, it decides to either move towards something or away from something. It is motivated simply by reward or threat.

How does understanding your brain help you have better conversations? Focus comes from conversations. And focus gives your conscious brain the power to channel energy, based on paying attention. Therefore, conversations are really the catalyst for action and impactful change.

Neurobiology of Human Networks (In-Groups)

Face-to-face social contact releases a wave of *dopamine* hits. When you add alcohol to the mix you can see why pubs are so popular! We can drink at home more cheaply, but this doesn't do it, neurobiologically speaking. Social interaction triggers *endorphins* which increase happiness and promote bonding.

When we are face-to-face *mirror neurons* light up in our brain to help us feel the joy and pain of others. Without this ability, there would be no empathy, there would be no rapport, there would be no relationships, there would be no co-operation, and there would be no collaboration. Humans are social animals. We *need* to feel we belong to our in-group. When we lose our sense of inclusion, we lose our identity. Our identity is the identity of the group we belong to. Our tribe is us. And the power of others in our tribe is profound as I emphasised in Chapter 2. We have no idea how much we are influenced subconsciously by the power of others. Our status in our in-group is linked to our success, to our very survival. Reputation matters.

Neurochemistry of Positive Conversations

Mental attitude has a profound effect on outcomes from conversations. When we choose our "sunny" brain we have a positive outlook and positive conversations usually follow. When we let our subconscious "rainy" brain surface we are in a negative state with negative consequences for our conversations.

Negative conversations increase slow release of the stress hormone *cortisol* which is produced in the *adrenal glands*. This major stress hormone triggers the fight or flight reaction to perceived danger. This causes long-term reduction in feeling of well-being.

Positive conversations driven by mindfulness, increase the release of the quick impact feel good hormone *oxytocin*, produced mainly in the *hypothalamus*, which activates networks in the *pre-frontal cortex* region of the brain where critical thinking and decision-making occur. This feeling of well-being promotes positive thinking. It is both a hormone and a neurotransmitter associated with bonding behaviours. Starting a conversation with a positive mindset produces the chemical "mix" of the neurological ingredients that fuel optimism and produce better outcomes. How your brain turns up is important. Mood is contagious.

Mirror Neurons

Researchers at the University of Parma discovered that when one person did a simple task another person watching had the same brain activity. These so-called "mirror neurons" located right below the *prefrontal cortex* increase our human capacity for bonding and empathy. *Mirror neurons*, as discussed in Chapter 1, are what enables us to have empathy, critical for brain friendly conversations.

Neuroscience of Listening

The *temporal lobe* is the part of your brain that produces your hearing. The *auditory cortex* is where the primary level of processing takes place. Your *frontal lobe* is for paying attention. The *limbic system* processes deep listening, the critical emotional content of the message.

Brain Friendly Conversations

Some Do's:

Do be clear about your intentions and the process—give them certainty
Do be humble—give people equal status
Do treat people fairly as you would want to be treated
Do demonstrate empathy—create some relatedness

Do make them feel really good about themselves—praise them!
Do make gentle eye contact when listening
Do lean forward from time to time to show interest

Some Don'ts:

Don't use your formal authority to exert your will—let them feel in control
Don't undermine, judge or criticise especially in front of their peer group
Don't fill the silences—hold the space
Don't interrupt or finish their sentences

Healthy Relationships

Our brains are socially wired to seek out healthy relationships to help us make more sense of our lives. The dynamics of relationships are based on mindsets, values, behaviours and interactions. Mindsets are the assumptions and beliefs that we hold. Values are our lifelong guiding principles. Behaviours are how we act, how we speak and how we listen. Interactions are how we approach disagreements and conflicts. The quality of results from relationships depends largely on the quality of our human interactions. Conversations involve many relationship-building elements, in particular: humanising—focussing on the person not the problem; expressing—speaking from the heart, not just the head; navigating—finding ways of resolving conflicts; aspiring—partnering new visions that generate new energy; imagining—new ways of seeing things; synchronising—aligning interests and actions; and co-creating future value.

Relationship-building skills include: testing assumptions, beliefs and values; checking understanding; sensitivity to personal wants and feelings; high levels of personal trust; emotional connectivity and natural rapport based on genuine empathy.

A successful relationship is one which individuals operate and collaborate from true partnership, as explained below.

True Partnership

People are always blaming their circumstances for what they are. I don't believe in circumstances. The people who get on in this world are the people who get up and look for the circumstances they want and if they can't find them they make them—George Bernard Shaw *Mrs. Warren's Profession* (a play first performed in London in 1902)

True partnership requires that we profoundly alter our connection with others. We shift from seeing other people as objects that can be moulded and manipulated to seeing people as human beings with whom we are already connected and related. The other person is not seen as someone who either takes power from us or is controlled by us, but as a companion in an evolving system.

True partnership is fundamentally about thinking about how best to relate to others: it is about how we can create new relationships, transform difficult relationships and make good relationships great. True partnership is about realising the power of changing a context. It is about becoming more proactive and less a victim of circumstances.

Unless we as individuals consciously intervene in the natural flow or "the drift" of life, the forces of power and control determine our lives and our destinies. We need to take control and start defining our lives by making our unique contribution. The job of transforming our world is up to each one of us (Fig. 6.1).

> We are the ones we've been waiting for. We are the change that we seek.—*Barack Obama*, commenting on Super Tuesday 2008.

Path of True Partnership—Parallel Mind Model

Connected **Conversations**—provide the *content* that creates a contribution to the wider group.

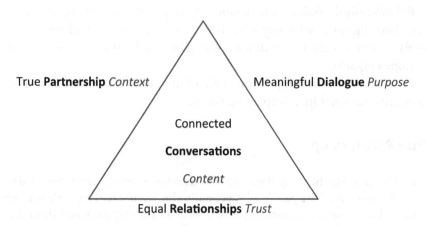

Fig. 6.1 The Parallel Mind Path of True Partnership

True **Partnership**—is based on a designed *context* and agreed accountability Meaningful **Dialogue**—is based on common *purpose* and passion and shared meaning.

Equal **Relationships**—are based on equal respect, *trust* and emotional connectivity.

True Partnership is an evolving and expanding system of interdependent individuals that relies on interconnectedness and interdependency. The power to change the context is recognised along with joint accountability for agreed outcomes. Success is determined by the quality of the relationship and connection. There are many truths and many paths therefore, listening empathically and speaking authentically is essential. The key skill is two-way communication based on honest, open and meaningful dialogue. The essential ingredient to making true partnerships work is trust based on equal respectful relationships.

Pause for thought

Who can you join in True Partnership that shares your vision?
What will be your shared context?

Meaningful Dialogue

Dialogue is the embrace of different points of view—thinking together, becoming aware of a flow of new possibilities—William Isaacs.

The quality of our lives is a function of our relatedness. **Meaningful dialogue** is a series of connected conversations that can be formal or informal. The word "dialogue" derives from two Greek words: *dia*, meaning "to show through" and *logos*, signifying "word" or "meaning". Dialogue is two or more people exchanging opinions on a particular subject.

Meaningful dialogue is a powerful tool that puts the principles and practices of true partnership into action. The meaning comes from the shared context. The very act of thinking depends on dialogue. Dialogue is literally thinking and talking together.

When introducing dialogue into meetings, we clarify values and assumptions. We focus on conflicts between values not people. Transference is an intrinsic part of human interaction and describes the process of projecting onto others' feelings based on our own values and belief systems.

Transference aspects of relationships are a common cause of misunderstandings. When we project our experience of who we are or how we see ourselves onto other peoples' values, it causes potential for conflict. On the other hand, dialogue can be a powerful tool to create coherence and alignment to find a shared direction to solve complex problems. But for simpler tasks it may only serve to slow down decision-making and delay progress. Autonomy is important—sometimes it is better to just let them get on with it! At its best dialogue takes us beyond collaboration to a new level of passionate co-creation.

Spontaneous Dialogue

It provides a chance to break down misunderstandings. It is almost a lost art so needs to be consciously worked on. Constant readiness is the key to success and empathy is the first critical step. You should be prepared psychologically to perform a gesture of empathy and be prepared to confront misunderstandings.

Planned Dialogue

You have to make dialogue happen. Dialogue transforms transactions into relationships. But before you can have dialogue, you need to have trust. Keep dialogue and decision-making separate. Give ground without compromising your values. Finding a common purpose and shared interests builds trust and creates a platform for meaningful dialogue.

Framing

Every conversation needs to be framed by asking the following questions: What is the opportunity? What is the challenge? What objectives should we set? What is a good outcome? What are the related issues? What are the relationship aspects? What issues can we eliminate that are beyond our control? What alternative thinking can we employ? Who else can we talk to?

Conversation Roadmap

Your conversation roadmap allows you to take the controls by planning and having better conversations that lead to more meaningful dialogue and true partnerships. Better conversations lead to better outcomes.

Conversation Roadmap Frame—My Three Cs to guide you through your conversations are:
Clarity, Confidence and Capabilities

Clarity

"If you don't know where you are going, then it hardly matters which road you take", said the rabbit to Alice in Lewis Carroll's *Alice's Adventures in Wonderland* 1865. Do you know where you are going? Do you know where your business is going? You need to be clear on the direction of your career and your business before you design your conversation roadmap to get you where you want to go. Otherwise the dialogue won't be meaningful. With greater clarity, each conversation can be planned to take into account the opportunities that present themselves, the outcomes desired and the objectives required to achieve them.

Confidence

Once you are clear about where you are going you have to have the confidence to design the dialogue you need to get you there. Dialogue means to create a setting where a group of people can maintain collective mindfulness. Dialogue gives people an opportunity to listen to themselves in the new context of a social group. Dialogue is the engine of your business, powering it forwards. Conversations should be collaborative rather than competitive so need to be based on a shared purpose, a common agenda and a mutual trust. Shared purpose is based on true partnership and provides the motivation and energy to change things. A common agenda ensures that everyone is confidently singing from the same hymn sheet! And last, but certainly not least, you need to trust your colleagues, they need to trust you. And trust is personal. You build it one personal conversation at a time. It is the hidden glue that you can't see, but you know when it is not there. Like oxygen. Without trust, nothing can be achieved. Without empathy, and lots of it, there can be no trust and a lack of confidence will follow. Empathy must be from the heart not the head.

Capabilities

With clear direction and a high level of trust, the challenge is to develop your capabilities and those of your organisation to deliver on the change you have agreed in your conversations. For your organisation to succeed in the digital age, it is essential your organisation culture is ethical; mindful; diverse; agile; innovative and disruptive.

Unblocking Conversational Roadblocks

Go from Me to We; remove your filters; watch the "drift" from your focus; stay on track; check understanding; summarise agreed action.

Pause for thought

Design a conversational roadmap for a talented follower to become a future leader of your organisation.

Developing Conversations

Developing conversations starts with designing the true partnership based on shared purpose; a common agenda and trust. Next, you have to frame the conversations by giving the dialogue some meaning and context. The energy in each conversation then needs to be harnessed to motivate individual action. The leaders need to connect the dots in each conversation to make sure that there is a focus on the common agreed purpose. All the time the conversations are progressing efforts must be made to develop relationships to improve trust between the parties and drive the agreed change. Trust is the fuel of change.

Conversation Skills

Developing conversations involves many skills including the following: observing, empathising, analysing, reasoning, challenging, expanding, summarising, coaching and transforming.

Conversational Ground Rules

Witness and acknowledge what is on other peoples' minds. Accept other peoples' emotions because they are a summary of their experiences. Understand others' styles; agree on the meaning of keywords; identify missing data; one speaker at a time; bring the issues to the table; keep discussions focussed; explain reasoning; invite the views of others; enquire the reasoning of others; don't hold back but beat up the issue not the person!

Conversational Mindsets The enemies of good conversations are potholes in your mind
  Your Checklist:

  not listening
  listening without hearing
  listening to what you want to hear
  distractions in your mind
  holding back
  starting at different points
  hidden agendas
  being locked into a box
  having a bee in your bonnet
  prematurely moving to action
  scoring debating points
  contrarianism
  inflated ego
  showboating
  group-think
  circular discussions

Pause for thought
List the conversation potholes you have fallen into

Communicating with the Listener in Mind

We need to believe in the messenger before we take away their message. In the ancient world of the Greek orators, the assembled crowd needed to be convinced in the appeal of the person competing for their attention before they could be convinced in their orator's message.

Aristotle understood the dynamics of this appeal. He understood there were three appeals that had to be accepted: the appeal of the person speaking; the appeal to the audience and the appeal of the message. Ethos, Pathos and Logos.

Ethos

Are they ethical? Do we believe they are a good person? Do we share their values?

Pathos

Does the messenger understand us and our world? Do they share our pain? Are they truly in our shoes? Or are they still in their own shoes?

If the person is authentic, communicates with the listener in mind and engages emotionally then we can believe in the messenger and take away the message. Trust is the issue. If we can trust the messenger, then we can trust the message.

Logos

What is their point? Why is their point the point? Does it solve a problem? My problem? Will it work?

To be an effective messenger, you need to communicate with the listener in mind, to use a receiver-driven communication style.

Receiver-driven communication is driven by the needs of the listener based on the feedback received by the speaker after they have spoken.

This feedback is received in the silence of the pause.

Communication requires the recipient to have space to process and consider what you have just said. Communication takes place in silence.

Critical Components of Communication

The biggest problem in communication is thinking it has been achieved.—attributed by many to George Bernard Shaw but no substantive evidence that he ever said this

There are two critical components of communication: content and emotional impact. The skill of an effective communicator is to bridge the two components for the intended audience with the right information and critically, the right delivery.

The Complete Communication Process

The speaker's intended message is not necessarily what the listener receives. The emotional tone of the delivery of the words, the context of the situation and the relationships, and the listener's own filters all colour code how the message is interpreted. These communication components can be seen in the above Parallel Mind Complete Communication Process Map (Fig. 6.2).

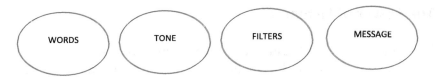

Fig. 6.2 The Parallel Mind Complete Communication Process Map

The words are the intended message. The tone is the emotional content. The filters determine how the message is received and include the context of the situation and the relationship between the parties.

The communication is what the listener receives, not what the speaker intended. But the responsibility of delivering the message always lies with the sender.

When you are delivering an important message bear in mind that the people who are receiving, it will receive it differently. All you can do is be sincere and authentic and use an empathic tone. A self-knowing leader connects personally with their audience. They hold true to who they are and what they believe. When they speak there is a connection between themselves and their work. Others see the link and are inspired.

Remember they must buy you before they buy your message. Your leadership presence is essential. Your listeners want to know who you are, what you stand for and the difference you want to make to the world. And they also want to know the difference you can make for them. Above all, they want to be given greater meaning to their work and lives.

Asking Powerful Questions Discovering Questions Categories

Agreeing assumptions
Discussing situations
Sharing feelings
Exploring ideas

Transforming Questions Categories

Provoking thoughts
Shifting perspectives
Dreaming possibilities
Building thoughts

The Power of Listening

Listening builds trust because it shows we care about the other person. It shows we want a balanced relationship. It shows we value the other person's contribution. It builds inter-dependency. Listening persuades people to co-operate. Listening is reciprocal, you listen to me and I will listen to you. When we stop listening, we lose our voice.

What stops us listening? Talking does! We can't listen when we are talking. To LISTEN as mentioned before we need to be SILENT. Why don't we listen? Is it our desire to feel confident in what we know? Is it our inability to acknowledge the full extent of our ignorance? Is it our need to feel we can give answers under pressure?

Is it a deep-rooted fear of losing control? Talking means being in control. Talking is being the master. Talking is hiding behind our professional mask. Reducing the risk of being discovered. Talking is judging rather than being judged. Listening is being the servant. Losing autonomy. Listening creates uncertainty. Listening is a threat. Will I be found out? Will I be treated fairly? Our brain protects our self-image. We fear that feedback may damage our ego, our social standing. There is more certainty in keeping our status quo.

Pause for thought

What stops you listening?

Why Should We Learn to Listen?

Listening gives someone a voice; listening is a silent witness; listening conversations can be enlightening and life-changing; listening gives us the best answers; listening is a two-way iterative learning process, we learn new things; listening gives others more confidence in us and themselves. Listening reveals your blind-spots and helps you grow; listening enables you to fully explore your own thoughts and challenge your own ideas.

What Can We Do to Listen?

Well a good start would be to stop talking! Be silent. The challenge in meetings is for us to let others speak four times more than we do. To do this you can use The Parallel Mind **PAIN** conversation framework. Start by asking them to talk about their **P**roblem. Help them **A**nalyse their problem. Help them understand the **I**mplications of not solving their problem. And lastly, give them the relief of imagining their pain could be **N**eutralised. They now have the tablet to take away their headache! **Listen, Diagnose**, then **Prescribe**.

The *Art* of Listening

The *art* of listening is: listening to the **unsaid**; listening with your **eyes**; listening with your **heart** and listening with your **mind**. Listening takes place in silence out of which real learning emerges.

Language can be a barrier to listening. The meaning people attach to words is coupled to their emotional experiences. There can be many words in one culture for something that has only one meaning in another. In the Zulu language, there are 37 words for green. Choose your words carefully when working across cultures!

As a leader and a coach, the more you listen to your clients; the more they will trust you. The more they trust you the more they feel safe to explore your ideas and share their ideas with you. You have less control but collaborate more. This conversation spectrum is represented in the Parallel Mind **Listening** Pyramid (Fig. 6.3).

Mindful Listening

Mindful listening allows you to *see more clearly* and get into a *state of flow*. Mindfulness is about focus and discipline. Cognitive control is a state of

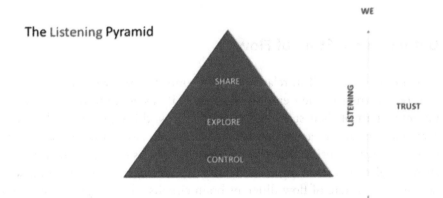

Fig. 6.3 The Parallel Mind Listening Pyramid Model

being, not doing. Being aware of your subconscious state and that of the other person. Mindfulness is about noticing inner signals and choosing a response, it is self-referencing. When you use your Parallel Mind your unconscious brain and conscious mind are in sync with each other. What is going on in my body right now? The more you notice your own experience, the more opportunities you have to be mindful. Mindfulness isn't difficult; the hard part is remembering to be mindful. It is something you need to practice every day.

Developing *Luminous Listening*

Luminosity is about developing awareness, "abiding in the state of clear light", in the words of The Dalai Lama. "Luminosity" is recognising the "luminous simplicity of mind behind the veils of thought", according to Matthieu Ricard in his book, *Happiness: A Guide to Developing Life's Most Important Skill.* It is when the freshness of the moment rises above the myriad of memories and future dreams.

Before you engage with your client clear your mind. Ask yourself, *who is my client and what is important to them?* Be truly present with your client. Pay attention. See what is there. Listen with your heart and your eyes. Pick up the emotional cues that your client is offering you.

When you improve your emotional sensitivity, you improve your powers of rational deduction because you are able to make more subtle valuations. When you step back and are truly present with your client you hear their music, not each instrument they are playing. You witness the miracle of another living, breathing human being. Attention creates synchronicity, *The dance.*

Getting into a State of Flow

Fully immerse yourself in relatedness and connectedness with the other person. Be a witness to their emotional journey. By listening to their story, you become a part of their story and part of their world. Humans are like mirrors, and we reflect each other. But you need to slow down to see things clearly. To really notice. There is no listener, only listening. Listening strips away social masks revealing true identity and feelings. Authenticity replaces facade. In this state of flow different brain circuits all fire together, synchronously. The brain changes itself by wiring together—a process called *neuroplasticity*, discussed in Theme I.

Your Business is listening to **hear**; listening to **understand**; listening to **care** and, above everything else, listening to **serve**. Listening is your Business.

Heedful Listening

Heedfulness means paying close attention. It means giving your full attention to someone when they are talking. And being heedful builds trust.

To be heedful when listening, you must eliminate all distractions and focus on the other person. They will feel you doing this and really appreciate you for choosing to care about them. There is nothing more powerful than listening deeply to someone.

Heedfulness is inspiring in a leader. When your leader truly listens to you, it makes you feel valued and important. They give you the feeling that you are important to them and in their care. They trust you and you trust them. And from this mutual trust comes opportunities to grow.

Different Coaching Conversations

The Marathon Challenges

My colleague Derek Benton inspired this idea for a different coaching conversation. He likes to run as his main form of exercise. Derek has turned sixty and, by his own admission, has never been an athletic person. He has completed two full marathons and several half-marathons over the past few years. Derek passionately believes that we all have the positive power to change our lives by focussing on our new challenges. And sometimes the challenges we choose for ourselves, or others choose for us, are extreme!

My extreme example of a *Leading by Coaching* conversation would be for you to persuade _everyone_ in your business to run a marathon (26.2 miles) within a 24-month period from announcing the goal. *On completion your company will pay £1000 to the favourite charity of each participant. _Everyone_*? Yes, is that not what corporate leaders do? They set a vision, a goal for everyone in the organisation, and look to everyone to get on with it, to deliver on the vision. You can see this playing out at the company "town hall" meeting and audio-visual conferences, webinars and Q&A sessions. Yes, there are those in the audience who have never run since childhood, some who may have physical impairment, and those who thought the whole idea was plain daft! Maybe together they form the silent (or not so) majority. But you are the leader and you have set the common goal. Your challenge is to engage your people and get them enthused, or at least willing. Change is personal. People see the need for change but don't like being changed. Organisations change one person at a time. And people change one conversation at a time. You are *Leading by Coaching* one conversation at a time.

So, start thinking about the coaching conversations to engage and enthuse everyone, to get them motivated, to achieve your goal for everyone—to run a marathon and follow in the fabled footsteps of the Greek soldier, Pheidippides, a messenger from the Battle of Marathon of 490 BC, who reported the victory to Athens.

Marathon exercise

How will you start the conversation?
How will you change the conversation for different personalities?
How will you deal with the, "no way"!?

Gestalt Coaching Conversations

The Gestalt approach to coaching conversations is to facilitate the search and movement towards wholeness, to help us understand our place in a turning world, connect the dots to complete the circle and see where we fit in. Only then can we move on.

The coach's power of presence, of witnessing the other person as a truly unique gift to humanity, drives the transformation of a greater conscious awareness. This emerging awareness is the focus of attention. Gestalt coaching is all about the here and now. The Gestalt coach holds the space, the silences, for people to understand their beliefs and values, where they come from and where they fit in.

Mindful Gestalt coaching is a systemic relationship-based approach that helps people understand their changing roles and responsibilities. It is fundamentally about the me/we constellation. It enables people to feel better about themselves and better about others, so they can move on to the next challenge that surfaces in their mind.

Communication takes place in the silences. And mindful coaching conversations are the place where the learning from the communication takes place, where new insights emerge, where new realities are reframed and created.

Mindful Coaching Conversations

Mindfulness transforms the coaching relationship. Mindfulness creates engagement. Mindfulness makes you aware of your own thoughts, feelings and sensations in the moment. Mindfulness is an attitude of allowing and acceptance. Mindfulness allows focussing closely on what is said and communicated non-verbally in the coaching session. Sometimes simply being heard and responded to mindfully is enough. Mindfulness is a non-reactive calm acceptance, cultivating an open-hearted presence. Mindfulness is being fully in the moment with and for the client.

The Power of Being Present

Be present when engaging in mindful coaching conversations. Truly present. You need to feel and share others pain. Above all, you need to show real empathy and compassion to build trust, to earn the right to be listened to just like the volunteers on the suicide hotlines did in Chapter 3. You develop a coaching relationship at the speed of trust.

What Is Mindfulness?

Mindfulness means staying present and observing thoughts and emotions without becoming distracted or influenced by them.

Mindfulness was defined by William James, the Harvard professor, in the 1890 edition of "Principles of Psychology", when he said, "mindfulness is the faculty of voluntarily bringing back a wandering attention over and over again and is the very root of judgment, character and will".

The ability to focus our minds by bringing our attention back to the present moment is the indispensable skill that enables us to take control of our lives, master ourselves and make progress.

Without focus on the present moment, our minds wander into the past or daydream about the future. Our thoughts and feelings seem to have a mind of their own. Pascal, the French mathematician and philosopher, understood this dilemma when he observed, "all of man's miseries stem from his inability to sit alone in a room".

Our minds tend to wander. And a wandering mind is very often an unhappy mind. The ability to think about what is not happening is a cognitive achievement that sometimes comes at the emotional cost of negative moods and anxiety.

The practice of mindfulness, which is more than 2500 years old in Eastern and Western Science, helps us deal with these problems effectively. In recent years, The, "Mindfulness Revolution" has exploded in the media and even in the scientific press. But how do you become more mindful?

First of all, you can practice mindfulness when doing anything from shovelling snow, cutting grass or walking the dog. I have been passionate about photography since boyhood, so I thought about how I could be more mindful in taking pictures. Instead of mindlessly taking digital pictures and deleting them without really thinking, I thought of an alternative. I followed the advice of Tracy Calder, Features Editor of Amateur Photographer, to focus on the space between objects when composing a picture. To make no distinction between space and form forces us to see everything as equal. You can try this yourself with your smartphone. Look at familiar objects in terms of the space around them and between them next time you find yourself with a few minutes to spare between meetings, travelling to work or on your way home. Mindfulness is a skill that needs to be mastered. It is the skill of paying close attention to what's happening in the present moment in the mind, body and external environment, rather than operating on automatic pilot. When we are being mindful, we are using our conscious mind rather than letting our unconscious mind direct proceedings oblivious to what is going on. We are using our Parallel Mind. We are the elephant and also the rider. And the rider is riding the elephant, not just being carried along where the elephant wants to go!

Second, thinking about your thinking, your ability to reflect on your mindfulness, to examine your mind is critical to your learning, and critical to a good coaching practice. Mindfulness opens up a greater awareness of your experiences. By developing the ability to live more consciously in the present moment, you experience the "power of now", being awake to what is actually going on.

Mindfulness practice starts by directing attention to our body. We experience our physicality in the context of the environment we find ourselves in. We begin to understand the close working relationship between the body and mind. We learn how to interrupt the cause-and-effect connection between our thoughts, feelings and our actions. We discover an increased ability to focus our mind consciously and to be mindful, to do the right thing at the right time in the right way, we respond rather than react. Mindfulness is the core ability that forms the basis of emotional intelligence.

You can be mindful anytime, anywhere. You just need to think about your thinking in the moment. You then become your thoughts.

Mindful Coaching Conversational Skills

To have more mindful coaching conversations:

choose to care about another person, so they feel less alone
be truly present with the other person
witnessing the other person as a unique human being
demonstrate empathic compassionate concern
listening deeply to who the person really is
see what your eyes miss, you see from your heart
achieve clarity by probing to reveal deeper truths
hold the space for insights to emerge
be silent and comfortable in the silences
connect by understanding peoples emotional drivers
appreciate peoples strengths and contributions
accept people unconditionally as they are
praise people to help them grow
transform people by helping them to move towards themselves
gain commitment to action.

Pause for thought
How can you become more mindful? More present in the moment?
What opportunities are there for you to shut out the noise around you and focus on your thoughts?

Conditioning

Condition your mind so that you don't react defensively to criticism. Instead, analyse what has been said to see if you can learn from it. Treating criticism as useful feedback is a high-level emotional control skill.

Leading with Your Brain in Mind

Neuro-Leadership Intelligence, you will remember from previous chapters, allows you to lead yourself and others through understanding how the brain works. Having strong **NLI** allows you to consciously choose brain-friendly behaviours that draw people towards you. **NLI** helps you have better relationships and more positive conversations that create change.

NLI is our ability to be in the moment, to be more aware of our own physical and emotional state and the physical and emotional state of others so we can steer conversations to better outcomes.

Mindsight

Mindsight is about using your **Neuro-Leadership Intelligence** skills to focus your brain, mind and relationships on a single intention. The power of mindsight is that it increases awareness and facilitates emergence through integration. A single point of focus.

Relationships and the Brain

Interactions with other people, according to Daniel J. Siege directly shape how the deep structures in the brain respond to safety or threats.

According to Siegel, in his 2017 book, "Mind", self-regulation appears to depend upon neural integration of emotions, thoughts and feelings. Mindsight is the capacity to reflect on mental states, self and others—the internal world of self and the external world of others. Metacognition is the ability to understand other peoples' minds. Self creates a sense of coherence and continuity over time. Communication patterns in relationships determine a healthy mind.

Engaging Conversations

A leader's prime responsibility is to define and describe the common purpose of the business. Getting people to see that purpose as positive to their personal interests and well-being is the art of leading and essential to getting things done. And why is it that people know what they should do, but don't do it? People will always confound! Jean-Paul Sartre wrote that, "Hell is other people", in the sense of the struggle to find the language to communicate and have yourself understood by others. Explaining ideas, concepts and instructions to people in a complex business operation is one version of hell but understanding and practising good basic coaching skills can go a long way in reducing friction and encouraging collaboration in the business.

> A wonderful fact to reflect upon, that every human creature is constituted to be that profound secret and mystery to every other—Charles Dickens, *A Tale of Two Cities* 1859

The Power of Story Telling

When you explore stories, understand emotions and find common purpose you build bridges.

Your brain is your story. In your parallel mind are your frozen memories, locked in your unconscious brain and your unfrozen thoughts in your conscious mind. Unfreezing more of your unconscious stories gives you more intuitive wisdom. It gives you the ability to be more *mindful,* to relate better to other people's stories. This is how we build relationships.

Be open-minded to the possibility that maybe we are wrong. Is there another side to the story? Can we improve our self-awareness and performance by getting some feedback?

A coaching relationship is fundamentally an exchange of stories for shared context and meaning. There are three stories: Yours, Theirs and Ours. Listen to their story, share your story and reframe both to connect on a human level.

Finding Your Story

The first thing to ask yourself when crafting your story is what point do I want to make? What do I want my story to teach or do? When you have identified the point or lesson you want to make, ask yourself when did I learn that lesson? When did the bulb light up? What story can you tell others so that they can learn from your experience?

Telling Your Story

Telling relevant stories defines who you are and the difference you want to make. What is your story? Why do you want to tell it? There are many different types of story, serious, funny, dramatic and moving. Stories can be about big events that are life changing or everyday stories that illuminate a lesson learned. Whatever the story you choose, the most important thing is that it is relevant to the point you want to make and relevant to your audience. It is the fit that makes a story powerful.

Landing Your Message

Passion persuades. If you are not enthusiastic, don't expect your audience to be. As we have seen before, emotions are contagious. You need to engage your audience by connecting with them. If they are not engaged, they will listen without hearing. Engage with yourself to be engaging with others. You can't be convincing unless you are convinced yourself. When you deliver your story, you must bring all of yourself to your delivery. You must show your emotions. They must see how much you care about the change you seek and how much you care about them. All their senses need to be stimulated by your energy. You must connect with their head and their heart.

They will get your message not from your words alone, but from the emotional profile of your voice, the congruence of its pleasantness, dynamism, competence, clarity, credibility and persuasiveness.

Your voice quality provides melodic emphasis to increase emotional involvement. Your pitch range, modulation, loudness and tempo all combine to let your emotions be heard. The music of your voice is in your intonation. The congruence of what you say and how you say it, together with your facial expressions and gestures, is your message. You are your message.

Difficult Conversations

Many conversations haven't taken place because we perceive them to be difficult. And the longer we put them off the more difficult they become. So, what constitutes a difficult conversation? And why do we put them off? A difficult conversation very often is one when you deliver bad news. Where there is a potential conflict, Where there are personal consequences of getting it wrong, We assume we know what the other person is going to say about us and we don't want to hear the truth! We fear our authority is going to be challenged. We fear we cannot control the outcome.

The common thread to all the above assumptions is fear. Fear of the unknown. And we know the brain doesn't like uncertainty. That's why it is unconsciously steering us away from having these difficult conversations.

Fear of confrontation drives the flight or fight response from the *Amygdala* in the *Limbic System*, the emotional centre of our primitive brain. Fear of what? Fear of damaging our reputation, of losing our social status. Fear of humiliation. Fear of rejection. Fear freezes our conscious thinking brain.

You probably know that fear is very often based on a false premise. **F**alse **E**xpectations **A**ppearing **R**eal. Learning to deal with our negative emotions and have our so-called difficult conversation requires courage. But finding the courage to have those difficult conversations is difficult! We have a choice: protect our precious ego or learn about ourselves and move on.

Difficult conversations are the bedrock of true partnerships based on mutual respect, understanding and shared purpose. Difficult conversations are learning conversations. Difficult conversations are coaching conversations. Difficult conversations should be everyday leadership conversations.

My colleague **Derek Benton** endured many difficult conversations during a decade of leading a declining growth business. This is his *Leading by Coaching* story. There are many valuable **insights** to be gleaned. I highlight and analyse what I believe to be some of the most important ones. I also highlight the essential skills he used to energise individuals and to keep team morale high.

> When confronted by stagnation, or decline in the top-line, there is very often an intense emotional response. Shock, denial, disbelief and anger follow as the results are viewed, then come the questioning and scramble for understanding that can feed panic and angst. People have all manner of reasoning for wanting not to change or address what is rational and obvious.
>
> Slowly there is acceptance of the situation, then a commitment to move on and deal with the business issues with steps to plan a new future direction. Somebody has to lead that.
>
> I would argue now that there is a greater need than ever to develop skills and behaviours in people to manage the increasing frequency, velocity and substance of business change. We must learn how to bring out the best in self-motivation for people to productively deal with transformation. If we are to be successful in creating continuity for a business organisation through shorter product life-cycles as markets and technology demands, managing out from one profitable position to another has to be the norm. **This requires leaders to meet the most basic human need that of finding purpose and meaning in life through work;** easy with the new and shiny, more challenging with the mature and not-so-glamorous.
>
> **I suggest and advocate building coaching skills for all business leaders and managers. Coaching is the main tool to help people use their skills, knowledge and creativity, without direction by developing an intuitive self-motivation.**
>
> **Coaching is no more or less than having a quality conversation or series of conversations. How do you develop these? I provide the following insights into what worked for me and why.**

If coaching is just a conversation or series of conversations, what are you going to talk about? And who are you going to talk to? And how? And when? What will ensure the quality of conversation(s). Subject matter for sure.

If the conversation is going to be about both parties' work and role in a stalled or declining business, in a business culture of winning, it is nonsensical to avoid knowing and explaining how you both feel about that. A mutual understanding of this most basic point must not be avoided. With that insight shared you can address almost anything.

All leadership takes up enormous amounts of energy, leading where impending failure is a goal, takes a different mindset. The leader needs, more than ever, to keep checking in with everyone on their levels of energy. There is just that more nurturing to do. You constantly have to nurture your people into a positive, forward-thinking mindset, to get anything done.

Quality of conversation means economy in conversation. Conversations that primarily have focus on mutually beneficial outcomes.

It goes without saying that any organisation is a reflection of the social behaviours of the individuals within. Wherever there are people there are passions, emotions, politics and competitions of ideas and influences.

Effective conversations are ones that produce insights to other viewpoints and your own. Success in coaching people can only come from their willingness share their thoughts. The leader coach's role is to put people at ease and their mindset firmly in "open".

Out of these conversations we individually, and as a team, built skills to self-direct, take ownership and find focus in difficult circumstances. **Coaching is exchange of energy between minds if it's nothing else.** The leader and the coachee both take something from the conversation.

The conversations we had within the team were built on what we could influence and how we could focus more on customer value given the resources were reducing. Conversations led staff to self-direct to explore options and make recommendations, put views in a business case style and advocate for change. Making the customer/client the centre of focus provided everyone with a degree of certainty about what was to be done.

The quality of conversation is perhaps the only thing a leader should concern themselves with if they want to influence, direct and manage change.

As a leader you need to listen a lot. I personally found the most effective tool in managing people was a weekly one on one meeting for each of my direct reports, where they set the agenda. The purpose of these staff meetings was a platform for coaching, self-motivation, building self confidence in their work and decisionmaking and identifying their own priorities and goals in their work (their agenda).

As a business leader, I do not believe that you can motivate people, but you can de-motivate people. Destruction appears to be much easier than construction, providing someone intentionally or unintentionally with uncertainty is a fast track to demotivation.

If you do not directly motivate, what do you do? You create the conditions for self-motivation to arise. That is a more sustainable and longer lasting contribution to individuals' performance at work.

The principal tool for the creation of the right conditions is an **authentic narrative**, that describes the purpose of the business, its value to customers/

clients, the value of the individual's work and contribution to the overall purpose together with the recognition of the uniqueness of collective endeavour and the rewards for the individuals and the enterprise.

The role of the leader is to shape the narrative and re-tell the story to the corporate audience and immediate business team, as often as required and on a personal a level as is possible. The narrative has to be authentic, by that I mean it has to be believable, and experienced. This again adds to the levels of certainty and it enables people to visualise how their work relates to the narrative. **This new narrative covered the essential elements of purpose.** Most importantly, it gave those directly in the business a certainty as to what we valued, recognition and status for work in managing the brand successfully.

Working in a declining business is not a very attractive proposition for a potential business leader. **The problem here is status, or loss of it.**

Conversations at the weekly staff one on one meeting were used to raise the above issue. Over time there grew an understanding of what was important to individuals about their work and working life. Through a series of conversations and encouragement to look to the future, explore career options and further skill development, had most staff trusting the coaching method. Getting levels of openness and honesty is not easy, but again being authentic about direction of the business and the challenges coming up, often helped people to self-select their options to stay or go.

We lead by providing autonomy to individuals and trust them to deliver with the minimum of direction.

By giving people more control over their work, at least for the majority who wanted to take it, their sense of autonomy and status were enhanced and engagement in the challenges maintained.

Difficult Conversations, Everywhere

There comes a point when the self-motivation of key people takes a hit, or when the financial stream is running dry. The conversations that begin here are inevitably about the endpoint.

In leading these difficult conversations, **I took the view that transparency was the best policy.** To be informed, enabled people to do the right thing. Self-interest is bound to kick in, and where possible to be supported. The conversations I found myself leading at this stage were all about **fairness**. People, regardless of how they viewed the impact on themselves, the customers, their colleagues, of the ultimate decline of the business, were able to act positively, if they experienced fair and **equal** treatment, and we kept the brand promise.

Helping individuals to analyse their own behaviour is the core value of coaching. An individual's level of relatedness to their team's work or the business team is proportionate to how they see the value of their own work, in that it gives them status within the group, certainty in purpose, and the will or motivation to act relatively autonomously. When something comes along to turn off the power, it's the final act. A leader's role is to help everyone mourn, helping all involved to **recognise the value of their contributions** to themselves, their colleagues, customers/clients and the continuity of the wider business; to celebrate.

How to Tackle a Difficult Conversation

Empathy is the answer. Put on the shoes of the other person. Ask yourself are you really and truly in their shoes or are you still wearing your own shoes?

"You never <u>really</u> know a person until you step inside their shoes"—Maya Angelou, *To Kill a Mocking Bird*.

Listening deeply to the other person will create more trust. People want to feel fully heard and understood.

And lastly, keep an open mind. Challenge your assumptions. Create a positive tone for the conversation Come to it with an open mind and create the conditions for mutually successful outcomes.

Start your conversation with something positive, for example praise, that is likely to encourage a towards response.

Difficult Conversations Are Learning Conversations

Difficult, but positive conversations, produce real insights in them that power innovation, the lifeblood of organisations. A truly diverse and innovative organisation is based on a collaborative leadership team enjoying a deep understanding of personal strengths, wants and motivations. Conversations that may seem difficult at the outset become easier when the parties open up in an engaging and honest way. This can only happen where there are deep mutually beneficial relationships based on higher levels of personal understanding and trust. With the right levels of personal trust constructive conflict can be managed better by using it as a catalyst for creative solutions. Individual strengths are developed where there is a constructive tension within organisations. Having difficult conversations requires courage but leads to finding better ways of doing things. You should have that difficult conversation as soon as you can. Courage is a competitive advantage.

Courageous Conversations

When you cannot control a situation, you feel vulnerable and nervous. You need courage to confront your fears and have that conversation. A courageous conversation is one you don't want to have! A confrontation you have been avoiding despite knowing deep down that you need to have it to resolve matters and move on. Very often it is insufficient relationships that prevent your difficult conversations taking place. These conversations may be with people higher or lower in the organisation hierarchy, you may perceive any conversation as a difficult one.

To move from protection to progress there are three internal conversations you need to have with yourself. The first conversation is about the facts. The second is about your feelings about others. The third is about how you feel about yourself.

The challenge is to have a learning conversation. Focus on the other person. What has happened from their point of view? Where does that leave them? How are they feeling?

We can then explain our position and how we are feeling. We should seek first to understand before we seek to be understood. Understanding people's interests and sharing feelings is a big step to resolving issues by having courageous conversations.

> **Pause for thought**
>
> What key relationship do you need to work on to pave the way for a courageous conversation?
> How can you build trust?

Straight Talking—Dealing with the "Elephant" in the Room

Courageous conversations require straight talking. We are often reluctant to challenge authority figures. We are reluctant to tackle the "Elephant" in the room. Excessive obedience and deference creates risk for organisations. Good leaders are approachable and create an open, psychologically safe space, where people are encouraged to speak up and do some straight talking. Our value and power lies in our ability to raise our consciousness about how we communicate. Our crisis as a culture is a crisis of insufficient consciousness. Organisations that have straight talking as a value change quicker and achieve more. Straight talking allows us to understand each other's roles and motivations better. It allows us to get the buy into who we are and what we want to achieve. Straight talking and a mindful coaching leadership style unlocks the potential of each member of the team. With the right mindsets, there are no difficult conversations only opportunities to grow. Everyone has a unique and valuable contribution to make.

Appraisal Conversation

Appraisal conversations require courage and straight talking. And starting on a positive note helps.

"Praise makes people grow". Victoria Brackett, formerly Managing Partner of Thomas Eggar law firm told me when I interviewed her for my book. She coached over 70 Partners through major change one conversation at a time. Her belief is that "Organisations change one person at a time". Change is personal. You can find a longer version of my interview with Victoria in Chapter 9.

To put them in a towards state appreciate exceptional performance and discretionary effort. Start with the positives. Talk about people's strengths. Thank them for their contribution. Ask them what went well and how they felt about it. Ask them what they struggled with and what support they want to deal with the issue better next time. Ask them what you can do as their leader to support their development and growth. Help them cope better with change by understanding better how they can change, how they can fit in with the new system.

Conflict and Conversations

Embrace conflict as a normal part of healthy relationships. Gestalt coaching brings greater awareness of the causes of conflict and creative ways to adapt and move on. There is a conflict potential in many difficult conversations. Having a brain-friendly approach minimises the threat of an away response and defensive behaviour.

Conflict renews and recharges relationships. It is a productive source of new energy. It creates opportunities to: remove obstacles in relationships; find creative solutions to difficult problems; facilitate change and growth; and leverage diversity.

Conflict recognises moments of truth. Conflict provides an opportunity to build deeper trust by empathising with people's pain.

Angry Client Conversations

Imagine you have heard and felt the voice of an angry client. How did the experience make you feel? Nervous? Anxious? Angry? Emotions are contagious. Maybe your client doesn't feel fully heard and understood! Maybe they just want you to show some empathy. To feel that you care about them.

What they need, above all else, is an empathic ear.

My Parallel Mind **ESCAPE** model (Fig. 6.4) below, provides a conversation frame to help you deal with a difficult client situation.

Collaborative Conversations

Collaboration is the idea that everyone works together, produces something better and with less effort. Collaborative conversations create something new. It is important, as Ben Emmens points out, in his excellent book *Conscious Collaboration*, to begin the conversation with the end in mind. Having a clear shared purpose is the critical success factor in any collaboration.

Different Personalities

You will remember in Chapter 2 I looked at how you could get on with different personalities by using the **DISC** personality profiling tool. The art of conversation is to recognise and adapt to different personalities and in different situations.

Empathy—put yourself in their shoes (get out of yours first)

Silence—shut up and listen to show you care to let them get it off their chest

Concern—show you care and want to help

Action—ask them what they want you to do, and what they will do, to remedy the situation and agree actions and timelines

Perspective—put the problem into perspective, for example by telling them, "this has never happened before".

Execution—make sure you do what you said you would do, and the client does their bit too, then tell them when you have done it

Fig. 6.4 The Parallel Mind ESCAPE Model

Thankfully we are not all the same! We are all unique human beings. We do however, generally speaking, have a dominant personality style as illustrated by The Rolling Stones rock band who have stayed together for over fifty years! The trick is to complement the other person's style rather than compete with it. The point here is that although the band members are clearly very different, they managed to stay together for five decades by having collaborative conversations.

Let's spend our lives together

The Rolling Stones have lived their lives together. But how do they manage to stay together for so long with all the pressures of fame and fortune? Their secret is they recognise their different personality styles and realise that their individual styles were a combined strength not a source for conflict.
So, what did they each bring to the group?

Director/Driver—Mick Jagger
Directors speak crisply using action verbs, talk about goals, care about the "bottom line", are always on the go and may seem insensitive. Mick is the driving force for the Rolling Stones success.

Influencer/Expresser—Keith Richard
Expressers speak rapidly, talk about ideas, use animated gestures, are entertaining, think out loud, may be imprecise. Keith is the creative spark.

Supporter/Harmoniser—Ronnie Wood
Harmonisers speak softly, talk about people, are sensitive to others, avoid conflict, are dedicated and loyal and may overcommit. Ronnie manages the egos!

Controller/Thinker—Bill Wyman
Thinkers speak carefully, talk about the details, are enquiring, often make lists, want things done "right" and may procrastinate. Bill gets the show on the road.

The meeting of two personalities is like the contact of two chemical substances: if there is any reaction, both are transformed—Carl Jung

Different Cultures, Different Conversations

I cannot stress enough the importance of cultural awareness and training when working across cultures. In addition to knowing how the brain functions in default mode you also need to be aware of the hard wiring that distinguishes behavioural preferences in one culture compared to another.

I have been working with diversity for the last fifteen years with my international clients. I have worked in many countries including the USA (New York, Washington DC, Houston), China (Hong Kong), Germany, Sweden, France, Belgium, Ireland, England, Wales, Scotland, Spain, Malta, Bulgaria, the Netherlands, Luxembourg and Switzerland.

I also had the privilege of leading an Intercultural Communication Programme at Munich University with over 200 students from all corners of the globe including China, South Korea, Russia, Latvia, Estonia, France, Spain, Poland, Ireland, Scotland and Turkey.

What has struck me most about this wonderful diversity is the common bond that is our shared humanity. We all have the same basic needs and we all are doing our best to survive, even thrive, on the planet. The problems are similar but the approaches to solving them differ culturally. Of course, identity is very important to people and cannot be denied. But, overwhelmingly, if you show some respect to your hosts in another country and make a sincere effort to fit in with their customs, they will welcome you with open arms and in most countries with a smile.

There is of course always a danger in stereotyping. We cannot exist without stereotyping. It gives us a point of reference when dealing with strangers.

The mind is always looking to simplify things and is good at creating patterns. Steven Pinker, in his book *How the Mind Works*, writes about how the brain, "puts people into mental boxes, gives each box a name, and thereafter treats the contents of the box the same". Unconscious basic assumptions are deeply embedded in our brains and are the source of unconscious bias.

And when we are under stress, we stereotype even more. We exaggerate our own culture to make things worse. Our emotional brain is taking over, and fear is putting us in an away state. We need to consciously take back the controls and override our primitive instincts.

The antidote is to take a step back and just observe. Notice how they do things. See what is similar and what is different. Human beings have the same needs but approach them differently. To mind the gap, you must see the gap first. The key is awareness. Observe their different approach to things. See behaviours through a cultural lens. You can then adapt your own behaviour to narrow the gap without being inauthentic. Your sincerity of good intentions is the most important thing to bear in mind. Understandably you can't always get it right all the time. And a good dose of empathy takes you a long way (Fig. 6.5).

Cultures collide when major cultural dimensions are opposed. Let's take the Time dimension for instance. In linear cultures like Germany, punctuality is important. Meetings should start on time. In multi-active cultures, like

When Cultures Collide: Time, Emotion, Uncertainty, Power

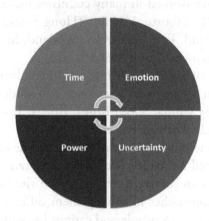

Fig. 6.5 The Parallel Mind Cultural Dimensions Model

Spain, relationships are more important, so everyone chats away (as I experienced) until all the guests arrive.

Turning to the dimension of Emotion, in some countries, like Finland, they do not show emotion outwardly and prefer long silences to connect with each other and nature. In Italy by contrast, they embrace each other publicly.

Next, we look at the Power dimension, in China hierarchy is important and the elders have a special place at the table. In the USA, making money is more important than any ascribed status.

Lastly, the cultural dimension of Uncertainty avoidance throws up some marked contrasts. In countries with high uncertainty avoidance like Germany, there are lots of rules that must be obeyed. There is no room for the maverick idiosyncratic Englishman upsetting the locals. The rules are the rules and apply to everyone!

Intercultural Communicating Styles

The English like to indulge in small talk and excel at vagueness and understatement. They inject a bit of humour to business proceedings and avoid any confrontation by keeping it calm, all "jolly nice chaps". The French love their language and eloquence is a powerful tool used by business leaders. Rhetoric and logical argument usually win the day. The Germans prefer directness before eloquence; truth before diplomacy; detail before the big picture. Americans want the big picture first. They like the hard sell and like to be entertained. The detail can come later if they are sold. The Dutch are even more direct than their German neighbours. Their focus is on efficient conveyance of facts and figures. For the Italians and Spanish, it is usually a discussion on football first for at least twenty minutes.

Listening Habits

The English are polite listeners who want a bit of humour and a slightly relaxed atmosphere. The French expect a logical presentation and debate everything. The Germans are good listeners who require a structured presentation filled with technical details. They take your presentation very seriously. The Dutch are cautious, even sceptical, listeners. They challenge you directly. The Italians are not such good listeners—they are too keen to fill pauses.

Presenting Styles

In the USA, sell yourself and your product first. They want to be impressed. So, impress them. The details can be discussed later. In Paris, you need to impress them with your logic and eloquence. And you must speak French! In Sweden, they want the facts and figures, and lots of them. They want to be convinced that your product is solid and so are you! Simple and elegant design is important, think IKEA. The Danish want modern design and quality. In Italy, style is important. Cars need to be beautiful and desirable.

Meeting Patterns

Meetings give individuals a chance to communicate. To use their speaking skills to have more influence. The use of speech—beyond the basic giving and receiving of information—is applied in diverse ways in different cultures. The Dutch agree by finding consensus. Germans persuade though linear logic. The French use eloquence as a weapon of persuasion. The Italians and the Spanish want to convince you personally with their bravado. Scandinavian cultures find their Latin friends rather overwhelming, especially the Finns who use silence as a form of speech. The English are prone to waffle and the Indians to flowery language. The Japanese like to stall and will go to great lengths to avoid losing face. The Chinese excel in ambiguity and send coded messages which confer status. The Americans want to sell you something and do a deal. Arabs want to exert their moral authority and position in their hierarchy. They want passionate rhetoric and strong eye contact. Russians are suspicious of authority and foreigners. Australians like informality and keep it all good mates.

Meetings can be short, long, boring or plain simply unnecessary. But whatever form they come in, you need to know the protocol, especially the critical beginning.

In Germany, people make a formal introduction, sit down and start. In Spain, things are not so simple or direct. Your meeting will not get going until 25–30 mins of small talk and everyone has arrived. I remember a coaching session I did in Madrid for some Partners in an international law firm. Their office overlooked the Bernabeau, home of Real Madrid, so the conversation inevitably centred on the fortunes of the men in white. In Japan, after the formal introduction, protocol seating, green tea, 15–20 min of harmonious pleasantries, the senior Japanese gives the signal to begin the meeting.

Leadership Styles

In the UK, the leader leads from within the team but is not a team member. Leaders in France are autocratic and often a product of the prestigious Grandes Ecole's, higher education establishments. The German leadership style is consensus driven but the leader usually sits in their own office and makes the final decisions. The Dutch leaders debate with their team extensively while Scandinavian leaders are the most egalitarian in the world. In Spain by contrast, leaders are autocratic and rely on their personal charisma to retain their loyal following. The Japanese leaders are highly consensus driven and it is difficult to see anyone making a decision. But the top executive ratifies the decision so has the final word. It is often a frustratingly slow process for Western business people. In the USA, leaders are free spirits who hire and fire at will. Failure is normally fatal, figuratively speaking.

You will find a more detailed analysis of cultural orientations in *Cross Cultural Communication, A Visual Approach*, by Richard D. Lewis which I referred to for the above text.

Leading Across Cultures

The key to leading successfully across cultures is to value and embrace diversity. Diversity drives innovation, builds bridges and connects you with your global clients. The important thing is to be sincere, empathic and extend the hand of friendship to build the critical trust (Fig. 6.6).

When coaching, you need to integrate three cultures. The culture of the profession; the culture of the organisation and the culture of the country. These cultures are like the intermeshing gears of a gearbox in a car. Unless they are in sync they will crash. And you need the oil of trust to make the gear changes smooth. In a law firm for instance, the professional cultures of lawyers and specialist support staff of HR, Finance and Marketing are quite distinct. The organisation culture based on firm history and values is, or should be, a common code of expected behaviours. And the national culture will be an embedded view of the world. Coaches help clients leverage cultural differences in all three cultural domains to find creative solutions.

In Summary

Conversations define our lives. Face-to-face interactions are best. The quality of results from relationships depends on the quality of our human interactions.

A true partnership grows out of connected relationships, meaningful dialogue and conversations that connect.

Fig. 6.6 The Parallel Mind Coaching Across Cultures Model

You need to trust the messenger before you trust their message. This requires Authenticity, Complete communication and Emotional engagement. Complete communication means it is receiver driven.

Communication happens when you are silent. You pause after you speak to give your listener(s) space to think about what you are saying.

Deep listening is active, engaged and full of care.

To be mindful means to be present and aware. To be mindful means to park distractions as they arise, so you can come back to them later without being diverted by them at a precise moment.

Conversations are perceived as difficult usually because of fear: False Expectations Appearing Real.

Different cultures have different listening styles, presenting styles and meeting patterns, so if you are interacting with a different culture, or with a mix of cultures, be aware you might wish to adjust or alter your own style, behaviours and attitude to fit in better with theirs.

Having effective everyday coaching conversations will be the meta skill for the leaders of the future.

Pause for Reflection

Take some serious time out to revisit and reflect on Themes One and Two before you start reading Theme Three. What more have you learned about yourself and how you lead and coach others? What did you learn about your leadership styles? What will you use from Gestalt principles to have better coaching conversations? How will you become more aware of the different cultural orientation of the nationalities you are working with? What are your key learnings from my book so far? What are your moments of personal truth?

Theme III follows and is about *Leading by Coaching* the next generation of leaders in your business. It examines the nature of leadership and change and looks at different leadership styles.

It looks at how you can influence the collective mind of your organisation by *Leading by Coaching* one conversation at a time. This section covers the nature of trusted leadership; leading change and mindful change. It is your personal guide to leading yourself, developing your signature presence as a leader coach, and leading others in everyday coaching conversations that drive impactful change in your business.

Theme III

Looking Beyond—*Leading*

Overview

Coaching in its most basic form is a conversation with a purpose. It can be formal or informal, it can take place anywhere and at any time.

Leading by Coaching joins up the latest empirical, observational and behavioural research into a framework for you to *think about your thinking* and expand your self-awareness on your journey to find your authentic voice as a leader.

In the first two themes of my book, I explored the science, the concepts and the practice necessary for you to have a deeper understanding of what it means to *think about your thinking*. Raising your conscious awareness will help you to have more engaging and impactful *Leading by Coaching* conversations.

Here in Theme III, I throw a spotlight on leaders' attitudes and behaviours that facilitate purposeful conversation that helps them lead sustainable change.

Their words and stories tell us something about who they are and what is important to them. Leaders reflect on what they think, say and do to lead themselves from the *inside out* and lead others from the *outside in*.

Here in Theme III, I act as an observer. You will gain insights on how the leaders I interviewed for my book expressed their *signature leader presence*. And how they put into practice the principles I put forward in the first two themes of my book.

Here in Theme III, I steer the two converging streams of conscious thought from the first two themes into a single stream, a powerful flow, a force for action and change. My "Theory of Everything", will help you develop the language you need to show yourself and articulate your *leader signature presence, Leading by Coaching* impactful change *one conversation at a time.*

7

Leading from the Inside Out

Introduction

The emphasis in Chapter 7 is on you the leader. Like diligent horticulturalists who plan their beautiful garden and carefully weed out unwanted plants, diligent leaders carefully weed out unwanted thoughts, so they can master the landscape of their mind to have maximum impact as a catalyst of change, leading from the inside out. I analyse the attributes and behaviours of business leaders I have interviewed and reflect on what is behind their thinking. I discuss different leadership styles, so you can define your unique leader signature presence. I showcase real-life examples of impactful leaders who dare to think differently. I provide you with an authentic leader checklist and a leadership behaviours self-awareness exercise to help you reflect on your impact as a leader. Essentially leadership is a coaching conversation about change.

Leading Yourself

I was half-listening to a gardening programme on the radio recently, in which an audience member asked the gardening expert to give an opinion on what the expert considered to be weeds in a garden. The listener was probably expecting a list of plant names considered to be the common enemies for the meticulous horticulturalist. The answer was surprising and thought-provoking: "A weed is any plant that is in the wrong place, not where you expect it to be, or where it is wanted".

© The Author(s) 2019
N. Marson, *Leading by Coaching*, https://doi.org/10.1007/978-3-319-76378-1_7

As with weeds, thoughts have a habit of growing unplanned and unwanted. Leading yourself is recognising the horticulturalist in you. The garden designer with a planting scheme that achieves the overall effect and vision you were looking for at any time of the year. Knowing that some plants are not in the right place at the right time calls for action, weeding. So too with thoughts and distractions. The quality of the leader's conversation in business matters because it is this that keeps the focus, energy and attention of others. Knowing your own capacity for distraction is central to recognising its capacity to confuse others. Thoughts not central to the design, spoken and communicated by you, in the wrong place at the wrong time, are potentially dangerous, whereas weeds are just unsightly.

We all get distracted; however, we may direct our thoughts through the power of our brain to focus and pay attention. In Chapter 3, I looked at the importance of self-awareness in finding your own authentic voice. Chapter 1 illuminated the knowledge from neuroscience on how thoughts are formed. We are our experiences, and how we choose to interpret the world through those experiences is our authentic selves. It is these self-regulating, self-reinforcing, thoughts in our mind that generally guide us and our actions.

Let us now pay attention to how this level of self-awareness is the key to understanding my concept of the Authentic Leader and how the Authentic Leader uses authenticity to shape conversations.

The Authentic Leader

Authentic leadership comes from a place of stillness. It is in the silence that we connect with our inner self. It is in silence that we have the stillness to think about our thinking. It is in the silence that we hold in our coaching conversations that we give others the space for their thinking to emerge, a space for learning. The monks know that in the silence of their monastery comes a stillness in which they can hear the voices of their thoughts. Wisdom comes from silent reflection.

And the silences in your *Leading by Coaching* conversations will allow you to connect on an emotional level with your followers. Silence has a powerful presence. But silence requires discipline. It is easier to fill the space than to hold the space. And good leaders hold the space for others to think about their thinking and see more.

Authenticity is a quality others must attribute. The attributes encountered by others and valued by them, make leadership credible and accepted.

Here are some leadership attributes that matter in building trust in ourselves as leaders. I describe each attribute and offer an explanation (in the shaded text) from The Neuroscience in Theme One.

Self-aware leaders realise their own worth. Firstly, they lead themselves in self-mastery. They understand their own innate strengths and value and this awareness gives them the confidence to lead. They accept themselves as they are, including their "imperfections". They empower themselves at the deepest level from a place of inner knowing and the acknowledgement (rather than validation) of others. They don't need to prove themselves but want to improve themselves. They are in a place of knowing and continually evolving. They operate from a clear set of personal values. They speak from personal experience and use their own words. Their authentic leader signature presence talks for them.

Authentic leaders have an emotional connection with their followers because they choose to care about their followers. Choosing to care creates an emotional connection that builds trust and loyalty. Conversations convey those emotions and actions reinforce those emotions.

Our unconscious brain is constantly organising our thoughts so that our conscious mind can be continuously developing self-knowledge. Realising that the mind controls the flow of information and energy within the brain and between brains, the self-aware leader seeks to reinforce positive experiences from social interactions.

Authentic leaders are great listeners. They never stop listening … and learning. They listen first and speak last. They really listen, and deeply. They listen to what is not being said. The feelings behind the facts. They realise that the true communication is what people take away and not what is said.

The self-aware leader practises focus and reflection. Improved listening and use of silence allow the unconscious brain to make the internal connections with past experiences and utilise its predictive quality to understand at a deeper level.

Authentic leaders coach and teach a new generation of talented people by gently nurturing and guiding them. They lead by coaching. They enable rather than control. Authentic leaders understand that coaching is a powerful process that can change people and the organisation itself. Authentic leaders collaborate, they have a *we* mindset. They engage in meaningful dialogue which according to William Isaacs, in the Art of Dialogue, is "the embrace of different points of view–thinking together, becoming aware of a flow of new possibilities". Authentic leaders develop true partnerships based on equal respect, shared values and goals.

Authentic leaders do not have all the answers, but they just keep on asking great questions! Authentic leaders improve people's thinking by asking, "What is your thinking on this?" They ask the right questions and focus on solutions not problems.

> The default state of the mind is to look for connections, and to make predictions, for the basis of action and physical behaviours. Seeking information from other minds is a shortcut to gaining experience.

Authentic leaders develop themselves. Authentic leaders look inwards at themselves before they look outwards at others. As the current Dalai Lama observed "the best way for a ruler to reign over his country is, first of all to rule himself". This introspection requires self-confidence and humility—an often-overlooked trait of a leader. It also requires self-compassion and emotional intelligence. By being more emotionally honest and expressing true feelings, others are encouraged to do likewise.

> No two brains are the same, but we all share the biological features of the brain. However, the internal wiring of our minds is as individual as we are numerous. Knowing that others think differently helps us to find confidence in introspection and reflection.

Authentic leaders inspire others to greatness. Authentic leaders are self-knowing; they inspire others with how they have personally overcome adversity. They tell stories of how an experience has shaped them. Authentic leaders articulate their life lessons in a way that resonates with the values, hopes and fears of their followers. Their stories are powerful because they use their emotions to tell them.

> The mind is the controller of energy generation within the brain and directs flows of new and existing information. Memory formation is more powerful when connecting and associating thoughts and ideas with emotions. Experiences appear to be stronger and more lasting. How we feel about an

idea or a thought is important to what we do with it. Stories, narratives, analogies, all help us connect quickly and deeply with others.

To use the example of the late Steve Jobs, founder of Apple Corp, he made leadership personal. At his commencement address delivered at Stanford University on 12 June 2005, he talked about how important it is to find what you love. Leaders like Jobs ignite a fire in others by sharing their passion and enthusiasm about the change they want to make in the world. And passion and enthusiasm are infectious. All the latest brain science tells us that these emotions are contagious. Leaders literally breathe life into others. Jobs' passions fired up the conversations in Apple.

What did Jobs do that made him an effective leader? For me he did several things extremely well. He bought extreme focus to his passion for product design and did not let much else distract him. Like the horticulturalist I mention above, he knew what the garden was going to look like all year round and started weeding out things in the wrong place. He also knew how he wanted people to feel about his products and was sure about the benefits that could enhance their lives. Lastly, I mention his ability to communicate and use narratives to engage others to share his ideas and values.

You lead by being, not doing; by developing, not directing. Always coming back to yourself. You will find a **Leader's Self-Awareness Exercise** at the end of this chapter as a starting point to reflect on what it might be like being led by you. You can use your answers to this checklist as a control point for feedback. You can then understand the gap between how you see yourself as a leader and how others actually experience your leadership.

To illustrate some of the points above, and I made in previous chapters, I want now to look at what others have said about leaders, leading and leadership. I want to examine what is innately "brain-friendly" in their comments and experiences. If you are going to improve the quality of conversations in business, it is useful to know what others think and how their experiences are influencing everyday conversation.

I interviewed a number of business leaders for this book. I wanted to find out about their business values and experiences.

I wanted to understand who they are as a person, as a leader and as a coach. And why their leadership style(s) motivate their followers.

The following is my abridged vinterview with **Joanne R Musselle**, Chief Underwriting Officer, **Hiscox Insurance.**

Which leader has had the most influence on your career? "My former boss, AXA Group CEO". "He trusted me, believed in me, taught me a technical approach, how to handle meetings, coached me and developed me professionally. Helped me grow personally".

What is important to you in Leaders?

"They believe in and live diversity". And that "You lead as you **are** and as you **do**". "They need to avoid unconscious bias and wilful blindness", as "Diversity drives innovation".

What is your business guiding principle?

"Key—Trust", Hiscox brand promise is "To tell you the truth—we assume you do" and "As good as our word".

What is your personal business ethos? "Values are important. Your personal values should be aligned to the corporate values of your employer if possible. Luckily, the **Hiscox** corporate values of **Courage; Integrity; Human**—empathy, fairness and respect; Excellent in **Execution Quality;** Open to **Challenge** and be Challenged, are in line with my personal values".

What drives your (leadership) behaviour?

"Fairness is the central core". "Equality—You are not better than anybody, but nobody is better than you". "Leaders need to give people the confidence to be all of themselves…To use all of their strengths".

How do you lead yourself?

"Core values" "Be authentic—be yourself at all times". "Do the right thing, however hard".

How do you lead others?

"Core principles: develop job; develop people". "Giving people the confidence to be themselves; checking in on emotional level; regular off sites", "Developing people to be the best people they can be; in a safe psychological space with high challenge". "Being tough but fair and constructive when giving feedback".

How do you lead your business?

"Blending leadership styles". "Developing people. Designing the job. Directing the business".

How would you like others to describe your leadership style?

"My leadership is personal. I want to do the best job I can do for you". "Discretionary effort is given to a person not a business".

When you read Joanne's answers a number of things jump out. Her former, influential boss provided her with the right conditions to grow in confidence and self-belief. He provided her with a degree of **autonomy** to act. And, like most people in business, Joanne expresses a desire for **certainty**, and consistency from her leaders. She recognises **trust** is required to lead and do business. She states that **fairness** is a quality she expects in dealings with others. As a leader, Joanne focusses on people, and the quality of her relationship with them—setting the right conditions for them to grow. It is a reflection of what she'd want for herself.

The language used by Joanne to talk about leading, is a mirror of what neuroscience tells us about what the brain looks for in a good working environment. Trust is given when there is a consistent pattern to the positive experience you have of others. The brain, as a prediction machine, looks for and wants to create certainty. It wants to control time and space—to have autonomy—to make the connections with new and existing information in memory. And it is constantly scanning for differences and variables in **social status** and threat status between self and others. It craves fairness.

The Trusted Leader

When we trust someone, the chemical *oxytocin* is released which makes us feel good. *Oxytocin* is a social lubricator. When leaders give us equal status the chemical *serotonin* is released. This makes us feel good about ourselves and our leaders. These two chemicals drive collaboration. They replace fear with reward. All progress is based on trust. Trust is not only about feeling trusted but also about trusting other people. *If you suspect a man, don't employ him. If you employ him, don't suspect him*—Chinese proverb.

Trust is a gut reaction and these gut feelings have a scientific basis. Some parts of the brain are unable to communicate directly with each other, so they use nerve clusters in the gastrointestinal tract as a relay. That is why we see from the heart and you should learn to trust your intuition. It is usually right. "Ever noticed that 'what the hell' is always the right decision?"—Marilyn Monroe

Trust is both seed and fruit of a culture with a common purpose and real passion. Trust flourishes in an environment of honesty—especially honest differences of opinion. Trust is corroded by hidden agendas. Trust requires integrity, which means being honest even when it doesn't suit you.

People follow leaders they trust. Leaders who are authentic. Leaders they can believe in personally as well as professionally. We all have had bosses we did not trust personally. Like many of us you held back. You did just enough but no more. You held back any discretionary effort you could have given. You chose just to do your job.

All motivation is intrinsically self-motivation. Your leader must instil a desire in you to go the extra mile. Productivity is directly linked to personal trust.

Personal trust is earned by trusting others first; by listening deeply; by witnessing people's suffering; by feeding back with kindness; by articulating the organisation's purpose clearly and giving people a clear idea of how they can contribute to the team.

The role of trusted leaders is a vitally important one. They give their followers a solid sense of themselves and their place in a changing world. Identity, purpose and meaning give people a greater sense of stability, security and well-being. People need to believe in their leaders to trust in them.

Coaching conversations help people join up the dots to find new ways of connecting with their in-group in an increasingly fluid social world.

We need to find new ways to increase our social well-being through stable relationships based on trust. It is ultimately our shared vulnerability as human beings that binds us together and provides a common narrative.

Pause for thought

How quickly do you trust others?
How quickly do people trust you?
How trustworthy are you as a leader?

The Mindful Leader

The ancient practice of mindfulness has its origins in Buddhism. In Pali language, native to the Indian subcontinent, "Sati" means mindfulness or awareness. It involves training the mind to be aware and pay attention on the present moment to thoughts, feelings and body sensations that arise, without judging. This practice gradually develops our capacity to respond rather than merely react to what's happening around and within us. The skill is to be able to focus our attention in the moment, to connect our senses to our immediate surroundings and to other people. Holding the space, being comfortable with silence, takes a lot of patience, discipline and practice.

It can be described as "falling awake". When we are mindful, we are fully alive, and we know it. We are able to act consciously, thoughtfully and from deep inside us, rather than react with kneejerk responses. For the Dalai Lama, mindfulness is the leader's way. Mindfulness helps choose the right action. The power of focus comes from our *pre-frontal cortex*, our conscious thinking brain and from the *hippocampus*, the emotional learning centre of our unconscious brain, the *limbic system*.

Every day the brain generates around 10,000 *stem cells* that split into two. One becomes a daughter line that continues making *stem cells*, and the other migrates to wherever it's needed in the brain for new learning. *Neurogenesis* adds power to our understanding of *neuroplasticity*, whereby the brain continually reshapes itself according to the experiences we have. Ideas come from insights. Insights raise *dopamine* levels that heighten attention in the learning process. The brain uses clearly defined central threads to make clear connections that fit into the learner's network maps. *Neurons that fire together wire together.* And constant reinforcement of ideas encodes the brain.

Mindfulness is a series of attention training practices and cognitive strategies that can help you detach yourself from unproductive thought patterns and behaviours. It involves learning to pay attention to the here and now, rather than worrying about the future or dwelling in the past. Mindfulness is about living in the light, being present, attentive and engaged. Being mindful means letting go and letting come, being authentic and purposeful, being self-aware and self-reflecting. It means creating a space to think. It means paying attention in the moment and without being judgemental.

Mindful leadership is about consciously experiencing the internal and external world. Mindful Leadership directs the attention of individuals and groups to a specific situation. It helps focus the mind on what is needed to complete the task. Mindful leadership finds the space to lead. It provides clarity and focus, creates a space for creativity and shows compassion and connectedness. Mindful leadership has the strength of character to display right conduct.

Mindful Leadership requires: resilience, fearless presence of mind, and unconditional responsibility. Mindful leadership is about "Vipassana", which in *Pali* means, "to see things as they really are". The Mindful leader looks beyond for what is actually there to gain insights. Mindful leadership requires mindful awareness. Mindful awareness requires you to choose something to notice.

A poor life this if, full of care, we have no time to stand and stare. W. H. Davies—*Leisure* 1911

Leading Others

What is leadership? A conversation. Leadership is a conversation. Quality conversations in business produce positive outcomes and changed perspectives. Conversation is not just communication; it sets the culture of the business. Conversation enforces the culture of the organisation, the way things get done. A quality conversation is a way of moving forward the goals of the organisation based on its values and strategic direction.

The social scientist Professor Albert Mehrabian studied what elements of expression create credibility. In his book, *Silent Messages*, he reported the results of a study in which business people were evaluated by listeners by the words they said, the tone of their voice (feelings, warmth, pitch, volume), and their body language. The latter was the most important in determining their credibility. How they looked when they spoke, how grounded and confident they appeared when they presented themselves, was more important than what they said and how they sounded. The audience is asking, *does the speaker truly believe in what they are saying?* Are you engaging, convincing and compelling. At the heart of any communication is that you express yourself honestly and authentically in a way that connects with your audience emotionally. The audience buys into you as the messenger before they will buy your message and take it away.

The leader as leader and as coach sets the example for brain-friendly communication. Quality conversations are supportive and motivating to followers. Communicating effectively, keeping an audience focussed on the important, as opposed to being distracted by the unimportant, requires self-awareness and discipline to weed out the distractions of the mind.

Leading Others in Conversation

Answering the Question: Why Should Anyone Want to Follow You?

Good leaders are self-aware, self-confident and assertive. They have found their unique signature leadership voice and are not afraid to use it. They recognise that leadership is about relationships. Good leadership is always about other people.

Leaders motivate and sustain performance in their people through their presence because they feel, in some way, connected to them on an emotional level. There is a sense of a shared identity, a feeling of belonging and deep personal trust in the relationship. There is a joy in a social connection and social intimacy. Leaders recognise that when people can fully engage with other people as one community, they are more likely to collaborate and be productive. Quality conversations instil and perpetuate the bonds of trust.

In simple terms what is important gets talked about and gets done—a shared collective consciousness in action.

I want to share the following story to illustrate this "one mind" togetherness.

The rise of the Swedish football club Ostersunds under English manager Graham Potter

A *leading change case study* based on a BBC Sport article published 18 November 2017

In July 2017, in Istanbul, a football miracle happened. The mighty **Galatasaray** lost their Europa League qualifier to **Ostersunds**, a small club in the Swedish lower divisions. On 22 February 2018 Ostersunds beat **Arsenal** in London in the Europa League second leg (round of 32), although they lost 4-2 on aggregate. They headed out of the Europa League, but they returned to Sweden with another famous win, this time at the Emirates.

Wind the clock back seven years to 2010, and the little Swedishs club side's fortunes were at rock bottom. They had just been relegated to the Swedish fourth tier with average gates of 500.

Ostersunds is not an ordinary football club. Their extraordinary achievements, on the pitch, including achieving promotion to the *Allsvenskan, the Swedish top flight, for the first time in 2016 and winning* the *Svenska Cupen* (Sweden's main cup competition), by beating the Swedish Champions Norrkoping 4-1 at their own ground in Ostersund, are underpinned by a unique approach to team-building off the pitch.

They have developed a "culture academy", where players sing, dance and act in front of an audience in an attempt to boost their performance ability. This has included staging a rock concert, at which Potter himself sang, and a performance of *Swan Lake*. He also encouraged writing and painting projects. These daunting challenges brought everyone together as a team.

The culture academy according to Graham *is a training method for decision-making and bravery. It also helps the players develop their self-awareness, motivation and empathy. You start to find out who is comfortable in uncomfortable situations, how different people cope differently with pressure, and how you can help them develop. I've done things I would never have done. We go out and integrate with the community in lots of ways. Our supporters are the most important thing for our football club. We started with 500 people at the game, and now we're averaging 6000 and there's a real feeling for the football club in the town.*

The rise of Ostersunds is a remarkable story of ambition, belief and courage. It demonstrates the power of togetherness driven by a shared purpose. It also shows how important it is to be human. Only when you show your vulnerabilities and celebrate your gifts can you go beyond your self-imposed boundaries, build on your character, and make your dreams a reality.

Graham Potter returned to UK football management in the Summer of 2018 to steer Swansea City to a return to the Premier League.

I imagine that his success involved many conversations and an unshakeable self-belief. Graham Potter took a gamble with his different coaching style and it paid off. The lesson for leading yourself lies in the power of focussing on your vision and sticking with it, motivating and delivering it through powerful conversations. This creates impactful change. Modern leadership is about strengthening the chain of command by delegating power rather than wielding it.

Those command and control scientific management principles espoused by Frederick Taylor in 1906—where fear is the primary motivation—are no longer relevant. Leading by listening, empowering and coaching is the new mantra—where purpose, passion and a common goal are the motivators.

The Russia 2018 World Cup has given Gareth Southgate and his authentic, caring leadership style a platform to show that football management has come of age. The English players thrived in reaching the Semi-Final because Southgate gave them personal responsibility to think for themselves and show their individual initiative and creativity.

Quality conversations make the difference.

Leading by Building a Quality Conversation Culture

Thinking Prior to Delivering Your Thinking

Check your emotional state when you feel under pressure. Good self-awareness involves honesty and means expressing your true feelings. Emotional intelligence gives you the ability to accurately identify your feelings. If you are emotionally honest with yourself, you become more self-accepting. Being emotionally honest with others encourages them to share their true feelings. Lack of emotional honesty leads to misunderstandings.

> Selective self-disclosure is a leadership skill. Emotional literacy is the ability to intervene with our own thinking to break bad habits. It is the ability to pick up emotions generated in different situations and work out where they came from. It is important to distinguish our emotions, so that we can learn what is driving us. We need to develop greater awareness of our internal observer, our emotional barometer.

Manage your stress through reflective thought. Calm your emotional brain down. Ask yourself, where is the stress coming from? Why are you reacting emotionally? Can you change your brain narrative to put things into perspective? Can you control when you feel anger or fear? It only takes six seconds to respond to your emotions rationally, rather than let your primitive brain hijack you. Ride the elephant!

Next time you present think about the venue, forum, and occasion. The physical space and the type of audience should impact your conversational style so you maximise your engagement.

Think deeply about your natural reaction when under threat.

In his book *Deep Survival: Who Lives, Who Dies, and Why*, Laurence Gonzales combines hard science and powerful storytelling to illuminate the mysteries of survival, whether in the wilderness or in meeting any of life's great challenges. Everyone has a mountain to climb. Everyone has a wilderness to conquer inside.

The survival lessons from Laurence, for staying out of trouble and dealing with it when it happens, are: perceive, believe, then act; Avoid impulsive behaviour and don't hurry. Know your stuff. Get the information. Be humble. When in doubt, bail out. The overarching, critical, and potentially life-saving lesson from "Deep Survival", is that you must listen to your inner voice, your intuition. It will tell you what you need to do to survive. Whatever your plan, be ready to abandon it. It is important to have a plan; however, you should always be planning because everything changes, all the time. Be agile, flexible and respond rather than react to your amygdala hijacked emotions. Trust your gut instincts from your unconscious brain and let evolutionary design protect you.

Reflect on the nature of trust. The invisible glue of trust builds confidence and gives people a feeling of safety and certainty that their brain craves. Trust is something we feel, an emotion that helps us co-operate and survive, especially in challenging circumstances. In the wilderness of the jungle and sometimes the work place/space.

When conversing about change, remember the initial reaction is emotional and biological rather than not logical. By linking change to purpose, you give people the compelling reason they need to change. The brain needs the *why* before the *what, how, when* and *where*.

Remember to use your coaching style as a good way to support your people through change. Be warm and authentic. Do not use the power of your formal status, be informal to put people at ease.

Organisations change one person at a time, *one conversation at a time*.

The Ethical Leader

Recent history is littered with unacceptable ethical behaviour from leaders of big business. Stories we still hear. I looked at the critical importance of ethics in Chapter 5, Leadership Coaching.

The need for more ethical leaders is paramount. We should care about ethical behaviour if we want business to be trusted by the public.

The ethical tone has to be set from the top, at Board level. Leaders need to be very clear what their personal values and virtues are. An ethical culture needs to be cultivated. An ethical culture is created by a series of actions and conversations by leaders, who are powerful role models. According to Professor Roger Steare, Corporate Philosopher in Residence at Cass Business School, "working culture is about purpose, meaning, values, creativity and humanity. The best possible working culture is close to the one we experience with family and friends". It is the responsibility of senior leaders and managers at the top of the organisation to set the right ethical tone.

My conversation with **Peter Large**, former Executive Director at the **Association of Chartered Certified Accountants (ACCA)** is a good example of a leader that sets the right ethical tone for his colleagues and members.

Peter thinks Governance issues are really leadership issues. "It's about doing the right thing for a sustainable business. Thinking ahead". Ethics is the foundation of the **ACCA** qualification.

The challenge of Authenticity is that there is always pressuring to stay on message, play it safe, avoid being a headline. So, leaders can be perceived as inauthentic, distant, and untrustworthy. Many senior leaders want to show who they are but don't know how to in public. They don't have the skills to communicate to diverse audience types.

Trust is the critical issue. The well-intentioned leader is a trust builder and business enabler. Trust is two-way: you need to trust people before they can trust you. Being trusted builds confidence in the trusted and in their leaders. Trust is reciprocal. And the foundation for trust is authenticity and empathy. Listening is the key driver for building trust. But people are not good listeners and the result is: damaged relationships; low morale; lack of trust and lost ideas. The cost to business is difficult to calculate (even by an accountant).

Leaders need to block out time in their busy week to listen to their people. Peter endeavours to engage in a range of formal and informal meetings with people at all levels. He also likes to hold informal question and answer sessions with teams—he enjoys the engagement. People want their leaders to be open and accessible. They don't expect their leaders to be perfect, but they do expect them to be honest. There is still too much emphasis on critical reasoning skills in isolation. Not enough time is spent on relationship-building. Human beings need to feel emotionally secure in their in-group.

The business case for ethical corporate cultures and frameworks is a strong one. Reputation at the end of the day is the most important asset of any business. Building trust with the public and the regulators is the most important task in constructing successful and sustainable businesses.

The Agile Leader

In the age of disruption nothing can be taken for granted. There is no room for complacency. Companies, even whole industries, can disappear overnight. This world of constant change requires leaders who are agile. Leaders who change faster and smarter than their competitors. Leaders who adapt quickly. Leaders who read the mood of their customers. Leaders who see opportunity in every threat. Leaders who can deal with ambiguity. Leaders who see beyond, see what others miss. Leaders who go where others dare not go. Leaders who impact change one conversation at a time.

Distributed Leadership

The shift away from command and control organisation structures towards more agile working involves a more distributed, agile leadership style.

Do we actually need leaders? What would happen if we didn't have any leaders? Thought-provoking questions, I think you will agree? The leadership question refuses to go away because communities have to make big decisions. Maybe a more enlightened approach is needed? Maybe a more distributed leadership model is required based on context and capabilities. Maybe shared values and a common code of behaviour can provide the basis of the agreed leadership principles that multiple leaders should follow. Leadership is moving towards becoming more about relationships and networks than elite leaders at the top of the organisation hierarchy. And trust is the glue that keeps the leadership matrix together. Building alliances with colleagues and stakeholders becomes more important than giving orders. Leadership in the future will be distributed, driven by culture and engagement. Everyone is a leader. Everyone is a coach.

Leadership is Personal

Leadership is intensely personal. According to **Tony Wright**, a Director at the London office of the global law firm **Latham & Watkins**, who

I interviewed for this book, "law firms at the end of the day are just a bunch of humans". In his firm there is a culture of self-driven, self-directed entrepreneurs, "partners are legal artists". They are all different, but all share the same one team ethos in a highly collaborative firm culture. The paradox is that leadership is both personal and shared at the same time.

The Inclusive Leader

The inclusive leader embraces diversity in every form. An inclusive, more diverse, open culture produces a smarter more engaged workforce. Exclusion damages relationships and demotivates people. Our social brain craves inclusion. Being excluded, like not getting invited to important meetings, can cause our brain to experience real pain similar to physical pain according to studies by The University of California, Los Angeles (UCLA).

> For my book, I interviewed Tangy C. Morgan, a senior advisor for the Prudential Regulatory Authority at the **Bank of England**. I was impressed by her thoughtful, inclusive approach to Financial Services Board composition. She is striving to encourage greater diversity of Insurance Company Boards to better reflect the diversity of the public they protect. Boards, in her view, should represent broad society, so that they can better understand the needs of the Public. Tangy believes passionately in the importance of ethical business and her approach can be summed up by her observation that "diversity is a fact, inclusion is a two-way conscious decision".

According to **Dominic Christian**, Global Chairman **Aon Benfield**, a leading global professional services firm, "Business should be less grey and more contemporary, more colourful, more visual, more alive, and more accessible".

My conversation with **Ingrid Waterfield** is a good example of a leader who is committed to gender and other diversity/inclusion issues.

> Ingrid is a Director at **KPMG** and advises clients across London and South–East regions on workforce issues. She led the recent Cracking the Code gender diversity research and leads KPMG's AGILE FUTURE FORUM. More recently, Ingrid is focussing on helping clients deal with their gender pay gap reporting requirements.
> She believes passionately that it is important to treat everyone as an individual. As a leader you should find out what motivates people personally and what are their future aspirations. Appreciating their individual contribution

Your Leader's Way

Leaders are expected to direct, give direction, measure, monitor and hold to account the actions of others and be responsible for their own. Most everyday conversations would revolve around those basic responsibilities. Leading yourself in changing the balance between how you direct and hold accountability starts with changing styles of conversation. Command conversations are a natural territory for leaders and can create uncertainty in followers if absent. Nurturing conversations—to produce self-directed learning and a greater sense of autonomy—may initially create uncertainty for both parties, however with patience may be more effective in producing desired outcomes.

I have explained how the brain creates memory and how the mind as the controller of information and energy across the brain works to produce efficient habits. The use of memory reduces the amount of energy needed to perform tasks. Once you have embedded a habit, like how you like to lead/behave as a leader, it is only possible to replace that habit with another. It is almost impossible to un-learn something.

You will only be motivated to change a habit if you find the new habit more efficient. Learning something new is hard and takes practice, like riding a bike for the first time. Eventually pay off comes after a lot of falling off your bike and getting back on.

Coaching people to direct themselves works because it is in sync with the nature of how the brain functions as a biological system.

Greater self-awareness allows us to be more conscious and effective in using our mind to control our energy and focus. Our innate survival instincts have produced a natural default to treat new information as threat first, potential reward second. This is how we process any new thinking and communication that comes to us from others. Leading yourself to overcome this biological mindset is the starting point for quality conversations.

Using conversation to recognise people's strengths and contributions reinforces positive behaviours and encourages change. Quality conversations focus on praise and future actions.

Leader's self-awareness exercise

Review and reflect on your leadership behaviours. When you have reflected deeply complete my self-awareness exercise by ticking the box, *rarely, sometimes*, or *usually* against the leadership behaviours listed. Be honest. Ask your colleagues to reflect and feedback on how they experience you. Mind the gap!

Leadership behaviours	Rarely	Sometimes	Usually
Leading Yourself			
Play to your strengths?			
Limit your weaknesses?			
Be aware of your own emotions in the moment?			
Practise self-tolerance and self-compassion?			
Set a personal example of your required behaviours?			
Ask for feedback on your leadership impact?			
Live your shared organisational values?			
Defend your personal guiding principles?			
Leading Others			
Listen deeply to other points of view?			
Show compassion and empathy?			
Use a developing style of coaching?			
Have open and honest conversations?			
Lead with conviction and passion?			
Communicate shared meaning and purpose?			
Appreciate and support team members?			
Give your people space to be creative			
Empower them to experiment?			
Tolerate their mistakes?			
Help people grow in their jobs?			
Are approachable most of the time?			
Praise people?			
Leading Your Business			
Scan for external threats and opportunities?			
Search for innovation in other industries?			
Are willing to take risks and try new approaches? support your people through difficult change?			
Develop high-trust relationships?			
Give your people stretching goals?			

In Summary

Leadership is an affair of the heart, leadership is personal. You lead, *one conversation at a time*, at the speed of trust, powered by empathy.

Authenticity is the lifeblood of trust. And authentic leadership comes only from a place of stillness. You lead from the inside out. Authentic leaders inspire others to find their authentic voice. Passion and enthusiasm are contagious and inspire others to act.

Ethical leaders set the tone from the top through their behaviour. Diversity and inclusiveness drive teamwork and power innovation.

Mindfulness—seeing things as they really are—is the leader's way. There is no single right way to lead—you can use many different styles depending on the situation.

All progress comes through quality coaching conversations.

8

Coaching Tomorrow's Leaders

Introduction

This chapter looks at how you can coach tomorrow's leaders by having more powerful everyday coaching conversations.

Being truly present and witnessing another human being, by listening deeply, has the power to transform their thinking. In this chapter, you will find tips for better listening and tips for better talking.

I also consider the power of questions for placement and clarification for effective conversations.

Straight talking and feedback can be catalysts to better awareness and relationships that lead to organisational progress and I give guidance here to having those challenging conversations.

The chapter examines how the coach can encourage different thinking by using the "seven thinking hats". It also analyses how diverse national and regional cultures have different starting points for their thinking—from another place; from another point of view.

This chapter concludes with a look at the changing world of work, the future of leadership and gives you a chance to reflect on your *Leading by Coaching* journey.

© The Author(s) 2019   **231**
N. Marson, *Leading by Coaching*, https://doi.org/10.1007/978-3-319-76378-1_8

Shaping the Future

Shaping the future will be a shared mission with followers, based on shared values, meaning and purpose. And this shared partnership will be powered by trust and deep relationships. In the new age of disruption, the human craving for social interaction, companionship and intimacy will be the only constant. The two critical questions for you as a leader are: How do people experience you? And how do people experience themselves in your presence? How your followers experience you, will define your leadership.

The meta skill of a leader in the future will be coaching people to learn how to deal with the complex challenges ahead. Supporting and developing young professionals now to be your future leaders.

Leaders will need to take us to places that we've never been before. If you are to step into the unknown, the place to begin is with the exploration of your inner territory. In the words of Henry David Thoreau "what lies behind us and what lies before us are small matters compared to what lies within us. And when you bring what is within you out into the world, miracles happen".

And you bring, as a leader, what lies *within you*—your signature presence—into your everyday coaching conversations. Because you help people change their thinking in your everyday conversations.

Everyday Coaching Conversations

Our lives are defined by our conversations. Our conversations have made us who we are. All our progress comes through our conversations. Conversations at home and conversations at work. Everyday conversations.

Coaching is a conversation with a purpose. Engaging conversations full of meaning are a catalyst to change.

Transformational coaching requires the coach to be a guide on the client's journey—being present; encouraging critical reflection; evoking new stories; helping the client map their values; identifying travelling styles.

A coach helps their client manage resistance to change. To understand and reframe resistance as learning. Resistance often shows up in different and unexpected ways. Better to confront people's concerns than dismiss them. Better to challenge their assumptions and help them open up positive opportunities.

Before You Can Have a Conversation with Somebody Else You Need to Have a Conversation with Yourself

Leading by Coaching, one conversation at a time, requires the use of your multiple intelligences as covered in Chapter 2. Working with all your intelligences—emotional, social, cultural and neuroleadership—is the technology of your mind and your competitive advantage. To do so effectively requires conscious awareness and discipline. You need to be consciously aware of your emotions and the emotions of others in the moment so that you can be mindful and do the right thing. You need to have the discipline of being silent in the silences. Not filling the space. Letting others fill the space. Creating space for others to think.

The Power of Being Present

People just want to be witnessed. Just listened to and understood. They just want someone to be there with them, to be there for them. Being present in the moment, giving people your full attention, so they feel recognised and motivated, commits people to you as a leader. When you are truly present as a leader you are able to spontaneously deal with what is there in front of you. You can dance figuratively with your client. And you can only reach out and connect to others if you are truly present with them. Being fully present in the moment is the first requirement of coaching. Being present is being alive, energised, able to express your emotions and feelings in the moment. Being present is showing empathy and connecting at a deep human level with your client, trying to understand what drives them internally.

> "At the still point of the turning world. Neither flesh nor fleshless; Neither from nor towards; at the still point, there the dance is, But neither arrest nor movement. And do not call it fixity.
> Where past and future are gathered. Neither movement from nor towards, Neither ascent nor decline. Except for the point, the still point, There would be no dance, and there is only the dance".
> T. S. Eliot *Four Quartets, Quartet Two: East Coker*[1]

Four Quartets are four interlinked meditations with the common theme being man's relationship with time, the universe, and the divine. *East Coker*

---

[1]Eliot, T. S. "East Coker." Four Quartets. Harcour: San Diego. 1947.

is described as a poem of late summer, earth and faith. As in the other poems of the *Four Quartets*, each of the five sections holds a theme that is common to each of the poems: time, experience, purgation, prayer and wholeness. Within the poem, Eliot emphasises the need for a journey and the need for inward change.

Power of Listening

Why Leaders Should Learn to Listen

> Leadership and learning are indispensable to each other. John F. Kennedy

Listening makes people feel respected and cared for, which inspires them to learn, grow and commit to action.

You only learn and grow from listening and getting feedback. Thinking through a complex issue can rarely be done well in isolated analysis. You can't fully explore your own thoughts and challenge your own ideas. Energise people by building on what they know, instead of exhausting them with what you know. Asking questions empowers people, giving advice stifles their motivation and creativity.

The best answers are in the minds of the people around you and mined from the conversations you have with them. Embrace the mystery of not knowing. Be vacant and vulnerable. Your best decisions will be made in conversation—a two-way iterative learning process. Saying I don't know gives others more confidence in you and in themselves.

Listening gives you more clarity about the decisions you need to make. Listening reveals your blind spots. Gives you the opportunity to recognise the value of completely new ideas. The brain needs to be surprised. Feeling absolute confidence in what you know is risky. Having all the answers is impossible. You cannot see all possibilities. There are many right answers. You have to have courage to deal with ambiguity.

Professional coaching is the ultimate opportunity to listen to someone deeply, and be listened to deeply, and can be an enlightening and life-changing experience for both parties. Listening is powerful because it gives people an opportunity to hear their own voice, to think about their thinking.

The Silences in your *Leading by Coaching* conversations:

- allow you to connect on an emotional level;
- create the space for you and others to think about their thinking;
- and for insights to emerge.

Everyday conversations should be listening conversations. So why do we find **it so hard to listen?**

Barriers to Listening

Fear is the barrier. Fear of seeing things as *they* are. Talking means being in control. Talking is being the master. Directing the conversation. Demonstrating mastery of your professional expertise. Hiding behind your professional mask. Preserving your status. Maintaining your ego.

Listening is being out of control. Listening is being the servant. Losing autonomy. Listening creates uncertainty. Listening, especially feedback, is a threat. We look for the facts that fit our view of the world. We see everything through our own unique filters. Our experiences. Our preferences. Who we are. We get what we expect. We see what we are looking for. We see things as *we* are.

I remember the Dilbert cartoon, where the boss admits that, *nothing I say in meetings actually means anything.* To which his young colleague replies, *then why do you talk?* The boss answers back, *I tried listening once. It was awful.* I think we can all recognise ourselves in the cartoon. Talking is so much easier than listening.

Deep listening takes place in silence. Communication happens in silence. Communication is the congruence of the words, the music (emotional tone of your voice), and the dance (how you look when you say the words). Choosing to care, empathy and compassion bring people to life. They feel witnessed, heard and understood.

What Great Listeners Do!

The word LISTEN contains exactly the same letters as the word SILENT. Whoever invented this word in the English language was telling us something! The Chinese picture for listening contains the symbols for eyes, ear, undivided attention and heart. Listening is about listening beyond the words to who the person is and what they need from you. What is going on with them. Keep your mouth shut! Listen to what is being said beyond the spoken words, tone of voice, body language, and posture. Listen to their non-verbal communication. That is their real communication. Communication takes place in the silences. Focus on what they are saying, not on your thoughts or how it affects you. Listen to how the person is thinking. Listen to the feelings behind the facts. Commit all your energy to the conversation you are having. Be interested; don't try to be interesting.

Talking about yourself lights up reward centres in the brain, just as narcotics do. Conversation should be a reciprocal exchange, in which each of you expresses an interest in the other. Ask good questions, it shows you are interested. Listen to see how you can help.

Practise reflective listening (as used by psychologist Carl Rogers) paraphrase your meaning of what is being said. Use positive body language and an enthusiastic tone. Don't pass judgement—be open-minded, see the world through the eyes of the other person. Practise, practise, practise!!!

My Tips for Better Listening

Tip 1: Be aware of your inner thoughts and feelings

Listen outside your thoughts. Switch off your internal chatter. Recognise your filters: Confirmation—*I know that;* Assessment—*I don't agree with that;* Pessimism—*It will never work.* Acknowledge your feelings in the moment. Be conscious of your inner body signals. What is it telling you about your internal state of being? How should you respond? What should you disclose?

Tip 2: Listen to what is unsaid

Never underestimate the importance of small talk in establishing rapport. Look for the non-verbal leakage. Betrayal oozes out of the pores of our skin. Listen with your eyes. "You know my method, Watson. It is founded upon the observation of trifles". Sherlock Holmes.

Tip 3: Focus on catching the ball

Focus on catching the ball, not hitting it straight back. Listen without immediately trying to say the next thing or connect the next dot. Focus on the big picture not the details. The client's destination not their journey. The impact of their emotions on their thinking. Their fears and aspirations; their pain and gain. You need to understand where they want to go before you can help them get there. Helping them reappraise, reframe and realign their expectations.

Diagnose first. Then prescribe. There is a natural bias to finding previous successful paths. Professionals of all disciplines including doctors, lawyers and accountants are all frantically searching through their previous successful matters to find precedents. And they do this despite knowing their client's circumstances are different and don't fit past experience.

Listening Is Your Business

Creating a listening business helps people deal with change and uncertainty with renewed energy. Listening conversations build trust. Listening conversations build collaboration. Listening conversations create openness for ideas to flourish. Listening conversations create new opportunities and pathways. What would happen if people really listened to each other? What problems could be solved? What could be achieved? What possibilities would be created?

Do you have a listening business? Do you listen to your clients and colleagues? Really listen?

Tips for Better Talking

You will remember from my ACE model in Chapter 6 that to build trust you need to be authentic, communicate with the listener in mind and engage emotionally. To talk better it follows that your body language and the emotional tone of your voice need to be in sync with your words. That is your communication needs to be congruent for you to be credible and believable.

The following hints and tips will help you get your message across more effectively.

Be specific; slow down; pause; notice what is important; make your point clearly; accentuate the positive; don't lose your client in the details; focus on their thinking not the issue. Improve your people's thinking by asking questions with the word thinking in it. For example: *What is your **thinking** on this?*

Put process before content; keep things simple; use simple words. Say it simply. "Everything should be made as simple as possible, but not simpler"—Albert Einstein.

The Power of Questions

Conversations are a unique source of creative interaction. Conversations can provide many layers of interaction. They can reduce risks of conflict by sending out feelers. Seeing what kind of response, you get. The greatest risk is rejection. Social exclusion is painful. Questions disarm the "mismatching" reflex in the brain. Questions test the water. Questions are much harder to mismatch than statements because they ask people to contribute to the conversation. Questions can leverage curiosity. Questions can uncover people's needs. Questions can create a sense of urgency. Questions can help establish a mutual agenda. Questions can provide emotional reassurance. Questions can test shared assumptions to avoid a false consensus. Questions can procure feedback. Open questions, like *what, how, why, when and where,* are a source of learning. Questions can uncover insights. Questions can produce innovation. Questions provide many layers of interaction that generate action. Closed questions, that require a yes or no response, help clients make decisions and commitments. Closed questions must be used with caution as psychologically you can fall into the trap of getting the answer that moves the client in the direction you want them to go.

It is important to listen carefully to questions, so you can answer them fully. Listening shows you care. Pause before you say anything to show you are thinking about your answer. By pausing before answering you are telling the questioner that their question was a good one and deserves your careful consideration.

Not listening, with your full attention, and noticing the non-verbal communication, can lead to misunderstandings and erode trust. And remember you can only coach at the speed of trust.

Questioning

Some **Opening** questions to get your conversation started:

How are you today?
How are you feeling today?
Thank you for staying late the last few nights
I appreciate your contribution to our project team You are making great progress, well done
What is on your mind?
What are you thinking about today? What is occupying your thoughts?

Some **Placement** questions to establish the context and purpose—what you are talking about—for the coaching conversation:

What do you want to achieve from this coaching?
How are you feeling about making some important decisions?
Why are you committing to having these coaching sessions?
What does success feel like?
Can you make it SMART? Specific Measurable Achievable Realistic Timely
How committed are you to change? On a scale of 1 to 10?
What is stopping it being a ten?
Where are you now?

How happy are you with your current situation?
What do you want to change?
Do you have control of your situation?
What can you change?
Whose permission do you need to move forward?

Some **Clarifying** questions to make sure there is a meeting of minds and common assumptions:

What do you think you can do to change your situation?
What is realistic?
What would be your priority?
What could be a first step?
Who can you rely on to help you?
What else would be important to you?
What have you decided to do?
Why is this important?
What are the external barriers?
How committed are you to taking the first step? On a scale 1 to 10?
What would have to happen for it to be a ten?
How will you feel when you have achieved your coaching goals?

Effective questioning is about asking the right questions, at the right time, in the right way, rather than following a list. The above questions are designed to get you started and inspire your thinking. Trust yourself to ask the right question at the right time by being truly present with your client and trusting your intuition! The **Parallel Mind Conversation pathway** is a visual reminder of the steps to follow in your coaching conversations. It is ok to deviate from the path but if you get lost you can get back on to it where you left off (Fig. 8.1).

Developing Tomorrow's Leaders

> One cannot teach a man anything. One can only enable him to learn from within himself. Galileo

The key to coaching for transformational change is mutual trust. A special relationship with someone where it is safe to bounce off ideas. Someone

Conversation pathway

Fig. 8.1 The Parallel Mind Conversation Pathway

you are not directly involved with day-to-day. Someone detached who can challenge your thinking. Someone who can help you think things through. Someone who can help you deal with the pressures and expectations of stakeholders to deliver exceptional performance. Your role as the coach is to hold the space for the client to think about their thinking. See things from different perspectives.

A coach can ask the coachee to put different thinking hats on. The dreamer. The realist. The critic. Using **Professor Edward De Bono's "Six Thinking Hats"** can help tomorrow's leaders see things from a different place; from a different point of view.

Each hat represents a distinct direction of thinking as identified with an assigned colour. The six directions are:

1. **Managing** Blue—what is the subject? what are we thinking about? what is the goal? can we look at the big picture. *What process does it need to go through?*
2. **Information** White—considering purely what information is available, what are the facts? *What do we know?*
3. **Emotions** Red—intuitive or instinctive gut reactions or statements of emotional feeling (but not any justification). *How does it feel?*
4. **Discernment Black**—logic applied to identifying reasons to be cautious and conservative. Practical, realistic. *Where are the barriers?*
5. **Optimistic response** Yellow—logic applied to identifying benefits, seeking harmony. Sees the brighter, sunny side of situations. *What can enable it?*
6. **Creativity** Green—statements of provocation and investigation, seeing where a thought goes. Thinks creatively, outside the box. *What are some creative alternatives?*

Coloured hats are used as metaphors for each thinking direction. Switching to a different thinking direction is symbolised by the act of putting on a different coloured hat, either literally or metaphorically. This metaphor of using an imaginary hat as a symbol for a different thinking direction was first mentioned by De Bono as early as 1971 in his book "Lateral Thinking for Management" when describing a brainstorming framework. These metaphors allow for a more complete and elaborate segregation of the thinking directions. The "Six Thinking Hats" indicate problems and solutions about an idea the thinker (coachee) may come up with. Changing hats forces people to see things from another perspective, another point of view. It requires a coach as a facilitator to maintain the discipline of sticking to the hat the coachee is wearing rather than reverting back to their everyday hat.

The Seventh Thinking Hat, Disruption Purple

I have added a seventh thinking hat—**Disruption Purple.** We live in the age of disruption. The coach should encourage the client to think about, *what happens if the rules no longer apply?* You want the client to put themselves in the shoes of potential disruptors. *How could you disrupt your industry like for instance* **Purple Bricks** *has disrupted the estate agent business model in the UK?* You can then ask the client, *what they could do to counter this threat? What could they do to be the disrupter? What is the threat? What is the opportunity?*

Reframing problems as desired solutions can be helpful. You don't necessarily have to remove the cause of a problem to come up with a way forward. When you are coaching a client, getting them to wear different thinking hats, you need to bear in mind the appetite for risk at an organisational cultural level and a national cultural level.

Every organisation has a different appetite for risk depending on their market position, historical origins, and personalities of the senior management, especially the CEO. You could ask the client how risk-adverse their organisation is, on a scale of 1–10. Silicon Valley doesn't operate like Lloyds of London!

Change is a political and behavioural process. An essential part of any change initiative in global organisations is understanding the cultural dynamics at play. Differences in thinking of other cultures need to be considered when discussing change initiatives with multicultural colleagues.

In my travels to different parts of the world, working with clients from different cultures, I have found beneath the superficial differences a profound sense that we are all alike and have the same needs. And emotions are at the heart of this common humanity. Emotions provide a universal language that creates a common bond that transcends religion and politics. We all interact with each other as people and talk, share perspectives and feelings. From dialogue comes TRUST. Tolerance, Respect, Understanding, Sincerity and Transparency. And with trust comes acceptance, appreciation and connection.

Trust is easier to build in your known environment than when dealing with people from another culture. In order to have everyday conversations across cultures that build trust, it is vitally important to understand how people from different parts of the world think.

I have developed a **framework** for approaching *Leading by Coaching* conversations with your colleagues across the globe. (For more detailed information, I recommend you read Richard D. Lewis, *When Cultures Collide: Managing Successfully Across Cultures*.)

When collaborating you should bear in mind the different ways people think in different cultures.

The different types of thinking can be grouped into my **Process, Preferences, & Movement framework**.

Process

This is the basic unconscious thinking process that drives how different cultures tackle similar problems. How the mind is conditioned.

In linear cultures, like Germany and Switzerland, people plan, schedule, organise, follow linear logic chains, do one thing at a time.

Multi-actives, like the Italians, are lively spontaneous and do lots of things at the same thing.

Reactives, like the Chinese and the Finns, listen quietly and calmly to other people's ideas, before doing anything.

High/Low Context
In high context cultures like Japan, decisions are made invisibly. To outsiders, it will not always be clear who the ultimate decision maker will be. The leader will be known to insiders and will be the one who ratifies any decision or agreement. In low context cultures, like Germany, the rules are the rules and it will be clear what the steps are before any decision can be made. And it will be clear who will make the decision.

Universalistic/Particularistic
In a universalistic culture, like Sweden, the rules are the rules. They apply to everyone and must be obeyed. If you in a car that is stopped by the police

for speeding and the officer asks whether your friend was driving too fast you will tell the truth.

In a particularistic culture, like Spain, relationships come before the rules. *Sorry officer, I didn't notice how fast she/he (friend) was travelling.*

High/Low Uncertainty Avoidance
In cultures with high uncertainty avoidance, like Japan and Switzerland, the status quo is usually the favoured route. If it works why change it? In cultures with low uncertainty avoidance like USA and China, risk is accepted much more easily. If we can make it better, let's do it!

Preferences

Preferences is about how different cultures prefer to be treated. How power is distributed, how emotions are displayed and how people communicate.

Hierarchical/Egalitarian
In hierarchical cultures, like France, there is a big distance between the powerful decision makers and the lower rungs of the organisational ladder. So, decisions must be referred up to the appropriate level of seniority. In more democratic, egalitarian cultures like Sweden and the Netherlands, there is a very flat structure and a lot of discussion among equals until the leader makes a final decision.

Masculine/Feminine
Hierarchical cultures are predominately masculine, and egalitarian are usually feminine.

In a masculine culture like the UK or US self-reliance is a quality seen as important in leaders. In feminine cultures like Sweden and the Netherlands, caring is more important, especially when people are struggling. Everyone rallies around to support the person get over their difficulty and move on.

Status—Ascribed/Achieved
In societies where status is ascribed, like China, status is given to people by virtue of their age, class, gender, family background or education. By way of contrast, are societies who give status based on their achievements, like Germany, where qualifications, titles and career achievements count much more.

Emotions—Affective/Neutral
In affective cultures, like Italy, people show their emotions, and display affection in full public view.

In neutral cultures, like Norway and Sweden, people hold back their emotions. They focus on the task in hand.

Direct/Indirect communication
In cultures, usually low context, with a direct communication style, again like Germany, you make it clear what you want. In cultures with an indirect communication style, like the UK, things are rather more ambiguous. You have to read the body language, you need to understand the relationships of the players, you need to keep it, as mentioned before, all "jolly nice chaps".

Movement

Movement is essentially how different cultures make decisions and move on.

Individual/Collective
In an individualistic culture like USA, the boss makes the decisions and people fall into line. If your client is from a collective culture like China, they will want to find consensus before making any decision.

Short/Long term
In cultures, like the USA, there is a short-term perspective. It is about making money today. Company results are reported quarterly. In cultures like China, there is a long-term perspective. It is about long-term relationships and sustainability.

Internal/External
External value systems are based on material recognition, the size of your house or car for instance is important in the USA. Internal value systems are based on personal character, your self-esteem and development is important in China.

Specific/Diffuse
In specific-oriented cultures, like Germany and Switzerland, your life at work is separated from your life outside work. Your boss has no influence on you outside your office. In Diffuse cultures, like, the USA, there is no separation of private and public space. One space diffuses itself into the other seamlessly. You are expected to defer to your boss if you meet in the supermarket. There is no barrier between work and personal life spaces.

Straight Talking

As discussed in Chapter 6, telling it straight takes a lot of emotional energy, but it needn't. It just needs the presence of mind and a bit of courage.

Giving timely feedback can be done informally, anytime—between meetings over a coffee or even walking together to the underground station. What is critically important is that it is delivered right. You need to adjust the feedback for the personality of the recipient and your relationship with them. And context defines everything. The last thing you want to do is erode the personal trust between you and your colleague. So, you should be transparent—be clear about your intentions—respect their feelings, try to understand their side of things, be sincere in wanting to help them, and be tolerant of diverse people and perspectives. So, the message is straight talking builds relationships because it improves transparency and increases the certainty the brain craves.

> I interviewed **Victoria Brackett**, who was then Managing Partner of **Thomas Eggar**, a regional law firm in South East England, for my book. She personally had coaching conversations with over seventy Partners to support them through change.
> Victoria directly empathises, encourages and praises others, and seeks to resolve emotional conflicts through communication: "Let's talk about it".
> *Organisations change one person at a time* she told me. Vicky had zero tolerance for *bad behaviours.* She had the personal courage to manage out six top fee earners because they would not buy into the new corporate culture of the firm. Attitude was more important than income. Work–life balance was also a very important value in the firm as demonstrated by Vicky's determination not to let her position at the top of her firm stop her being a good mum.

Victoria's message to anyone who finds it difficult to start a "difficult" conversation, is to just start one, with the words, "Let's talk about it".

Challenging Conversations

To really find your voice and challenge people in power, or to deliver critical feedback, you have to manage your anxiety of losing control of a situation. You may be tempted to use your formal authority. We all, well most of us, share the neurotic need of wanting to be liked and no one wants to be criticised or embarrassed. Having these personally challenging conversations runs the risk of upsetting the status quo and damaging your status within your group.

Dealing with "challenging", awkward conversations requires a heady cocktail of courage, assertiveness, self-confidence and self-reliance. A leader's duty is to help their followers find and use their voice. Recognising this individuality requires leaders to have the courage to engage in conversations that may not be easy or may reveal something personally challenging to deal with. You can revisit some techniques for starting these "challenging" or "difficult" conversations and finishing them with win/win outcomes in Chapter 6.

The power of honest conversations to heal is incalculable. Honesty is an expression of personal integrity. In professional service firms, everything is dependent on personal interaction. Honesty is the foundation of good relationships with clients and colleagues. Lawyers and accountants are trained to spot what is wrong and get things right. They need to avoid making mistakes 100% of the time. The consequences of getting it wrong are potentially disastrous. This makes them insecure. Fear of the unknown stops honest conversations. They are happy to criticise but not to be criticised. To judge but not to be judged. To be the one with the power and control. They don't like to give feedback in case they get it back.

It is important to say the unsayable, to speak the truth, to tell it as it is.

Say it straight or it will come out crooked!

The Gift of Feedback

Feedback is the mother of invention. It is the fuel of the learning organisation. Feedback can drive strategic intent. Feedback should be appreciated, learned from, acted on and shared. Reactions to receiving feedback can be open or closed. An opportunity or a threat. Critical feedback should always be given with kindness. Always ask yourself how you would like to receive it. The aim should always be to increase someone's confidence, not reduce it. Negative feedback increases activity in the *amygdala* that releases stress-producing hormones and neurotransmitters that interrupt logical thinking in the *pre-frontal cortex*. A brain-friendly way to give feedback is the sandwich technique. First give at least three positive feedbacks and a strong belief in peoples' qualities. Then give the negative criticism with sensitivity. The filling in the sandwich. Then finally increase their emotional well-being by being optimistic and enthusiastic about their future. Agree a doable action plan and get them to commit to a first step. This should help you to deliver the improvement you are seeking while at the same time protecting their fragile ego from going into flight mode! Making them feel psychologically secure. Giving and receiving feedback positively is an important skill of a leader and a coach.

Making It Personal

When you are Chairman of a combined law firm with over 60 offices in more than 30 countries, remembering people's names is challenging but nonetheless important. It is a good example of the critical human non-essentials that keep the togetherness in the firm and reduce conflict to a minimum. **Paul Smith**, the former Chairman of **Eversheds Sutherland**, embodies this personal style of leadership. Below is a transcript of my interview with Paul during the last year in his ambassadorial role.

Leadership interview Paul Smith, former Chairman Eversheds Sutherland LLP

Nick
What is your role in the Firm?
Paul
Ambassador for the Firm, Chair of The Board, and a voice for the Partners
Nick
What do you do as Ambassador for the Firm?
Paul
Internal—
Keeping togetherness—I always make it personal and try to remember names. I want them to look forward to my visit not tidy the files on their desks—Father Christmas is coming to see us!
External—
Getting business; developing the brand; helping establish the "global footprint" of the Firm
Nick
What do you do as Chair of the Board?
Paul
Reporting on Executive Council meetings and balancing the future of the Firm
Nick
What are your roles as the Partners' voice?
Paul
Listening and feeding back to Management their aspirations and concerns Resolving rare disputes, upholding the special democratic culture of the Firm
Nick
Tell me about the Pro Bono work you do personally
Paul
I like to inspire young people from humble backgrounds to reach for the sky. I want to be a role model for what can be achieved with ambition, hard work and application.
I also speak at student conferences
Nick
How do you lead yourself?

Paul
> I have been heavily influenced by my Mentors, especially an 80-year-old law-yer from Denver, Colorado
>
> I have committed myself to continuous personal improvement. My curios-ity is endless, and I actively encourage people to approach me—stop me in the lifts!
>
> I make sure that there are no disasters on my watch—you can't control events, but you can navigate them safely

Nick
> How do you lead others?

Paul
> Constantly communicating the Firm's progress
> Constantly re-enforcing the Firm's values
> Constantly supporting, mentoring and coaching the Firm's Partners

Nick
> How do you lead the Firm?

Paul
> Delivering my Chairman's Manifesto—doing what I promised to do
> Not being a "kick the tyres" Chairman
> Guiding, monitoring and communicating the direction of the Firm
> Educating Partners to focus on profitability

Nick
> What will be your legacy to the firm as Chairman?

Paul
> Helping the firm grow, by helping to win business
> Overseeing a successful US merger

Nick
> What advice would you give to the new Chair?

Paul
> Be remembered for something game changing
> Advance the job—always be engaging, communicating and leading
> Be lucky!

Change Is Complex

Change is complex. People are operating in a complex social system of power coalitions with a multitude of personalities, emotional drivers and egos. The goal is emotional equilibrium. Organisational change always has personal implications. People ask themselves, *how will change impact on me? Will it give me less or more control? Are their threats to my social status?* People need to feel listened to. They need to be witnessed. They need to feel fully heard and understood. They need to feel that someone cares about them. They need to feel that someone is there to help through the painful process of change. Organisations change one person at a time, *one conversation at a time.*

Leading by Coaching is a powerful process. If done systematically it can change the organisation's culture. Personal development and growth improve performance and provide a competitive edge. *Leading by Coaching* helps organisations to respond more quickly to change and become more sustainable.

The Changing World of Work

Mark Watkins of jump shift leadership and professional behaviour change skills coaching, based in New Zealand, www.jumpshift.co.nz, shares the following vision for *Leading by Coaching* in the changing world of work.

The past does not equal the future. Today's **V**olatile, **U**ncertain, **C**omplex and **A**mbiguous world is complex and chaotic, where there is no linear relationship between cause and effect. This requires leaders who are adaptable, learn fast, balance trade-offs within decisions and reflect, learn and grow.

Simple and complicated roles will be automated. The complex and chaotic world of work requires pattern recognition, sense making and intuition—deeply human traits.

The top 6 skills identified in *The Future of Jobs Report, World Economic Forum* as needed in 2020 are (1) Complex problem solving, (2) Critical thinking, (3) Creativity, (4) People Management, (5) Coordinating others, and (6) Emotional Intelligence. At the same time, the top emerging jobs can be summed up as (1) Data Scientists and (2) Yoga teachers!

The Creative Shift

Solving twenty-first-century problems is going to require a shift in thinking from the thinking that was responsible for them. Artificially intelligent thinking machines will replace humans in many traditional jobs, but we shy away from discussion of what this means. The world of work will be very different for our children. As a leader will you help people define the jobs they want rather than let current jobs define them?

McKinsey Global Institute's report on automation says that jobs comprised of predictable, repetitive physical tasks are most likely to be partially or fully replaced by automation in the near future.[2] But technologies exist

---

[2]Manyika, J. et al. (2017, January). *Harnessing automation for a future that works*. Retrieved from McKinsey Global Institute: https://www.mckinsey.com/featured-insights/digital-disruption/harnessing-automation-for-a-future-that-works.

today that are able to do cognitive tasks. Just as our ancestors learned how to create and work with tools, we need to learn how to work along with machines and emerging technologies creatively.

Heraclitus in the fifth-century BC found that the problem with trying to understand the world was that it keeps changing all the time. He remarked "that you cannot step twice into the same river".[3] What he meant was that by the time you take the second step, the river has flowed on, so even just one second later the water is different. We will need to find new rivers to step into and they will be flowing faster and changing course at an unprecedented rate.

And the workplace itself is changing. At the Milan LinkedIn office, the company is experimenting by using different rooms to represent five typical locations in Italy (a theatre, a restaurant, a tailor's shop, a cellar and a garden): the aim is to explore how to design rooms, so they are best suited to different work tasks. They found that certain designs can help or hinder how well different tasks are undertaken. For example, the more a room stimulated senses, the better it seemed to be for learning and individual tasks, but the poorer for group tasks.[4] Welcome to your new world of work!

Your followers will look to you for ideas: for how they can use creativity to generate productivity; for how they can use purpose and passion to power performance; for how they can ensure well-being.

What does this all mean for developing leaders? Nick Petrie, of *The Centre of Creative Leadership*, suggests that vertical development is required to build a leaders' capacity. Knowing more "stuff" isn't as important as applying it meaningfully within your context. They call this the "knowing and doing gap". Wisdom is knowledge applied. Three key elements to unlock this in leaders are: **Heat moments**: Where you are literally in over your head, here your current capability is not sufficient to solve the challenges. To do so requires thinking differently. **Colliding Perspectives**: Leveraging diversity of people, thoughts and new thinking and integrating this into your own **Reflection**: Self-reflecting, being asked questions to challenge your perspective, coaching.

All three requires social support and feeling psychologically safe, allowing you to take risks, stretch and learn from your mistakes.

And therefore, so what for coaching? Considering the evidence above, leadership in the VUCA world partners beautifully with coaching.

---

[3]*Heraclitus.* (2007, February 8). Retrieved from Stanford Encyclopedia of Philosophy: https://plato. stanford.edu/entries/heraclitus/.

[4]Charbauski, R. (n.d.). *LinkedIn Designs Office for the 5 Senses.* Retrieved from Steelcase: https://www. steelcase.com/research/articles/topics/informal-spaces/linkedin-designs-new-workplaces-five-senses/.

The Future of Leadership

In tomorrow's company leaders will have influence rather than power. And they will exercise their influence through a networked world. They will have influence only if they communicate across social media platforms in a relevant, meaningful and aspirational way.

Leaders' relationships will be personal, driven by purpose and meaning and based on high levels of emotional connectivity and trust. By bringing together your learning you will be well on your way to finding, and articulating your unique signature presence as a leader and as a coach. How tomorrow's leaders' experience your signature presence in your *Leading by Coaching* conversations may well define your leadership legacy.

Your *Leading by Coaching* Checklist

Here is my list of questions for you to self-reflect on your *Leading by Coaching* conversations:

Do you:
coach your talented people to help them develop their full potential?
create space for tomorrow's leaders to grow through self-directed learning?
help them find their voice by dimming yours?
win their hearts by demonstrating empathic concern?
give your followers an opportunity for professional mastery and control over their work?
encourage your people to fail and learn by failing?
empower them to make decisions and so feel autonomous?
trust your people with early responsibility and challenging projects?
make them responsible for the outcome of projects with the minimum of direction?
support your people by giving them unconditional positive regard and the benefit of any doubts?
foster emotional commitment by developing closer social bonds that result in *emotional contagion?*
generate a sense of hope and excitement about the future?
provide your people with a clear sense of identity and belonging?
recognise and make visible to your team discretionary efforts?
understand the neurological impact of your leadership on the brains of your followers?
practise deep and compassionate listening?

9

Leading Impactful Change

Introduction

This chapter answers the question: how can I have more impact as a leader? By having coaching conversations that offer insights and fresh thinking, plus the energy and desire to act.

I explain what these positive conversations look like, and how to avoid the brain's default "away" reaction by using "towards" inducing couplings of words and emotions that create open learning.

In this chapter I explain how the brain is plastic and can, with the right conversations, break hardwired habits and create new neural pathways if there is a clear vision, strong self motivation and enough repetition/ reinforcement.

I investigate how the brain deals with change and how you can use this knowledge to impact change in your organisation, one conversation at a time.

The Parallel Mind neurological framework for SAFE change is introduced.

I look at the psychology of change from the different perspectives of me and we and analyse why change fails and how you can avoid the pitfalls. Critically, I outline the conditions needed for sustainable change.

The brain science behind why story telling is a powerful tool for change is explored.

I review the change insights from a number of high-profile case studies that demonstrate the role of "difficult" conversations in leading impactful

© The Author(s) 2019
N. Marson, *Leading by Coaching*, https://doi.org/10.1007/978-3-319-76378-1_9

change and end with some questions you can use to navigate those "difficult" conversations.

This chapter looks at agile organisations and how they use coaching to accelerate change.

The chapter also looks at leading change across cultures with the help of some powerful learning from a major transatlantic law firm merger.

By the end of this chapter you will be able to develop and articulate your unique *signature presence* as a leader and as a coach.

The purpose of a business is to create demand for its products and services. A sustainable business adds emotional connection to rational purchasing decisions. The heart rules the head when choosing one brand over another. And the pace of change is relentless even for market leaders, as Bill Gates showed when he said that "Microsoft is always two years away from failure". In 2018 Microsoft is once again the king of the tech industry. Satya Nadella has made Microsoft an investor's favourite again. But how did he turn the tech giant around? Find out later in this chapter!

Your job as a leader is to deliver impactful change to your organisation. And to do this you need to understand the nature of change, the change process and how you can coach your people through change, one conversation at a time.

The Brain and Change

Most of us like the predictability of some routine in our lives. Our brain craves certainty. But we live on an unstable, violent and turbulent planet. So, we accept that things change and get on with our lives as best we can. The human species has developed its dominance on planet earth by being the animal most able to adapt to its changing environment. Our brains are very agile. We can deal with change although we don't like unpleasant changes. Exotic holidays are one thing; being caught up in a monsoon is another. What we really don't like is being changed by other people. We don't like the idea that they have power over us. We want to chart our own voyage and be the captain of our own ship. We resist being changed. Resistance to being changed is normal. The psychological reaction to change is overwhelmingly negative to begin with and becomes positive later if given positive conditions for change. Change is biological not logical. Change is pain for the brain. Organisational change outside our control means that our brain cannot predict with any certainty what is going to happen to us. To the brain bad news is better than no news. We want to be told it straight. We can then plan our survival. Important insights from neuroscience research reveal how our brain works when faced with uncertainty. The *thalamus* monitors the traffic in the brain, constantly scanning for potential hazards. When the *thalamus* perceives a risk, it alerts the *amygdala*, which oversees protecting us from danger, pushing us to fight or flight. When there is an *amygdala* hijack, there is a changed physiology. Increased heart rate, increased blood pressure, the brain is preparing for battle. It is responsible for our instinctive and primordial reactions to stay alive. The *cortex* is responsible for rational analysis, assessing and evaluating the data in order to make logical decisions.

SAFE Change

The brain needs to feel safe. Safety comes from certainty. The brain seeks to control its environment. The emotional centre in our brain, the *limbic system*, provides us with an early warning for any threats either real, or perceived, to our safety.

The brain is a prediction making machine continuously weighing up the odds of survival and responding with a simple binary, "towards or away" decision when confronted with uncertainty. Jeffrey Schwartz, the scientist who inspired David Rock to write his ground-breaking book "Your Brain at Work" and who is the father of the Neuroscience movement, called the brain an "error detection machine" in his influential book, *The Mind and the Brain*. Neurons light up to focus on our mistakes and thus the brain is also a "self-checking mechanism". The brain is also, according to Dan Siegel (2012), in his *Pocket Guide to Interpersonal Neurobiology*, an "anticipation machine". Our ability to anticipate and make predictions about the future is the crux of intelligence.

SAFE change is a simple and powerful Parallel Mind Model variant on David Rock's SCARF Model. It will provide you with a framework for coaching people through change that promotes psychological safety (Fig. 9.1).

Social Status

We feel safer in social groups. And we feel safer in our chosen social groups if we have status and that status is clearly recognised by the other members of the group.

The Parallel Mind SAFE Change
Framework:

Social status,
Autonomy,
Fairness, and
Emotional engagement.

Fig. 9.1   The Parallel Mind **SAFE** Change Framework

Status gives us more power and, therefore, more control over the resources we need to survive. Status makes us feel safe.

Autonomy

People inherently are nervous of perceived threats and so are wary of change and uncertainty. But we tolerate our changing environment and adapt to fit into our new circumstances. Our primitive *basal ganglia*, the brain's control centre, soon works out the new routines that restore equilibrium. This automatic pilot system in the brain saves us using the *prefrontal cortex* thinking brain in the neocortex which is extremely energy hungry. Our brain resets its cruise control and off we go again!

But despite a reluctant acceptance of change, our brain as mentioned before strongly resists being changed by other people. We want to control our own destiny, not be in the power of others. We want to retain our autonomy.

Fairness

We all want to be treated fairly. Ever been in a queue and someone pushes in front of you? How did that make you feel? I expect you or someone else probably said something like, "Can't you see there's a queue here?" Or perhaps, "You should queue just like everyone else". Fairness is important to your brain.

Emotional Engagement

People want to be engaged and to be shown some empathy. Relatedness is important to the social brain and trust is the core issue. If you don't engage with your client and show them empathy, they won't trust you.

People's hearts rule their heads when it comes to their psychological safety. Emotion is more powerful than logic. BREXIT is a good example of SAFE change at work. People chose to protect their psychological safety over their Economic security.

The Psychology of Change—Me, We and the Power of Others

The first cycle of negative feelings starts with denial and anger. We say to ourselves this is not happening; it cannot be real. We then feel confused and isolated. We frantically try to make sense of what is going on. Our brains are desperately trying to make sense of their new surroundings. Trying to find new meaning and purpose. We feel isolated in our social group. We start asking ourselves who is still a friend and who now has become a competitor Who can I trust? We become depressed. We are in crisis. We are paralysed.

Our conscious thinking is frozen. Our emotional brains are in control. We are powerless to think of a solution to the dilemma we find ourselves in. We need help! Help from our bosses to give us some power back. Some control over our lives. We need to feel that someone cares about us and our happiness. Someone to talk to us as a unique individual. We are not a cost on a spreadsheet. We are flesh and blood, a body of emotions. Change is personal to us. We need to be consulted, listened to. We need to feel that our vote counts. We need to feel that change is fair. That someone is showing us some empathy. We need someone to coach us through the change, to show us how we can change and fit in. Organisations change one person at a time.

Social Pain and Change

Social exclusion is as painful for the brain as physical pain. There is a need for social connection at work. UCLA research, using MRI scans, showed that being left out of a game of catch activates the pain network in the brain. I felt the pain when I was dropped once from the school football team. I felt like an outcast. Socially excluded. Not part of the A team in both senses. I was desperate to get back into the team, to rejoin my tribe. Research shows that we warm to people who are more familiar to us. Our brains process thoughts about out-groups in a different way than our in-groups. There is less activation of the *medial prefrontal cortex* inclining us to see those in out-groups as more objects than humans. Our brains lead us to be biased, to take shortcuts towards our in-groups and away from perceived out-groups. Unconscious bias training is not enough to change the way our brains put people into convenient boxes. We need systems in the workplace at every level to mitigate our biases. There is a neuroscience basis for connection. *Cortisol* is released when stressed; *serotonin* makes us less fearful; *dopamine* gives us pleasure when we relate to someone in a social setting; *oxytocin* makes us feel calm when we are with someone we trust.

Changing Your Business *One Conversation at a Time*

Our lives are defined by our conversations. Our conversations have made us who we are. All our progress comes through our everyday conversations, at home and at work.

The pre-conditions for successful conversations include: authenticity; sincerity; honesty; empathy; compassion; openness and common language. Coupling between words and emotions triggers towards or away response and different brains, translation differently. To avoid getting a default away threat response—the brain is a prediction making machine—you need to put it in a towards reward response. Create a positive start to your conversation—praise, empathy, concern, equal power and status—all these gestures will help put people into a receptive and relaxed state. Give control to the other person. Ask them what they want to achieve. Focus on common values, shared agendas and interests. Don't assume you have common assumptions—define what is important to you and ask what is important to them.

No two brains are the same, we fill our reality gaps to make our own meaning and find relatedness. Cultural preferences also fill gaps, so be aware that someone else's reality may not be yours. It is how you make people feel that is most important.

You've got to get into their minds—become a part of their story. Deep listening, witnessing and understanding key behaviour—shows you care. Silence gives stillness to the brain to allow thoughts to develop—the monks know the power of silence to harvest their thoughts. When you listen to someone, they can hear themselves. They become consciously aware of their thinking.

Sharing their pain is cathartic and builds emotional bonds. At the end of the day all people really want is to feel fully heard and understood as human beings. When we are more comfortable with the silences in our coaching conversations, we become more consciously competent in having effective coaching conversations. We become masters of our conversations instead of hostage to fortune. We are more ready, willing and able to have those difficult conversations that we have been putting off.

And effective conversations give people the energy to act in alignment with our shared interests.

How to Have More Effective Coaching Conversations

You are your message so how you look—your body language and facial expressions—communicate a lot about your intentions and frame of mind. Relax and smile. This will, as previously discussed in Theme I, cause their brain to release the chemical transmitter *dopamine*, the feeling good social hormone. Smiling also helps you feel less stressed. When you smile, other people feel less stressed too. Maintaining eye contact builds confidence and trust. The critical thing with eye contact is not how much but when. You should maintain soft eye contact when they are talking. It is not as important when you are talking as long as you make eye contact at the beginning, to make sure you have their attention, and at the end of talking, to make sure they got what you said. Tilting your head forward slightly reduces your power over others by indicating deference and humility. This will help remove any real, or perceived gaps, in status. Mimicking gently the other person's expressions—returning a smile—will help them get a sense you are understanding how they are feeling. Be careful not to overdo it though as this will make you look inauthentic.

Coaching Dilemmas

A dilemma is a situation in which a difficult choice has to be made between two or more alternatives, especially equally undesirable ones. Dilemma derives from the Greek word meaning "double proposition".

Coaching can be helpful in tackling ethical dilemmas people have at work. An **ethical** dilemma is one in which a person has to choose between two options, both of which are morally correct but in conflict. Ethics and morals are inseparable. They both deal with questions of right and wrong. What constitutes **ethical** behaviour is determined by societal or cultural norms.

Using the Gestalt changing chairs technique, example in Chapter 4, the client can see both sides of the argument more clearly. They are then in a position to see ways they can resolve their dilemma. Gestalt coaching is about finding creative solutions in the search of wholeness, finding the best way for people to stay in harmony with the system they are part of.

Building a Coaching Culture

Skilling leaders as coaches give organisations an internal coaching system capability and a competitive advantage. Better coaching skills result in better engagement and higher individual performance levels as evidenced in the following **John Deere** case study.

How Coaching Lifted Engagement at John Deere. A NeuroLeadership Institute case study

Why coaching?

In a global organisation like John Deere, the brand name of Deere & Company, an American corporation that manufactures agricultural machinery, there is always pressure from competitors driving organisational performance. This organisational drive for performance puts significant pressure on people to perform individually. Coaching provides a thinking space for creative workers to come up with smarter ways of working. Leadership transitions, pivotal to the future success of the organisation, are also accelerated by coaching interventions.

Why an internal coaching system?

Training and developing a team of internal coaches builds the skills for better formal coaching engagements, and everyday coaching conversations it also provides a context rich—on demand—coaching resource.

Who gets coaching?

Employees at all levels.

What coaching methods?

Brain-based coaching methods.

What has been the impact of the global coaching programme?

- Increased engagement
- Improved leadership skills
- Better conversations
- Improved relationships
- More confidence as leaders
- Greater happiness at work

What are the organisational benefits of neuroscience-based conversations?

- Improved everyday interactions by understanding the drivers of social threat and reward.

- Behavioural change facilitated insights
- A growth mindset to develop others

Summary

The leaders at John Deere found that investing in learning how to coach their employees more effectively improved not just formal coaching sessions but also everyday coaching conversations.

Engagement of leaders and employees increased and so did productivity. Accelerating the organisation coaching vision has made work more meaningful and organisational performance has improved as a consequence.

Feedback on the programme

"His change in conversation style helps me better apply my thinking about solutions and participate to choose the best one. I have more trust and respect for my manager as a result".

Building Trust *One Conversation at a Time*

Leaders are trust-builders. You lead at the speed of trust. High-trust relationships help people to feel safe, proud and included. A safe organisational environment created through mutual trust enhances creativity, encourages collaboration and improves the quality of decision-making. The space of trust, of feeling trusted, and trusting others, creates a reciprocity of vulnerability. Leaders who make themselves vulnerable to their followers. Followers who make themselves vulnerable to their leaders. Leaders who allow their followers to show vulnerability. Followers who allow their leaders to show vulnerability. Vulnerability builds trust. Leaders who build trust bring to the surface what has remained hidden, in order to be perceived as human, personal and relational. A spirit of benevolence prevails in an organisation full of trust. Good will towards colleagues and clients is the fuel of highly collaborative organisations. Trust and respect go hand in hand. We need to respect a person before we can trust that person and equally, we need to trust a person before we can respect that person.

Leaders build trust by behaving consistently and with integrity. By constantly communicating a collective vision in an authentic way. By always being authentic, whatever the situation and the leadership style required in the moment. Leaders build trust by sharing power; by giving people more control over their lives. The brain wants autonomy, so good leaders empower their people. They consult team members when making decisions. The brain wants fairness, so good leaders set and follow the same set of rules consistently. The social brain wants status, so good leaders delegate, recognise and celebrate achievements. The social brain also wants to feel it belongs in its chosen social group, so a good leader exhibits shared values. Relatedness is important to the brain and the good leader builds strong personal bonds with their followers. The emotional brain needs empathy, so good leaders choose to care for their followers and demonstrate concern. Empathic concern is a key attribute of successful leaders. Empathic literacy, explicit understanding of what someone else feels and thinks at any given moment, is the key skill for leaders of change. A 2018 survey by YouGov, as part of the *UK Working Lives* project, found that one in five employees rated their relationship with their managers negatively. And a quarter of workers said their job negatively affected their mental health. I believe that all leaders have a duty of care to provide a psychologically safe and positive working environment. Not only it is the right thing to do morally but it also makes good business sense too. Healthy workers are happy and productive workers.

What Trusted Leaders Do

Trust may be invisible, but it is a most valuable commodity. As John Kotter says, "It is impossible to estimate how many good ideas are abandoned every day as a result of difficult to manage relationships".[1]

As discussed in Chapter 7, being trusted and trustworthy are critically important attributes of an impactful leader. The trustworthy leader, according to a September 2014 research report from Bath University, is human, relationship-focussed and personal. People gauge trustworthiness on the basis of that person's leadership actions and practice. Trusted leaders put relationships at the heart of everything they do. Participants overwhelmingly shared the importance of relationships in their experiences. They act like real people engaging with real people. When leaders take on a relational mindset, they create a sense of inclusion and support for their employees. Authenticity is the lifeblood of trust. Authentic leaders know who they are and so do their followers. Their leadership is their life story. Trusted leaders enable mutual responsibility. They recognise and develop uniqueness. They know that diversity powers innovation. Above all, trusted leaders build a trust bank, one conversation at a time; one gesture of kindness at a time. Every conversation full of trust builds the leaders' radius of trust and, therefore, influence. Trusted leaders build deep relationships by being authentic,

---

[1]Kotter, J. P. (1995, May). Leading Change: Why Transformation Efforts Fail. *Harvard Business Review*. Retrieved from Harvard Business Review: https://hbr.org/1995/05/leading-change-why-transformation-efforts-fail-2.

communicating with their listeners in mind and engaging at an emotional level. They recognise the power of empathy to drive their organisation forward. They know that every step presents an opportunity, but every opportunity harbours a risk. And they know trust helps people forget the "but". Trust-building behaviours, being authentic, communicating with the listener in mind and engaging emotionally, can be represented simply in the Parallel Mind **ACE** Trusted Leader Model, see Theme I, Chapter 3, Finding your authentic voice as a leader.

No one is perfect in relationships but, if we pay attention we can at least focus on putting more positive investments in our trust bank.

> **Pause for thought**
>
> Think of a leader in your organisation you trust. Why do you trust them? What is it that they do?
> How do they make you feel?
> Write a list of all the things you do to build trust with your followers. Reflect at the end of every day on your behaviours as a trusted leader.
> Write down your TRUST BUILDERS and your TRUST BUSTERS and do more of the former and less of the latter the next day.

Conditions for Change

The oldest and strongest emotion of mankind is fear, and the oldest and strongest kind of fear is fear of the unknown. Good leaders recognise that change is emotional not rational. They know that people are not intrinsically interested in the corporation's strategic opportunity. They know what drives people emotionally is safety. The brain needs certainty. The brain needs a safe environment, so it can predict the future with more certainty. As mentioned before the brain is a prediction making machine continuously scanning the horizon for danger, making the right calls for survival. It likes habits because it knows that they are safe. Any change in routines introduces risk. Risk to survival in a physical and a social sense. The brain as mentioned before feels the pain of social exclusion as much as the pain of a physical assault. We are social animals wired to collaborate and co-operate in social in-groups. We need to feel safe within our working group. We need to have status and the power that infers. Power is control. Control means we can be more certain about outcomes.

Good leaders instinctively know what their people need from them. They engage emotionally with their followers. They communicate and connect on the same emotional level. They tune into the same emotional wavelength. There is an emotional resonance between leader and follower. They make their followers feel included and valued. They give them confidence by delegating responsibility for key tasks. They support their followers by helping them adapt to the new conditions with as much certainty as it is possible to give. The certainty that their commute won't be disrupted, their working hours won't be longer and that they will be fully supported to learn any new skills required for a change of role.

By creating more certainty, with honest and sensitive communication, good leaders of change help their followers change their behaviours. They coach people to grow into their new world and develop their skills and broaden their range of competencies.

Good leaders choose to care, and people follow leaders who they believe care about them. Satya Nadella chose to care about his people. This is one of the main reasons he so successfully mastered the reorientation at Microsoft. Nadella knew how to use the mostly unused skills of empathy and compassion. Compassionate treatment of colleagues motivated people to change faster. Satya realised that feelings are the critical factor in change processes. Empathy is about understanding and connecting emotionally with another human being. Compassion is about reaching out and helping them deal with their situation. Empathy is the first step on the path to compassion. And compassion is a competitive advantage as proven by the resurgence of Microsoft.

Leadership Journey—Sian Fisher CEO The Chartered Insurance Institute (appointed 2016)

Sian Fisher took the helm at the Chartered Insurance Institute with a mandate for change. This is her leading change story after a year in the role.

Nick

What were the challenges you saw when you started your new leadership journey with the CII?

Sian

Looking in was a cathartic process of talking together about: who we are; who we want to become; what is working; what isn't working; what could be better; what should be our purpose; what should be our target operating model; what should be our key processes

Nick

What about the external environment?

Sian

Looking out I could see some tough challenges ahead. We needed to create a compelling reason to exist that people could believe in; craft an engaging narrative; work on personal motives and encourage people to own the vision and fill the leadership vacuum.

Nick
>How did you get people to embrace the change that was needed?

Sian
>Importance of getting **everyone** on board by: listening; engaging; consulting and having fun
>Importance of letting people air their views and **respecting** their position
>Importance of being **constructive** without personalising

Nick
>How important is diversity in your vision for a new CII?

Sian
>Importance of **Diversity**: listening to as many different voices as possible; widening the pool; getting new angles and ideas; stretching capability
>Importance and effectiveness of everyone rowing in the **same direction** for the **benefit** of **all**

Nick
>How are you keeping people engaged in the change process?

Sian
>Empathy; engagement; education; excitement

Nick
>What are your guiding principles for developing people?

Sian
>Honesty; transparency; challenge; and feedback

Nick
>What is your Leadership Signature?

Sian
>Whatever your skills, you are always going to be more effective, if you believe and care about what you are doing.

In September 2018, the CII moved out of its listed building into brand new offices in Lombard Street in the heart of the City of London. The new address symbolises Sian's commitment to modernise the CII and make it more relevant to its members, the wider insurance market and the general public.

Compelling Story

The rational brain also needs to be engaged. There needs to be a compelling reason to change as is the case with the Chartered Insurance Institute above. A compelling story that people get. The so-called "burning platform" compelling reason to change. As Jack Welch, former CEO General Electric, succinctly puts it, "change before you have to" and "control your own destiny, before somebody else does". You need to give people a compelling reason to change direction. A certainty about the consequences of inaction. Lao Tzu, in his classic book, The *Art of War*, stated the blindingly obvious observation that, "if you do not change direction, you may end up where you are heading". The obvious needs to be spelt out. A compelling story forces action to ensure a happy ending. Or at least not a disastrous one. It is something bigger than all of us. Survival or something to be proud of and worth making sacrifices for.

You must frame your story as a journey—your story—dramatic, experiential, evocative, persuasive, engaging, connecting and inspirational. Richard Turere, a 13-year-old Masai boy, told his dramatic and truly inspirational story at a TED talk, "My *lion lights* invention that made peace with lions". He told his captivated audience how the use of solar panels linked to a car battery protected his family's livestock in Kitengela on the edge of Nairobi National park in Kenya and without harming the lions.

Storytelling and Brain Science

The reason Richard's story lesson sticks is that it is embedded in your mind as a motion picture which arouses emotions and throws up images. Emotions of fear of hungry lions, of joy of finding a solution that protects the cattle and the lions. Images of Africa, the light and the landscape. Stories help the brain recognise patterns and synthesise. Stories are a pathway to understanding.

Our brain records our life as two selves of one story. Our experiencing self and our remembering self. Our experiencing self is like a stranger observing us. Our remembering self-records significant events and memorable moments. What we notice we remember. The brain composes stories for future reference. A library of stories from a lifetime of learning to refer to when making decisions.

Organisational storytelling provides a powerful metaphor for who we are, where we come from and what we stand for. Stories travel across organisations and provide the cultural glue that binds everyone together.

Role Modelling

Leaders who model the behaviour that they want to see are daily change catalysts, like Mahatma Gandhi, "We but mirror the world. All the tendencies present in the outer world are to be found in the world of our body. If we could change ourselves, the tendencies in the world would also change". Walk the talk if you want to be taken seriously. Be personally credible if you want to be believed and followed. You need to believe your story and in yourself as a leader. "You must first be convinced if you are to be convincing", as Winston Churchill put it.

Reinforcing Mechanisms

For change to stick, you need to reinforce your compelling change story. You cannot communicate it in too many ways or too often. Have a clear message and keep repeating it in a consistent way. Reinforce the desired changes in behaviour by rewarding good behaviours and punishing bad behaviours. Recognise and reward examples of good behaviours.

Capability-Building

Every great company or product started with a dream. What if we could communicate across oceans without cables? What if we could see someone smiling in a country the other side of the world? What if we could find a cure to cancer? What if they said we couldn't build a supersonic airliner and then we built Concorde?

Capability-building in organisations is about thinking about the needs of customers. What capabilities will we need to serve our customers in the future. Without growing capabilities there may be no future for the company. Growing capability is about staying relevant to our customers' world. Staying relevant to their evolving aspirations. It is about challenging our assumptions and suspending our beliefs. It is about having a dream and making it a reality. When he was just 16, Albert Einstein performed his famous thought experiment. He visualised travelling alongside a beam of light. This is where his theory of general relativity had its early birth.

Imagination is more important than knowledge—Albert Einstein

The Agile Organisation

I looked at the agile leader as a style of leadership that is a catalyst for change in Chapter 7. I now want to look at the agile organisation which is emerging as the new dominant organisational business model in the age of disruption. The organisation is morphing from a machine into an agile, living organism. Quick changes and flexible resources have replaced bureaucracy. Hierarchy and silos have been replaced by a focus on action based on a shared mission. Teams built on accountability have replaced command and control instructions. Gallup research has found that if an organisation aspires to be agile, its culture must have the right mindset. And the quality of its managers will determine whether the culture of the organisation is agile. Managers who have continuous conversations with their employees. Managers who engage and develop their people effectively. Managers who believe strongly in the purpose and values of their organisation. An agile mentality that adapts quickly to changing customer needs is driven ultimately by the employee experience.

According to McKinsey's Report January 2018, there are five trademarks of agile organisations.

1. Strategy—based on shared purpose and vision
2. Structure—network of empowered teams
3. Rapid decision and learning cycles—information transparency
4. Dynamic people model—that ignites passion based on community learning
5. Next-generation—enabling technology[2]

Agile organisations provide changing products and services that meet changing customer aspirations and competitive landscapes. Agile organisa- tions integrate new technology to deliver seamless solutions to customers. Agile organisations thrive in the rapidly changing world of big challenges and big opportunities. Agile organisations use coaching conversations to develop tomorrow's leaders.

How Agile Is Your Organisation?

The following case study will give you examples of the agile organisation in action and I hope it inspires you to think of ways you can make your organisation more agile.

> **The Agile Organisation—Case study: ING[3]**
>
> **ING**, the Dutch banking group, achieved a remarkable transformation by realising they were first and foremost a technology company, and then a bank. Financial services was the product offering, but the driver of their cutting-edge delivery was Information Technology.
>
> So how did ING, the Dutch banking group, achieve such a remarkable transformation?

---

[2]Aghina, Wouter et al. (2018, January). *The five trademarks of agile organizations*. Retrieved from McKinsey & Company: https://www.mckinsey.com/business-functions/organization/our-insights/the-five-trademarks-of-agile-organizations.

[3]Based on an article from Extracted from an article in *McKinsey Quarterly*, January 2017. https://www.mckinsey.com/industries/financial-services/our-insights/ings-agile-transformation.

Their "agile" model, which began in June 2015, started with establishing "tribes" made up of "squads". This agility was provided by multidisciplinary teams comprising a mix of specialists all focused on making the customers' journey with ING as smooth as possible.

Each *tribe* has a coach for individuals and squads to create high-performing teams. The squad, the basis of the new agile organisation, is self-steering and autonomous. It comprises representatives of different functions working in a single location and, critically, has "end-to-end" responsibility for achieving client-related objectives. Each squad must agree its purpose and how to measure its impact on clients. It also decides on how to manage its daily activities.

The new ING agile working system is only effective because the new ING culture is part of the transformation. The behaviour required to implement the agile system includes customer centricity, ownership and empowerment. Culture needs to be rooted and reflected in everything an organisation in transformation does.

This approach has already improved employee engagement and boosted productivity.

Breaking down silos, in terms of both organisational structure and office design, created more open communication channels facilitated by more open spaces for informal interaction.

Leadership, determination and teamwork changed ING for good. Seeing mistakes as learning increased the appetite for risk and accelerated innovation. And most importantly, agility plus purpose has created a better customer experience and kept ING ahead of its competitors.

The Connection Culture

One of the most powerful aspects of business is how a feeling of connection between management, employees and customers provides a competitive advantage. Only if people, who are part of the business, feel a sense of connection with the business, and each other, will the potential of the business be realised. Connection provides a sense of well-being, reduces stress and makes us more trusting.

In 2013, my son Christopher had a life-saving kidney transplant at Guy's Hospital in London. The staff in the Renal Unit—everyone from the consultant surgeon who performed the operation, to the receptionist that booked our appointments—had a warm disposition and optimistic attitude that lifted our spirits and gave us hope. We felt connected to them and they, it seemed, felt connected to us. They chose to care about Christopher and our concern for his well-being. Five years later we still feel that sense of care, compassion and connection when we visit the Guy's Renal Out-Patients' clinic.

Establishing a connection culture isn't rocket science, but how many organisations really pull it off? Does yours?

Change Insights

When it comes to successful change in organisations, the critical factor is team dynamics.

Google set out to find out what makes a Google team effective and got some surprising answers. Who is in the team mattered less than how the team members interacted, how their work was structured and tellingly, how their contributions were viewed. The Google people team called their project Aristotle.[4]

Google learned that there are five key dynamics that set successful teams apart from other teams at Google:

1. Psychological safety: Can we take risks in this team without feeling insecure or embarrassed?
2. Dependability: Can we count on each other to do high quality work on time?
3. Structure & clarity: Are goals, roles and execution plans in our team clear?
4. Meaning of work: Are we working on something that is important to us personally?
5. Impact of work: Do we fundamentally believe that the work we're doing matters? Are we making a difference that makes a difference worth making?

Psychological safety was found to be clearly the most important dynamic found by the Google team. Team members who felt safe to take risks and be vulnerable in front of their teammates were happier, more creative and more productive. They also stayed longer with Google.

Psychological safety is so important that it underpins the other four dynamics. So how come? Well, ask yourself how many times have you been in a meeting and not spoken up because you were afraid to look stupid,

---

[4]Duhigg, C. (2016, February 25th). *What Google Learned From Its Quest to Build the Perfect Team*. Retrieved from The New York Times Magazine: https://www.nytimes.com/2016/02/28/magazine/what-google-learned-from-its-quest-to-build-the-perfect-team.html.

especially in front of more senior members of your team? Our biggest fear is social exclusion to lose our status within our in-group. This feeling of being outcast causes us pain. Psychological pain, as you now know, is just as painful as physical main when processed by our emotional brain. When we are severely threatened, we can have an *amygdala* attack. This is the brain's fight or flight response to danger. *Amygdala* triggers in the workplace include lack of respect, being treated unfairly and lack of appreciation, believing you are not being listened to and treated with scorn. We can have more emotional control when threatened by being more self-aware of our moods, by talking to ourselves about our feelings, by being more aware of the moods of others and by showing empathy.

The following real-life case study about a **major change to the work space** gives an insightful account, based on the perceptions of the change leader, of the challenges he faced *Leading by Coaching* a team through a difficult change process.

Lessons in leading change

Few of us go through our careers without being part of a business restructure of some sort. And we know that physical changes to people's working environment can have a deep and lasting psychological impact on the dynamics of relationships, social groups and the leader's credibility. Loss of status, or perceived loss of status, arising from changes in job titles and reporting lines is a threat to the brain and people experience real pain dealing with it. Our relative position in our immediate social group is a key factor in our ability to survive and thrive in the work place.

Change is a very personal experience. Everyone experiences change differently. Change is an emotional roller coaster ride that needs a lot of one to one coaching conversations to calm down the *limbic system*, the emotional centre of the brain. Very often organisational change is felt by those directly affected as being forcibly imposed. As I mentioned before the brain wants autonomy, to feel in control. The brain craves certainty. It wants to be able to predict what is going to happen next. Being out of control feels dangerous and unsettling or even threatening. If we must change then our brain must know the deep reason why, before getting to grips with the rationality of the how. Emotion is more powerful than logic. As a leader you must win the heart before the mind.

Make a compelling case for change

Each change requires a compelling case and a *Leading by Coaching* conversations style to engage the whole team to accept and support the change. Only then you can achieve a successful implementation. You need a clear and concise story-line that can be adapted to stand testing with all the relevant audiences. It should be remembered that resisting change is normal, and your followers will have less personal interest in the proposed changes than you do. They will also have less contextual information, so spend more time on the essential story-line. Don't shy away from more complex story-lines, share the colour of the complexities. You are working with clever people, so do not dumb down your messages and be open to challenges. More information, rather than less, will help people understand the difficult context in which a decision is being made. Openness also builds the trust in the leader that is so critical to implementing successful change. Above all don't underestimate your people and bear in mind they will talk to each other.

Communicate using a coaching style

Communicate as early and as honestly as is realistically possible. Provide information that is meaningful and helpful to those receiving it. Go beyond sticking to the corporate messaging. Anticipate and address personal implications before being asked. Engage in everyday conversation and give people an opportunity to contribute their views and let off steam. Also talk to individuals as much as possible, especially with those who have influence with the wider group. Show empathy whilst at the same time being firm on the case for change. Be clear on what is, and is not, for discussion. Don't raise expectations and don't say or do anything that might compromise a future decision. Don't try to distance yourself from the change decision although it is perfectly fine to admit that there are inevitably pros and cons. Don't say you personally have a different view. Avoid anything that will be distancing yourself from the management's change decision, you are the management in the eyes of your people. You will lose respect if they think that you are imposing on them something you don't believe in yourself. This can seem an obvious point to make, but often this aspect is overlooked. The real challenge is to be authentic and show empathy without wavering on the case for change. In reality leaders have to help their teams to accept change and this is not possible if the teams at times feel that their leaders are resisting the change themselves. You cannot have one set of rules for yourself and another for everyone else.

Leader's dilemma

A big issue for leaders is what they can do if they really do not support the change. You are likely to encounter such situations at some point in your career. How do you resolve the challenge of honesty and authenticity versus corporate loyalty? When the change is unlawful or unethical the leader should challenge the Board in an appropriate way and step down if the change is critical and there is no alternative course of action to retain respect as a leader. Where the change is legal and ethical, you might not welcome the change but can accept it as a necessary means to an end. You can then reframe the change to create your own personal story that fits your values and belief system. It all comes down finally to a matter of integrity and personal principles.

Always leading by example

Your values must do your talking. You should lead from the inside out. Who you are, is how you lead. You are the change you seek. You will maintain the trust you enjoy as a leader by being transparent, respectful, understandinging, sincere and tolerant. Empathy and authenticity are your calling cards. Share your personal journey—this is authentic and can help others by seeing that you are going through a difficult and painful change process yourself. Demonstrate empathy but avoid token symbolism. Explain reasoning and address challenges head-on. If the leader has a reputation for being honest, people will find the leader more credible and believable. They will appreciate that approach and may find it refreshingly different in an age of fake news. People want a caring but also a strong leader when it comes to representing their interests inside and outside the organisation.

Change is hard but providing it is lead one conversation at a time with integrity, openness, fairness—showing empathy and compassion—it can be implemented successfully and with the leader's reputation enhanced.

Final thought

Imagine you are moving your team from a Listed building (that supported a silo mentality) to a shiny new open plan office. Think about the coaching conversations you would plan with your people to lead them through this change. How would you approach coaching and supporting them through their personal psychological challenges?

Leading Innovation

"Innovate or die" is the tenet that underpins most businesses in the age of disruption. Massive household companies like Kodak and Polaroid, just to take one industry, got close to going out of business because they failed to read the tea leaves in their markets. They didn't see that digital imaging would capture the public imagination so quickly. Innovation has to be led from the top. You need to create a culture of questioning and challenging to drive innovation. It is better to disrupt yourself internally than being disrupted externally.

Innovation Change Process

Innovation is observing, questioning, associating, experimenting, networking, failing and succeeding.

Courage is a competitive advantage. To get bigger you must get braver. Big ideas require bold leadership. Failing and succeeding are two sides of the same coin. You only learn from your mistakes. There is no failure only feedback.

Ed Catmull, President of Pixar, was asked what piece of advice he would give to his 20-year-old self. He refused saying, 'he would not want to give himself advice that would have helped him avoid a mistake that is part of what he is today". What response would you have given?

The **CASS/CII** research project, that I lead on behalf of the Chartered Insurance Institute with Dr. Robert Davies of Cass Business School, looked at the role of leaders in driving innovation in their organisations.

We discovered using a more participative, coaching leadership style which is helpful in building an innovative corporate culture especially when it comes to motivating Millennials. Change is an emotional journey. Motivation should come from the top and innovation from the bottom. Corporate leaders' role is to clear the path for change and remove the barriers. To create the spaces for employees to come together socially to learn and innovate, one conversation at a time.

> You can do almost everything if you can suspend beliefs—**Marna Whittington**, COO AGI

Only 2% of law firms are driving innovation according to their clients, as researched in the annual *Winmark Survey* in 2017. My research team at Cass found that leaders who used a palette of innovation types led more innovative organisations. Their innovation went beyond the usual product and process focus to innovate with their own people to increase intrinsic motivation. At one law firm, the staff thank the management for their music! The firm set up choirs and offered music lessons. These innovative initiatives boosted staff morale and lowered stress levels.

Client Innovation

The best innovation arguably is client led. Only the client experiences, your products and services, so it stands to reason that they will have the best insights into how you can improve them. Connections and conversations provide the fuel for innovation. It is the relationships between people that power the insights and ideas that produce innovation. Customer innovation starts with "intimacy", getting close to the client. When you get close they tell you things that customer surveys never do. They want a say, to be involved and engaged. From "intimacy" comes insights out of which comes ideas, inventions and innovation.

I interviewed a Managing Director of a top five global investment bank as part of my CASS business school research into leadership and innovation. She told me she has a conference call every Monday with her Country Heads to discuss client feedback. They can, therefore, react much quicker than their competitors to improve their client service delivery. That is why they rarely lose an institutional client.

Context is critical. New leaders need to match strategy to the situation. Align interests. Create coalitions. Agree goals. Establish priorities.

Most businesses will need to radically redesign the way they work to survive and thrive in a rapidly changing world. The biggest enemy to change is not changing your success assumptions. Most universal truths, according to Tarun Khanna of Harvard Business School, play out differently in different contexts. For innovation to work in different cultural environments, you will need to drop assumptions about what has worked in the past, and then experiment to see what actually works in the present and is sustainable. You will need the ability to understand the limits of your knowledge, so you can apply it to different environments. You will need to pay attention to context at multiple levels. Time bound, geographical, historical, institutional, cultural, political, economic, social and technological. You will have to examine what you do from a macro and a micro level.

Innovation must add relevant value to both parties. A great idea stays a great idea unless it can be translated commercially into a new solution, or a better solution, that solves a problem for the customer or satisfies a customer desire. Innovation is the voice of the customer. The innovation needs to be integrated into the product effectively and efficiently. It is the execution that separates the great companies like Apple from the rest.

Client concentricity starts with listening to clients, finding out what they want, and then translating these wants into relevant and valuable products that can be delivered consistently with high quality.

A good example of client concentric innovation can be seen in my Allianz Global Investors case study which was part of the CASS/CII Leadership Innovation research outlined earlier in this chapter. It is also a great corporate change story.

Allianz Global Investors Case Study Overview

The transformation of AGI from good to great—a story about the journey to find, and be, the authentic voice of the AGI client. And the critical things that the AGI leaders did to create the innovation that made the change possible.

"Allianz Global Investors can be anything it wants to be—if it really wants to be it" **Marna Whittington**, Global COO AGI

This case study is the story of business excellence in a disruptive age. A story about vision, courage and leading innovation.

In 2004 AGI one of the world's top five asset managers didn't know who it was. The critical question was: *What did* AGI *clients want* AGI *to be?* And where could AGI find the authentic voice of AGI clients? AGI needed a client value proposition. The new AGI DNA. And the Client Value Proposition needed to be aligned to a new Employee Value Proposition.

AGI has gone from good to great.

AGI **Learning Points**

"Change is an emotional journey"—John Kotter

Employees
You can't change the client experience without changing the employees experience first
Need to find the employees authentic voice
Employees want to know who they are
Employees need a sense of purpose
Employees want to be full of pride
Employee value proposition is essential
A new type of conversation needs to take place between the company and its employees—a listening conversation
Clients
Authentic voice of the client must always be heard
You sometimes have to look in new places to find the authentic voice of your clients
Clients want to know who you are
Clients want solutions optimised to their own business
Clients want a partnership mentality
Clients want professional service expertise—product expertise is no longer enough
A new form of value creation is required and needs to be implemented in a holistic way
A consistently delivered single unifying idea should drive the client experience
Client value propositions required for the Group and modified for main customer sectors
Starting the train
Someone has to start the train
Attract an informal following of like-minded colleagues
You need compelling outside evidence that the train is on the wrong track
Without a compelling, rational and emotionally charged reason to change people don't change
External research creates an upward challenge
Research should be an internal and external learning process
Need to change the client and employee experience
Getting everyone on-board
The innovation is in how you manage people to get on the train
Two side bottom-up and outside-in approach is needed to overcome the common barriers to transformation
Finding the shared DNA or "glue" binds everyone together
A sense of connection and community allows everyone to live the ethos and values
A powerful force to unite all layers of management is needed to launch the transformation process
Communicate at an emotional level—people respond better if they are pulled rather than being pushed
Never underestimate the power of the informal group to influence the formal organisation
Keeping the train on track
Change is a structured approach not a communication exercise
Don't be afraid to say "stop!" if a critical barrier needs to be overcome

It is important to understand the link between thoughts, feelings and actions

Leaders

Leaders must be passionate about the business

Leaders must persuade others, have and display a sincere belief that they are doing the right thing

Leaders must convince management that they are listening and committed to change

Leaders need to move from a they mind-set to a "we" mind-set

Leaders must all stand up for the Group client proposition

There must be an emotional connection between leaders and followers

Leaders excitement about the future vision creates focus and a sense of urgency

Board needs to be a team with a common goal not a fragmented group of individuals with separate interests

Why Change Fails

> When there is possession, there must be loss of possession; when there is a gathering together, there must be a scattering—this is the constant principle in things—Li Qingzhao, 1132 AD

Impermanence is a fact of life and yet we find it hard to accept change and move on. The various estimates given as to the percentage of failed change programmes, range from 70% (A study by John P. Kotter, Harvard Business Review, 1995) to 95% (In a 2014 Deloitte study, the reported aggregate success rate from more than 5000 innovations was less than 5%). Only the resilient see it through. So, why do so many well-intentioned change initiatives fail? There is no easy, single answer. Change fails for a multitude of reasons.

My research indicates that change fails because of a lack of: buy-in; belief; desire; appetite; purpose; meaning; passion; enthusiasm; courage; empathy; understanding; patience, execution; integration; **listening**; exploring; creativity; constructive tension; teamwork; partnership; openness; dialogue, coaching, co-creating; relatedness; lack of flexibility, **sensitivity**, sincerity; **trust**, transparency; tolerance, respect; **engagement**; lack of connection; and poor communication. And last, but not least, a lack of fairness or perceived fairness, "the greatest dent to morale is when there is a sense of unfairness, inequality and injustice"—General Eisenhower.

An Institute for Employment Studies 2018 report found that employees could be highly engaged with their job but not their company, and vice versa.

This meant that HR strategies designed to boost engagement, necessary for change, were not having the required results. Organisations oversimplify the concept of employee engagement and need to really listen to the needs of their employees.

Pause for Reflection
If you think back to a failed change initiative, you were leading or being led you will identify with some, or many, of the reasons listed above why success was elusive. You may have your own thoughts on why so many change initiatives fail.

Change or Die

When cardiac patients are told after a bypass to "change or die", you would expect them to change. But nine out of ten don't change. We like to think that crisis and fear motivate people to change but studies have shown that even in the change or die situation, most people can't change. So, what is going on here? What is the psychology behind this startling fact? One reason is that when people are pushed, they resist. Without intrinsic motivation, people will not persevere. They need to be engaged through the heart, not the head. People are not rational, they are emotional beings. You have to make an emotional connection with them that inspires a new sense of hope. Alan Deutschman, in his book *Change or Die*, says extensive research has shown that the most successful change actually begins with an emotionally significant relationship followed by reframing and repetition. Change is about learning and trust. Who do you trust to coach you? The emotional link to your coach is the critical factor in change. Change is an emotional roller coaster learning journey. We can change but we need to learn from other people. But before we can learn, we need to feel that they believe we can change. If you want people to change, believe in them and help them get their voice back again.

Purposeful Change

Change is hard, change is personal. We want to know why we should change. Our brain wants to know what the purpose of change is. Purpose is powerful.

Changing Minds

Leading change in the digital age is hard. It is easy to get stuck and to feel overwhelmed. However, neuroscience research can be used to give you new perspectives on leading change. There is a gap between our conscious intentions and our unconscious behaviour. The unconscious mind is hardwired to resist change. It is a lot bigger and stronger than the conscious mind and has been honed over millions of years of evolution. Our brain is driven by basic responses towards pleasure or away from pain, based on external stimuli processed by the *limbic system* the emotional centre of the brain. When it senses a threat, the *amygdala* hijacks our conscious brain. This primitive knee-jerk reaction puts us in automatic fight or flight model; we are hijacked by fear which often isn't rational. False expectations appearing real. There are three things you can do to lead your mind in the direction you want to go: set a clear direction; motivate unconscious minds; and clear the path.

When the unconscious and conscious parts of the brain are working together in harmony, a powerful dual processor core creates optimal performance. A Parallel Mind. Being humble and setting the right leadership tone puts people at ease and reduces the status threat. Providing clear communication of expectations helps to increase certainty. Letting others take charge and make decisions increases their autonomy.

Your brain is a self-organising emergent system. Every day, hundreds of thousands of synapses are released into the brain as a free-learning resource to make new connections. The brain is constantly adapting to a changing environment in search of wholeness, to find a natural order. Learning is an emotional experience; we learn best when we are engaged. The *hippocampus*, responsible for memory, sits inside the *limbic system*, the emotional centre of the brain. Optimal learning is a social activity; we learn best when we are in small groups. So, leaders should create a multitude of informal opportunities for followers to learn together.

Insight is central to long-term change, but each person needs to have their own insight and not just listen to their leader's insight. To encourage thinking, leaders need to ask questions with the word "think" in them. Attention drives change and is the active ingredient for changing the brain. A leader's job is to help others to think better for themselves.

Mindful Change

We are too busy, like Pooh Bear in Chapter 4, bumping along to change our habits. Too busy doing the same old things, in the same old ways, to think about our thinking. Too busy trying to find clear water in our muddy pond. Too busy swimming around in our goldfish bowl blissfully unaware of who is looking in. Too many distractions to focus on what's truly important to us rather than what is urgent for somebody else. To be effective leaders of change, we need to focus on what is important. We need to direct our thinking. We need to be consciously aware of our thinking in the moment. We need to be mindful. To see our seeing. To pay attention. Notice what is there. Focus. Stay with the silence. Observe what is emerging. Harvest the insights. Insights provide the energy for firing and rewiring our brain. Forging new neural pathways. Breaking the old habits. Our brains are naturally hardwired to resist change. Our unconscious emotional brains crave safety. So, to embrace change, you have to focus your conscious brain. First, you need to have the intention to do something. Then, you need to pay attention to what you want to do. Next, you need to do it. Then, repeat the process. Attention density changes the brain. Every time you pay attention to something, the *neurons* in your brain fire and your neural paths rewire. The brain is plastic, wired to change to meet the challenges of a constantly changing environment. But if you want to be in charge, you need to be mindful. Attention is the key that unlocks your free will; it is the gate-keeper to your awareness. Consciousness acts as a "bright spot" on the stage, directed by the selective spotlight of attention. Mindfulness can activate wilfully directed attention. For Buddhists, it is the moment of restraint that allows mindful awareness to take hold and deepen. Directed mental force stops the grinding machines of the unconscious. Mindfulness is falling awake, getting out of your own way and paying attention in the moment.

Transformational Leadership

In the age of disruption, emergent leadership will be the new way of leading. Holding the emerging space for others to think better will be a key skill. Your ability to lead others may well depend on your ability to lead yourself. To consciously intervene, do things in a timely and mindful way. In essence, develop a greater level of cognitive control. Observing your own thoughts is central to your ability to choose between the active and the passive, to switch from autopilot to taking control. Being more present and self-aware, in the moment, leads to a state of "letting come", allowing you to consciously participate in a larger field of change. Honing your ability to observe your inner experience, to think about your thinking, to see what you're seeing, to imagine different futures, to connect the dots in search of wholeness and, above all to be mindful, will be the future leader's way.

Leading Change Across Cultures

Transcultural leaders need to be curious about other cultures and customs. They value diversity, gender, race, religion, nationality, sexual orientation, culture and personality type. They are ambitious learners, compulsive listeners. They are intellectually curious. They want to know what is going on in the rest of the world. They are open and optimistic. They embrace change and are not afraid to fail.

Marianne Motherby was Global Counsel for **Deutsche Bahn** when I worked with her and her international team. I was impressed by Marianne's authenticity as a person, as a coach and as a leader. She combined intellectual power with humility and sensitivity. In her fireside chat, she put forward a number of powerful principles that have stayed with me. The main principles are: if you want your people to be happy, give them a smile (a day without a smile is a lost day) and keep your promises; if you are not sure you can deliver, promise only that you will do your very best; overselling undermines your credibility; practise what you preach; your message is in how you act; you are the message, more so than what you say; be sincere and show empathy; encourage your people to give you honest feedback; be prepared to say I was wrong and I am sorry; use personal power not organisational position; egalitarianism and hierarchy can sit together; appreciate people and give helpful feedback; give them space to make mistakes while striving for excellence; and openness for different perspectives is a catalyst for positive change. Marianne leads by example.

Diverse Communication Styles

Cross-cultural communication is two sides of the same coin. On the one side, misunderstandings and on the other, opportunities. Communication style is the way in which we communicate, a pattern of verbal and nonverbal behaviours that comprise our preferred ways of giving and receiving information in a specific situation. Communication needs to be authentic, intentional and empathic to allow it to be well received in any culture.

To be interculturally competent, communicators need to be themselves and make every effort to understand the other person. It is important to have a shared context and goals. Behaviours need to be adapted to meet the cultural needs of others. Small differences should be noticed as part of a larger communication style. Sincerity is the key to establishing trust.

Post-merger Cultural Adjustments

Values often get lost in cross-cultural translation. Cross-cultural translation is listening to how things are said, and what is not said. Communication is in the *in between.*

A post-merger cultural values integration programme can be helpful to improving understanding and creating a cultural resonance for effective collaboration. Values set the right tone and allow consistent decision-making. Core values guide good behaviour, flag up unacceptable behaviour and can be applied in day to day dealings. Values provide a common narrative for the combined business. A common meaningful dialogue in the business is based on shared understanding, agreed outcomes and connected conversations. A true partnership.

A post-merger cultural value integration programme consists of three parts: values audit; values alignment; and values in action system. Values audit consists of agreeing desired core values; guiding cultural principles; the best values from each organisation; desired behaviours and new values. Values alignment includes externally facilitated workshops across the business. The external consultants' role is translating cultural differences and building consensus on a small number of critical core values binding the organisations together. The workshops also provide an opportunity to meet new colleagues, share experiences and discuss the new vision for the combined organisation. The success of the workshops can be seen in delegates, commitment to follow and promote core values; communicate those values to the wider organisation; and by so doing, create a strong sense of shared ownership. A values in action system consists of a series of cross-cultural gatherings, both formal and informal, and projects that focus on delivering cultural insightful value to the organisation.

The positive impact and competitive advantage of conversations across cultures through integrating employees across the planet, is the glittering prize from a merger or acquisition. But, sadly, the prize often remains elusive. Unable to be grasped very often as a result of a lack of trust, the challenge for leaders is to create the right listening culture that promotes trust and collaboration. They need to create a "boundarylessness" organisation in the words of Jack Welch, the former CEO of General Electric. The reflective conversations between global colleagues in co-operative relationships are crucial in making possible the creative dialogue that leads to innovative ideas. Informality and a soft culture build trust and intimacy, the essential social lubricant of emotional expression for cross-border innovation.

Neil May, who advised the Lovells Board on the merger with Hogan & Hartson, gives his account below, of the strategic transatlantic law firm initiative in his following case study written for this book.

Hogan & Hartson and Lovells Merger Case Study by Neil May

At the end of 2009 Lovells and Hogan & Hartson went to their partnerships with a proposal to come together to create a Top 10 global law firm with some $1.7bn in revenue. Strategically while Lovells and Hogan & Hartson were successful businesses their growth was squeezed from stronger firms above and from others encroaching from below, and both lacked the depth and reach to win some mandates on their own. The resulting combination, a "merger of equals" in May 2010, was widely seen as one of the most successful mergers: why?

Lovells had been considering a merger as one route forwards for several years, providing it was with the right partner. The merger proposal put to partners was very clear on the areas of strength it would create and honest about those practices that would gain less. The combination was proposed as a step forwards, but by no means a magic wand that would solve everything.

Management outlined the alternatives to combining the firms and why this particular combination was the favoured path. In other words, the proposal to partners addressed the rationale side of why we should do this, why now, and why not doing it was worse than the stresses that would arise from doing it. Importantly the focus was on creating an entity that functioned from the outset as one integrated firm, not as a collection of separate businesses. The more there was a sense of being one firm, of one large tribe, the more reassured the emotional mind would be.

The merger documentation was comprehensive. It gave an overview of the impact on each practice area and outlined risks and the extent to which they could be mitigated. It laid out in detail what the firm would look like in terms of its vision, management structures, the individuals on the executive team, partnership processes (including appointment of new partners, voting rights and remuneration from a single profit pool), branding and the combined client base. It also examined the finances of the firm and how the firm would operate from a structural perspective.

In general lawyers have an unusually high need for autonomy and high levels of scepticism—to the extent of being somewhat suspicious of the worth of management in comparison to the obvious value of being a good lawyer giving good legal advice. The approach to the combination provided logical and emotional reassurance by demonstrating management had indeed considered the proposal robustly. There was therefore trust that the recommendation was in both firms' interests, not that this was the result of hubris. Both CEOs were seen as authentic and demonstrating integrity.

This approach also addressed several themes we have raised in this book, in particular the need to reduce levels of uncertainty when facing change. You must address in parallel the logical mind, and the unconscious emotional mind, the latter being far stronger than the rational part that thinks it is in control. The firms held an integration retreat for some 60 or so influential people in February 2010.

This was not restricted to the Executive or heads of areas, but rather included key sector and client partners, as well as key operational staff. Traditionally change models seek a small guiding team, but while control is needed success tends to require many change agents, not just the usual management suspects. As well as increasing your capacity and touch points, this approach also provides social support across the network: humans are creatures that need to feel relatedness to others. The retreat used an external facilitator, and we considered the lessons from professional service firm mergers, from other business trans-Atlantic combinations, as well as post-merger integration and culture.

A key reason many strategic initiatives fail is because they are not sufficiently exciting to generate the energy and commitment needed to overcome the inevitable problems that will arise on the journey. This applies to business plans as much as to mergers and is a major weakness of many so-called vision statements. In this respect a key first task is to gain enough energy for action. Change needs to become part of life, part of the day job, rather than something separate. It does not result from management memos.

Yet it is in the day job where weariness and general non-engagement will arise. As any coach will attest, you need to help people to recreate energy if you are to keep them on the path. In classical change management this involves celebrating wins, but more widely it should be seen in terms of managing energy levels rather than ticking off project management milestones. However, a further challenge in practice is these wins are often somewhat remote from the day-to-day life of individuals, so while positive they are only partly felt. In a large business with many sub groups a surprisingly large amount of effort is needed to collate all these wins, so they can be shared and connect with individuals so that collaboration feels real.

It is common in mergers for management to claim firms have similar cultures, and Hogan Lovells was typical in saying this. At the retreat we actively considered culture using the McKinsey 7s framework. This brought some differences into the open, so we could discuss them. Primarily Hogan & Hartson leant more strongly towards up-or-out people management and had stronger centralised management decision making, while Lovells had more strongly developed systems, larger professional support functions, and more experience of mergers.

There was clearly a degree of difference between the higher level of consultation partners sought in Lovells and the more hierarchical authority given to management in Hogan & Hartson, and it was recognised this could be a source of low-level irritation until a new mid-point settled. Similarly, business support staff in Lovells were more likely to take the lead in advising the partnership on priorities, whereas in Hogan & Hartson it was more usual for partners to lead. For example, Lovells would be slower and more conservative in allowing the spread of mobile devices beyond Blackberries with Bring Your Own Devices, while in the US partners were more likely to simply want the support functions to connect their iPhone. Creating a new mix between control and flexibility was probably a better position for both predecessor firms. Importantly the firms' cultures were both informal and collegiate rather than being sharp elbowed.

Changing your business one conversation at a time is difficult when the organisation is large and geographically spread across continents. Different nationalities naturally have different perspectives, ways of working, and levels of cultural individuality: that is simply a reality. Making use of these differences is an important element of becoming greater than the separate parts and at the same time should be of benefit in dealing with clients across different jurisdictions.

For launch day a video was produced of staff in offices celebrating the creation of the new firm. Culturally we knew different groups would have different views about creating a video, but even those who originally, we doubtful admitted it did enthuse people across the firm. It provided an opportunity for many people to have conversations, but also to reach out to others. In general US law firms were more likely to present a conservative brand, with muted colours such mulberry red. Perhaps most frequent in the video was the goodwill shown towards the new branding, with Hogan & Hartson transitioning to the Lovells' vibrant lime green branding, and a degree of shock and humour along the lines of "it's very green". In creating the new we need to allow a sense of closure of the old, a Gestalt, so people could move on.

Another aspect of introducing a large number of people with certain ways of working to another large group with different ways is that there will be a large number of instances where people bump-up against others who approach things quite differently. That makes a large combination much harder than absorbing a smaller group. The positive side of this is that interactions help build experience that builds the new combination, as we all learn how others think. However, systemically it is at these boundaries where puzzlement, friction and drag will occur, and the larger the number of groups the larger the number of potential points where this will happen. This is one aspect of organisational change that is too often forgotten. In practice we found these were more likely to arise in relation to aspects of management and operations than when partners were working together on clients.

We should also expect any merger to impact an individual's *status*. It will affect their relationships and their power and support networks—in other words their psychological state. A merger means people start to work for a new firm but without having emotionally chosen to leave their existing firm. This tends not to cause too many issues where an individual's hierarchical position is not put under threat, but we should always expect it cause resistance when they do, it is a threat.

Hogan Lovells made fair headway in addressing such concerns, but because they relate to the behaviour of large numbers of individuals in their own local markets such things are never easy. Pragmatically, management expected people to resolve such low-level frustration, but with the benefit of hindsight perhaps a greater level of skill in how people can have effective conversations, at the heart of this book, would have been beneficial. This is not to ignore the peculiarity of partnerships, which require considerable management time to be spent on smoothing out issues amongst co-owners: it is simply a recognition that a more widely dispersed skill across the firm in having effective conversations would be valuable. Better conversations create better business, and they reduce sapping energy from dealing with friction.

From a *Gestalt* coaching perspective, we see value in holding people at the point where they stay with problems, rather than shying away. This builds *awareness* and as a result *options* emerge for how they can respond. Often in organisational change initiatives it is only when there is sufficient motive to change (such as when the current state becomes sufficiently frustrating) that any resulting action occurs. Allowing this feedback to surface requires building an environment where people feel *truly safe*, so they can raise concerns or share uncertainties without fear of attack.

Safety and security matter psychologically. When we feel criticised we produce higher levels of cortisol, which diverts energy away from the thinking towards the protecting brain. We are likely to perceive greater levels of negative judgement than was intended. Importantly these effects can last many hours, which then imprints unhelpful memories, which affects future behaviour. This is why being highly skilled in your interactions with others matters.

It may help to illustrate this with an example. The new firm was primarily run on practice lines. Onto this was overlaid geographical, sector and client teams, creating a classic matrix. Matrixes, we know, have inherent tensions. The concept that the number of things we can hold in focus at any one time has moved over 50 years from +5 towards 1–3 as our understanding of neuroscience has grown. A matrix structure will present conflicts but generally with insufficient rules to aid easy and certain decision making.

Over the first couple of years the firm wanted to develop its industry sector strength but found the industry heads uncertain over their level of authority, and unclear how senior management might give emphasis over resource conflicts in prioritisation. For example, a sector might identify a client that was important to that sector, but it might be less important or profitable for an individual practice or an office, or at least a lower priority for where that group should direct its limited discretionary effort. This aspect needed to be revisited a few times openly in order to help partners find a way forward. Similar uncertainty arose in relation to the power of Office Managing Partners and again this was best tackled through empathy and open discussion.

Since such uncertainty is a natural part of matrix structures, it also links to how individuals believe they are being appraised, which affects their status. People want to make the decisions they believe management would feel are the right ones, but complexity means the optimal business choice may not always be obvious to individuals. This brings us full circle, back to trust in management, particularly where some management committee may decide how your performance should relate to your compensation, which happens in a merit-based system.

A criticism is sometimes made that spending all this time in dialogue with people diverts management attention away from 'more important' things. Certainly, there is a danger it can crowd out the more critical strategic issues, and part of management's role is to balance multiple agendas and prioritising where to spend their limited time now. However, what actually makes a difference in transitions is maximising the involvement of staff in decision making, managing the interface between groups, and phasing the change process to build momentum.

A final comment on change relates to best practice. As part of the combination the firm created Co-heads, yet best practice according to many business school models is you should create single roles and deal with any pain up-front while you have momentum. However, Hogan Lovells deliberately chose to have joint heads instead, because it was critical that people felt they were being led, and appraised, by someone who understood them and their market. This reflects the need for safety and fairness we have explored earlier in the book.

A downside is that joint roles are likely to introduce some lag into the progress, but both individuals and businesses tend to change in a series of steps and pauses. It was expected that after a few years as the frustrations inherent in joint management structures might then be felt, so partners would be confident enough to move to single heads. That move then provides the new single head management team with the opportunity and support to take the next step forwards.

Fundamentally, success depends upon people being willing to go out of their way to be patiently helpful to others and to be aware of how they come across in treating others, who hopefully will reciprocate positive behaviour. The way you interact—knowing how to have effective conversations—is at the core of this.

Strategic Post-merger Success Factors

From a strategic perspective, post-merger success factors include: complimentary markets, clients and offerings; shared vision, aspirations, purpose, passion and values; plus, common behaviours, benefits and rewards.

Strategy change process consists of: realising, reviewing, reevaluating, reinventing, refocusing, reshaping, realigning and refreshing.

People change process consists of: re-enthusing; reconnecting; re-energising, redeveloping, recognising and rewarding.

Hogan Lovells LLP has become a successful transatlantic law firm merger. I spent some time talking with the Global CEO **Steve Immelt** to see how he leads a firm with over 800 Partners worldwide.

Interview with Steve Immelt CEO, Hogan Lovells LLP

Nick *What is your vision for Hogan Lovells?*
Steve *Hogan Lovells is a bold distinctive law firm creating valuable solutions for clients*
Nick *How do you define as valuable?*
Steve *Doing premium work, helping clients deal with complex multi-jurisdictional challenges using a one Hogan Lovells collaborative approach—complex problems require one team solutions*
Nick *How would you describe leadership in Hogan Lovells?*
Steve *Distributed. Everyone is a "licensed leader" and can reach out to every part of the firm*
Nick *What is your main competitive advantage?*
Steve *Our people focus. We have a very good people development team. Emphasis is on non-legal skills. We have a very good people development team who have won awards for their training programmes.*
Nick *What are the enablers of progress?*

> **Steve** *Collaboration through day to day connection; Everyday Leading by Coaching style not a directive telling style; Giving people space to think; Listening to people, really listening, to understand them and show you care*
> **Nick** *What are the barriers to progress?*
> **Steve** *Not enough straight talking; People don't know how to have "difficult" conversations; Lawyers are uncomfortable with feedback—often insecure; Stick to their in-group; Cultural misunderstandings*
> **Nick** *How would you describe your leadership style?*
> **Steve** *Get clients and colleagues excited about what we can do together*
> *With 800 Partners leadership has to be intentional and direct—"You can't tell people too many times your core message". Straight talking but with sensitivity; Important to listen to your "internal voice"—keeping in touch with your feelings*
> **Nick** *Final thoughts?*
> **Steve** *Quality of relationships are critical to the firm's success; Need to partner with clients—understand where they want to go and go with them on their journey; It is a firm imperative to have an industry practice area matrix approach to add real value by helping our clients navigate an ever more complex world.*

When Professionals Have to Lead

Leaders in professional service firms are invisible. They lead by stealth. They are on the surface reluctant leaders. Their skill as leaders is to mask their ambition behind the plurality of the firm. They operate in a leadership constellation of up to 14 key influencers. A Senior Executive DYAD of Managing Partner and Senior Partner, or sometimes CEO and Chairman, with up to 6 people is running the firm. A DYAD is the centre of the leadership constellation around which revolves Partner influencers; Practice Heads; Heads of Services; and other influencers. A DYAD operates, according to Laura Empson, Professor in the Management of Professional Service Firms and Director of the Centre for Professional Service Firms at Cass Business School, part of City University London, on the basis of intuitive collaboration, structured coordination, negotiated co-habitation and careful co-operation.

According to Professor Empson, this plural leadership model depends on discrete invisible leaders who are informal, apolitical and operate under a cloak of ambiguity. These inner leaders, a hidden hierarchy, are sophisticated political operators who lead without leading. Power is highly contingent on creating a general consensus. The game is about influence. Everyone who has influence is trying to influence the others who also have influence.

An effective PSF leader according to Professor Empson's research: understands the complexities and subtleties of a PSF; is able to identify and navigate the leadership constellation; is highly respected for their professional skills and cutting it with clients; does not appear to be seeking power; is able to attract and inspire autonomous followers; has a strong personal vision and ability to communicate it; has a deep belief in the values of the firm and its roots; is able to build consensus and act decisively; transfer responsibility but intervene selectively; and is comfortable with ambiguity and conflict.

> As Senior Partner and Managing Partner, we have absolutely no constitutional power whatsoever… there is nothing in the Partnership Agreement which says you can do this, or you have powers to do that… So, we were elected to that post but there is no mention anywhere of what the role is, what powers we have, which is fine… So, you govern by your mandate and your personal credibility and authority, not by virtue of some kind of constitutional power that's given to you—Senior Partner International Law Firm
>
> When I took on the role I looked forward to getting my hands on the levers of power. But when I moved into my office. I realised there were no levers—just a desk—Senior Partner Accountancy "Big Four"[5]

The legal industry tends to lag behind other industries when it comes to innovation, but things are changing if my interview with **David Coupe** of **EC3 Legal** is anything to go by.

David Coupe

is Senior Partner of "**EC3 Legal**, The Insurance Law Firm", which he founded. He dared to be different. He wanted to offer clients something different. A law firm based on a better client satisfaction. A law firm based on long term relationships. A law firm based on friendships and cross referrals. A business based on innovation-based solutions to complex problems. David told me that business is about risk and intuition. He has also set up a consultancy business, in 2017, because the opportunity is there.

Leadership in changing markets, he says, "is simply about reading the tea leaves early; understanding what the tea leaves may mean; making sure you are the one making the tea and offering the tea and sugar. Strangely the second cup of tea is never as good as the first, and never received as well".

When it comes to leadership he says it is about your colleagues believing in you as a leader, trusting you to drive the car. "Someone has to drive when it's raining on the motorway, when you can't see where you are going because of

---

[5]Leading professionals: Power, politics, and prima donnas 2017 by Laura Empson.

the spray from lorries, people in the car have to trust you will get them home safely. And sometimes you have to stop the car because it is too dangerous".

It is important to value disruptive talent. Make people feel loved. Help people grow on their life journey. Give them something to believe in, something better over the horizon.

David's final thoughts for future leaders are, "Find a vision. Plan for it. Test it. Don't be afraid to change it. Be always planning and adjusting and stay nimble. Opportunities are taken by the ready and brave".

Developing Your Unique Coach Signature

Who I am is, enough in itself is the basis of my coaching. Who you are as a person is how you coach. You coach from the emotional well of your deepest experiences. You bring everything that has made you who you are to every moment you are present with your coachee. Your unique coach signature. We coach from our wounds and vulnerabilities not our greatness. We should express our humanity, not "coach". The soul longs to express itself and to be heard and seen. "I want to do for you what the spring does for the cherry trees"—Pablo Neruda, Chilean poet, diplomat, politician and Nobel prize winner for Literature.

Developing your unique coach signature style is about using your authentic voice to help your coachee to find and use theirs. Expressing your soul encourages your coachee to express theirs. To express the essence of who they are and the difference they want to make. Your unique coach style is your authentic signature presence, your *dance* with your client. Gestalt coaching is an exchange of what it is to be human. An emotional connection based on a high level of personal trust and rapport. The quality of your relationship is the most important factor in the quality of your coaching. Understanding the context of your coaching is also critical in helping the person find wholeness and move on.

The **Dance** is where the context of the coaching, the authentic signature presence of the coach and the coachee all come together in one powerful expression of humanity. **The Parallel Mind Coaching *Dance* Model** brings these components together (Fig. 9.2).

Authentic Signature Presence

My signature coach presence is built on my life journey and my executive leadership experience in Financial Services. In my personal life supporting my son Christopher, who suffered brain damage at birth, taught me the

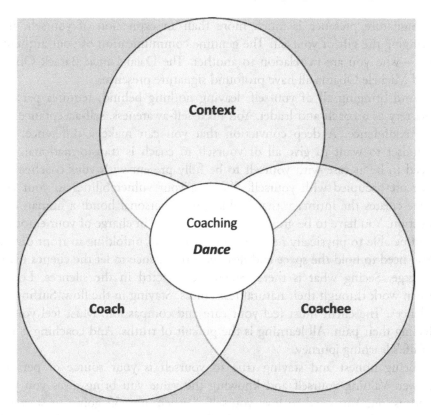

Fig. 9.2 The Parallel Mind Coaching *Dance* Model

importance of witnessing, empathy and compassion. In my business life, I recognise the importance of focussing on people's strengths. Above all else I believe that there is nothing to be gained by holding back. Open dialogue with constructive and positive feedback only creates opportunities to learn and grow. My challenge as a coach is to help the people I coach, produce reasoned thought by challenging their thinking. My coaching experience has taught me that the ability to absorb new thoughts and insights comes from reflection. And reflection requires focus on listening to self and others. My confidence as a coach comes from the courage to confront and lay bare my human vulnerabilities. My purpose as a coach is to encourage others to see the opportunity in adversity and create new paths, one conversation at a time.

You are the instrument of your coaching. Bringing the whole of yourself to the "dance" of coaching with your coachee is the catalyst to change. Only the interplay of sensing and moving in the moment contains the dance of a coach's authentic signature presence.

Signature presence is much more than an expression of yourself, it is bringing the gift of yourself. The genuine communication of your authentic self—who you are in relation to another. The Dalai Lama; Barack Obama and Michele Obama all have profound signature presence.

And bringing all of yourself, leaving nothing behind, requires personal mastery as a coach and leader. You need self-awareness, self-acceptance and self-confidence. A deep conviction that you can make a difference. The mindset to want to give all of yourself to coach is transformational. You need to be at ease with yourself to be fully present with your coachee and not pre-occupied with yourself. Showing your vulnerabilities to your coachee creates the intimacy that builds a deep personal bond: a human connection. You have to be grounded in your values, in charge of your emotions and be able to physically respond to the situation unfolding in front of you. You need to hold the space and deal with the silence to let the client's truths emerge. Seeing what is there. Staying connected in the silences. Letting them work through their natural resistances. Staying in the flow. Surfing the silences. The client must feel your care and compassion. Must feel you are feeling their pain. All learning is the pursuit of truths. And coaching is part of life's learning journey.

Being honest and staying true to yourself is your source of personal power. Valuing yourself and knowing the value you bring gives you your permission. You need to love yourself. "When are you going to start loving yourself?"—June Carter from *Walk the line*, Life Story of Johnny Cash. Being whole is what allows you to be a transformational coach. You coach with backbone and heart. The backbone to say what you feel and the heart to reach out with compassion. Human dignity and value is at the centre of coaching. Truly, "we are fearfully and wonderfully made"—Psalm 139:14. Coaching is about shared humanity and the insight and liberation that come from the gift of our presence as coaches when we are truly present with our clients. Creative adaptation and adjustment are the essential functions of the self. Learning about yourself is the only way to care for yourself, *Medicus curat, natura sanat!* Meaning, A doctor cures but nature heals. Hippocrates Latin motto.

And you need the communication skills to connect. The communication style to match who you are within the relational context. You need to flex your tone, posture and language to build a deep rapport. To express your emotional responses, it is not enough to feel emotion—you have to show it. To communicate successfully as a coach, you need to use your voice and body language. Use a pause, with eye contact in the silence, after you speak to say, *did you get that?* Looking at people in silence shows you care. It is a technique that I coach my senior clients in. It is used by Barack Obama to connect emotionally with his audience. Use statements with "I" in them, to provoke a response, rather than always asking questions. Statements like, *I think you are holding back, I wonder if there is something else*, Or, combining a statement with a question, *I noticed that… what do you think about that?*

You need a high degree of emotional intelligence to be aware of your emotions in the moment and be able to manage them. And emotional intelligence includes having an empathic response, being aware and managing your emotions and a healthy optimism helps too!

Being present in the moment is central to *Gestalt*. To use yourself as a coaching instrument, you must be fully alive, fully awake and fully alert. You need to bring all of yourself to your coachee. Staying with them in their stuckness and holding the space for self-learning to emerge is at the heart of the *Gestalt* coaching system. One of the themes of *Gestalt* is assimilation. Any organism, including the human organism, grows by assimilating from the environment what it needs for its growth. Only by assimilation can an organism be unified into a new whole. Assimilation needs a state of awareness. Awareness is characterised by contact, by sensing and excitement. *Gestalt* formation always accompanies awareness. We do not see three isolated points, we make a triangle out of them. We see a picture not the dots that make up the screen. Forming and completing *Gestalts* is the normal process of the healthy mind. Any incomplete *Gestalt* represents an "unfinished situation" that demands attention and closure to allow new *Gestalts* to be formed. The German *Gestalt* translates as meaningful organised whole. The human mind is a meaning making machine perpetually trying to make sense of its environment. Trying to fit in. So, coaching essentially is about helping people adapt, complete their unfinished *Gestalts*, fit into their changed system and move on.

Gestalt is about human experience, learning by understanding what is going on in the here and now. You can't become a competent Gestalt coach by reading my book although it should be a good starting point. I do hope however, I have inspired you to seriously consider getting trained as a Gestalt coach to master yourself as the instrument of your coaching.

The Reflective Practitioner

Barack Obama said he is most productive in solitude. Silence then words. Eloquence takes time. As he came to the end of his tenure as President, he shared his daily rituals with *The New York Times*. The biggest surprise was the importance he placed on finding quiet time. He felt he is at his most productive in silence. Almost every night that he was in the White House, Mr. Obama had dinner at 6:30 with his wife and daughters and then withdrew to the Treaty Room, his private office down the hall from his bedroom on the second floor of the White House residence. There, his closest aides said, he spent four or five hours, largely by himself.

What can you do to make yourself more productive in your solitude? You can do three things:

1. Find your space—carve out your quiet time
2. Honour your time—stick to your schedule!
3. Create boundaries—have the discipline to say no to the competing demands of others.

If the former President of the USA could create the space to find some solitude to reflect, then so can you! When will you find some quiet time in your week?

Neuroscience reveals the nourishing benefits that silence has on your brain. We already know that too much noise is not good for our brains or our bodies. Research has linked noise pollution to sleep loss, high blood pressure and heart disease. Neuroscientists are now uncovering the benefits of the absence of noise to our brains. When your brain is at rest, it gathers and sorts information. It literally self-reflects! Your brain's *auditory cortex* remains hard at work even in silence. It retrieves the memory of music and lyrics for instance. Your brain creates an illusion of sound. Scientists have found that silence helps you generate new cells that split into neurons that integrate into the *hippocampus*, the learning centre of your brain.

We should take more quiet time to think and reflect. Introversion can make us powerful leaders.

Developing your signature presence as a leader coach requires time and the space to reflect.

Reflections on Silence

In your hectic life, silence is a vital resource like pure water. Refreshing and invigorating. Silence calms your body, turns up the volume on your inner thoughts and retunes you to your outer world. Your brain is chattering away to itself in the quiet. Your brain works in silent spaces to encrypt information into neurons that generate thoughts and actions. The surface of the sea may look calm, but it is never truly still.

The brain has a quiet default mode situated in the *prefrontal cortex* that keeps it constantly active, alert for danger and always processing information. The brain uses this default mode to allow you to self-reflect. In your reflective silences your brain is busy integrating external and internal information into a conscious space, fitting you into your turning world. Finding quiet places in your busy life allows you to reflect deeply, in effect to talk to yourself. To get to know yourself better.

In your *Leading by Coaching* conversations, silences prompt cell development in the *hippocampus*, the brain region responsible for learning.

Two-minute silent pauses in your conversations, based on neuro-silence research, are the most powerful for calming the mind to enable your client to think about their thinking effectively.

Neuroscience tells us that silence is not empty. There is a lot going on in your brain to help you make sense of a crazy world!

Silence may not be tangible, but it has a powerful presence and a distinctive quality. In the words of the marketing slogan of Ronkko, a watch company based in Finland, "Handmade in Finnish Silence".

Your *Leading by Coaching* Journey

Each of us has an Inner Critic. It's that voice you hear telling you that you can't do something you want to do. It is the voice of anxiety, fear and doubt. Your Inner Critic talks down to you. You are going to fail because you are not good enough to succeed, it tells you. Your Inner Critic protects you from harming your fragile ego, your precious self-image. It says, stop, hold back and be safe. The voice of your Inner Coach is much more positive. It tells you that you can do it. It is full of hope and opportunity. It knows perfection is a goal that cannot be attained and strives for excellence. It knows that you have to fail many times before you can succeed. It knows that all learning comes from trying something new and finding out what you need to do to make the experience better next time. Becoming the best version of your imperfect self is going to need you to free yourself from fear of the unknown and self-doubt. Leaders are made not born. You control the voices in your head. The more positive thoughts you plant, the more you water them and give them sunshine, the more you weed out your negative thoughts, the more your garden will grow into the beautiful garden you imagined and dreamed of. To flourish as a leader, you need to have the mindset of a horticulturist. Plan your garden. Give your plants the best chance to grow. Pull your weeds. Choose your thoughts carefully and cultivate them with love. Accept yourself as you are. Be honest about your weaknesses and be responsible for your actions. Never let anyone define who you are. You are fighting your private war in your mind. Control your thoughts with all the will-power you can muster because your thoughts become your leader's journey; your thoughts become your leader's destiny; and ultimately your thoughts become your leader's legacy.

Before you continue your leadership journey, ask yourself:

How can I introduce Leading by Coaching principles into everyday conversations?
Where does Leading by Coaching fit into my leadership?
Where can I start implementing it? When is it appropriate to use it? Do I need permission?
Who in the organisation needs to give me permission to use it? What support do I need? Coach training?
How can I establish a Leading by Coaching culture in my organisation?
What in-house coaching resource do I have access to? How can this capability be developed?
How can our external coach pool be developed? Do our external coaches understand our organisation culture and strategic goals?
What are the advantages of a Leading by Coaching culture to the organisation? Where in the organisation can it have the most impact?
Who in the organisation can benefit the most?
Who needs to buy into the Leading by Coaching concept?
Who needs to be involved to make it work?

In Summary

You change your business *one conversation at a time.*

Coaching conversations can be anytime, anywhere. They can be formal or informal.

The conversation pathway gives you a framework for your coaching conversations.

Building a coaching culture and upskilling leaders, as coaches, gives organisations an internal coaching system capability and a competitive advantage. Better coaching skills result in better engagement, higher individual performance levels and greater loyalty.

Leaders are trust-builders, building trust one conversation at a time.

The agile organisation is emerging as the new dominant business model in the age of disruption.

Cross-cultural communication is two sides of the same coin. On the one side, misunderstandings and on the other, opportunities.

Who you are is how you coach. Your unique signature presence. You are the instrument of your coaching.

Coaching takes place in the *dance* where context, coach and coachee all come together.

Finding some quiet time to reflect on your *Leading by Coaching* helps your brain think about its thinking and consolidates your learning.

My Final Thoughts

My mission in writing this book is to facilitate a happier, psychologically safer and more productive work place where people listen to each other and choose to care.

Leading by Coaching helps create a better working environment because it encourages better conversations that lead to better outcomes. Tomorrow's leaders want to be trusted and developed, not controlled and directed. They want to use all their talents to create a better world. They need leaders who believe in them and who nurture their growth and support their development. Leaders who listen with compassionate empathy. They can then express who they truly are and bring all their creativity to solving the increasingly complex problems we all face. The old command and control organisation is starting to creak. It lacks the agility and adaptability of the instant feedback social media platforms. The only redemption for established business will be faster reaction times driven by a more open listening conversation culture that encourages, recognises and rewards, challenges to the status quo.

Organisations that embrace such an open *Leading by Coaching* culture will, I believe, attract and develop more talent and, thereby, create a more competitive, sustainable business. *Leading by Coaching*, tomorrow's leaders, *one conversation at a time*.

Leading

We need a new way of leading our organisations. We need to make being human the centre of enterprise. Business should be based on trust and accountability rather than hierarchy and coercion.

We need to change how we organise the world of work. We need to give everyone permission to be a leader. Everyone can be a leader of change by being the change they seek.

Social groups at work are, like all living organisms in the natural world, self-organising. So, leaders should set the direction, clear the path and get out of the way. People don't want to be managed but they do want to be engaged. The CEO should be the Chief Engaging Officer!

Coaching

Helping people find and use their authentic voice is my mission as a coach. Seeing people, I have coached become whole and happy again has given me much joy. I wish you much joy in your coaching too.

Coaching is a hard road to travel along. My experience of coaching has been a sometimes-painful journey of discovery about myself. You have to look in at yourself before you can look out for others and look beyond for your business.

You don't coach people, you sit with them and witness their story. You listen deeply, share their pain and help build their confidence by believing in them. But first you need to believe in yourself. And no person is an island. You too need someone who believes in you and supports you. That is why it is good to find an experienced mentor in your business and a qualified coach supervisor.

The most important thing to remember when *Leading by Coaching* is that you are winning the hearts of young leaders by demonstrating empathic concern for their well-being. And with 47% of British workers, according to Investors in People, looking to move jobs in 2018 and nearly half citing poor management as the main reason, developing your people has never been more important to your business.

Allowing people to fail and show their vulnerabilities by making it ok by showing your vulnerabilities, selectively, allows a creative culture to breathe. Fear stifles creativity. Not being afraid to admit your own failures encourages other people to try new things. Accepting failure should be a normal part of the learning process that encourages personal risk. And without any risk, there can be no reward. No one ever achieved anything game changing without putting their skin into the game. Ask Richard Branson.

And "don't worry about reaching perfection, you'll never get there", according to the painter Salvador Dali. *And* "being right is overrated. You just need to know why you are right", according to Albert Einstein.

Excellence should be your goal. Being wrong and knowing why you are wrong should be your aim. Thomas Edison had 200 failed attempts before he had a successful light bulb! He learned something from every failure. You have to fail to succeed. Try, try and try again. Winston Churchill, apparently said, "success consists of going from failure to failure without loss of enthusiasm".

The Power of Coaching

> No power on earth can stop an idea whose time has come. Victor Hugo, French writer 1802–1885.

Coaching works because it is self-directed learning. It allows individuals to harness their authentic selves, knowledge and energy and direct it, focus it, to a purpose. Purpose arises from insights that appear to be spontaneous, yet dependent on feedback and stimuli from others, especially their coach. Self-direction is making sense out of the chaos in the mind, seeing the path to take and making choices to move along that chosen way.

Leading by Coaching

Mastering yourself and being a master of your *Leading by Coaching* conversations will help you in your quest of developing and growing tomorrow's leaders beyond their self-imposed boundaries.

Leaders have impactful conversations by combining self-mastery with a deep understanding of the brain at work; Gestalt coaching in action; and meaningful use of language—words and their emotional significance.

A leader also needs to be aware of the overriding nature of self-organisation in humans. Self-organisation is a guiding principle in living organisms. It arises in observable chemical interactions incorporated in the building blocks of life. Self-organisation in humans is a powerful driver manifesting itself in free will and independence.

Coaching plays to exploring and building on the overriding principle of self-organisation and free spirit. And Gestalt coaching methodology helps people find a safe harbour in an unpredictable sea through encouraging their journey back home to themselves. Helping them search and find closure and a return to wholeness. Helping them find their true authentic self. Guiding them gently to find new ways of making their purpose relevant to the changing system they are part of.

Coaching conversations provide a platform for exploration of self and the wider system. Questioning and encouraging insights that help find closure but ultimately being drawn for the need for autonomy. Our presence as a coach, and another human being sharing the joy and suffering that is human existence, inspires a true expression of self. We bring a precious gift as a coach.

Reflections on My Coaching Journey—"Who I Am Is Enough in Itself"

After more than a decade of coaching I realise, more than ever, that the only thing that matters is to bring all of yourself to your coaching. Opening yourself up makes you vulnerable and requires courage. But if you cannot, or you are not prepared to do this, then you cannot give permission for the person you are coaching to do the same. Coaching is scary. It takes courage to take off your professional mask and disclose your true identity. The fear of being found out. The fear of being judged. The fear of being found to be wanting.

My Gestalt coach training taught me the power of being truly present with my client as a fellow human being. This can only happen when I give myself permission to be myself. Only then can I ask their permission to witness them and share their journey. Permission is important in coaching. And it builds intimacy. And intimacy builds trust. You coach at the speed of trust. But you must trust yourself before they can trust you. Before every coaching session, I repeat those life-changing words, "who I am is enough in itself". All I can do is turn up, be myself and be present with my client. All my clients want from me is to just listen to them. To listen to who they are, witness their story and share their pain. And help them move on.

My Personal Message to You

I hope my book has inspired you to have more and better conversations with the people you lead.

I hope my book will inspire you to coach tomorrow's leaders to find their authentic voice and use it to create a happier, psychologically safer and more productive world of work.

Above all I hope this book will give you the confidence to bring all of yourself to your coaching conversations.

Thank you for listening to my voice. I truly hope I have helped you find your voice, so you can help others find theirs.

A book can only go so far in developing your awareness and skills as a coach. So, to provide you with a practical next step, I have developed, with my colleagues Derek Benton and Neil May, a Parallel Mind *Leading by Coaching* programme.

During the programme you will have a safe place to develop your unique coach signature. You will develop your skills by practising your coaching, seeing your performances played back and getting feedback from your fellow coaches and the course faculty. The learning will come from the silences in your coaching, interacting with your peers and reflecting on your coaching.

An outline of the programme can be found at www.leadingbycoaching. com.

Coaching is never easy but always rewarding. Lead every day by having courageous coaching conversations that inspire and develop your followers to become the future leaders of your business. Your *Leading by Coaching* conversations will allow you to have more impact as a leader and become your leader's legacy.

I wish you every success and joy *Leading by Coaching one conversation at a time*.

Nick Marson December 2018.

I would love to hear from you. Email me at nickmarson@parallel-mind. com.

Epilogue

The sun is setting over the Tibetan mountains. An orange glow gently lights the ancient stonework. There is a stillness in the air. The Monks retire from their prayer and ready themselves for slumber. Tomorrow the same sun will rise again in the east and flood the monastery with sunlight. But it is not the sunlight that illuminates their thoughts, it is their silence.

© The Editor(s) (if applicable) and The Author(s),
under exclusive license to Springer Nature Switzerland AG 2019
N. Marson, *Leading by Coaching*, https://doi.org/10.1007/978-3-319-76378-1

Inspirations for My Book

This book has grown out of many conversations and I have been inspired by many diverse sources. These sources range from the philosophical to the scientific. Suggestions for further reading follow. One of the best guides on our incredible journey into the brain and out of the mind has been **David Rock** who brilliantly translated the pioneering work of **Jeffrey M. Schwartz** in his seminal work, *The Mind and The Brain*.

As a leading figure, it is no surprise that **Albert Einstein** is often referenced. From him, I learned the importance of *Gedankenexperiment* (thought experiments) of dreaming. The unconscious mind is a world of dreams that surface in your thoughts and motivates your actions.

My research into the latest scientific breakthroughs of our understanding of the inner workings of the brain have inevitably led me to the work of **Daniel J. Siegel** whose, "Pocket Guide to Interpersonal Neurobiology" is a beautifully written integrative Handbook of the Mind. His latest book, *Mind*, in the words of *Emotional Intelligence* author **Daniel Goleman** "widens our world with this mind-opening and mind-bending exploration of mind itself. From a journey through *Mind* emerges a compelling sense of our connection to each other, and to the universe". Dan Siegel is a true pioneer in applying the latest science to well-being, education and public policy. A deeper understanding of the social nature of the brain led me to the work of **Matthew D. Lieberman**, a pioneer of the new field of social cognitive neuroscience in his book *Social*, which explores how our brain engages in social activity. A sensitive, fair, socially cohesive workplace ethos make a great difference to the motivation, productivity and well-being of employees.

© The Editor(s) (if applicable) and The Author(s),
under exclusive license to Springer Nature Switzerland AG 2019
N. Marson, *Leading by Coaching*, https://doi.org/10.1007/978-3-319-76378-1

The brain is also profoundly emotional. We feel before we think: passion drives reason, emotion is more powerful than logic. In his book, *The Emotional Brain*, **Joseph LeDoux** suggests that emotions are biological functions of the nervous system. The challenge for mankind is how to better integrate cognition and emotion: our emotions should be the servant of our thinking and actions not their master.

In *The Power of Others*, **Michael Bond** explores peer pressure, groupthink, and how the people around us shape everything we do in ways that we are often not consciously aware of. Our behaviour is influenced far more by others than we'd like to imagine. We are not our thoughts, it seems.

No investigation of neuroscience would be complete without understanding your inner Chimp—your best friend or your worst enemy. *The Chimp Paradox* is a powerful mind management model that can help you become a happy, confident, healthier and more successful person. **Professor Steve Peters** explains the struggle that takes place within your mind and then shows how to apply this understanding in every area of your life, so that you can: recognise how your mind is working; understand and manage your emotions and thoughts; manage yourself and become the person you would like to be.

Abraham Maslow's *Hierarchy of Needs* and **Carl Rogers'** *Self Actualisation* help us examine our lives and search for a higher purpose. **Don Clifton's** *Strengths* based psychology helps us to assess and capitalise on our unique gifts and so lead a more satisfying and successful life. And **David Kolb's** Experiential Learning Model gives us a framework to experience, learn and reflect—to be a life-long reflective practitioner.

In his thought-provoking and accessible book, *The Consolations of Philosophy*, **Alain De Botton** suggests that the birth of philosophy started at the death of Socrates who was condemned to be executed by the people of Athens for failing to worship the city's gods, of introducing religious novelties and of corrupting the young men of Athens. In Plato's account of his trial, he had defiantly told the jury: "So long as I draw breath and have my faculties, I shall never stop practising philosophy and exhorting you and elucidating the truth for everyone I meet". Socrates crime was challenging his people's thinking. If thinking is a crime, then we should all be criminals. Philosophy is relevant to students of business because it challenges them to think and challenges their received wisdom.

Leading by Coaching crosses all frontiers, it has no boundaries and is universally applicable. Translating the principles put forward in this book across cultures has been gained from working in many different countries. My cultural bible is *When Cultures Collide* by **Richard D. Lewis** who was working at Rolls Royce International, at the same time, I was running an international presentation skills course.

Gestalt principles are the foundation of my coaching. I discovered this powerful thought system when I attended The Academy of Executive Coaching Advanced Executive Coaching Programme run by **John Leary Joyce** whose book, *The Fertile Void*, is a classic work on Gestalt Coaching.

Gestalt Coaching is powerful because it focusses on the here and now, what is going on in our bodies and minds in the moment, what is driving our sensations and thoughts. Insights emerge in the silences. We learn how we can find closure and become whole again by adapting creatively to fit better into our changing world. As **T. S. Eliot** wrote in Four Quartets: "We shall not cease from exploration / And the end of all our exploring / Will be to arrive where we started /And know the place for the first time".

The father of Gestalt therapy, **Frederick Perls**, has given me the psychological understanding of how we develop an awareness of self and grow as a person. The starting premise of Gestalt is that experience begins at the contact boundary (the boundary between 'me' and 'not me'). Gestalt methodology allows us to examine the nature of that experience before going on to investigate the various obstacles that stand in the way of maturation and growth. Gestalt stresses the need for completion of unfinished situations, so we can move on to new experiences. I have found that my Gestalt-based coaching has often been transformative and, in some cases, life-changing for my clients and for me too.

Peter Senge in his powerful book, *Presence*, starts with understanding the nature of wholes and parts and their interrelatedness. Our normal way of thinking deceives us into thinking, wholes are made up of many parts, like the components of a machine. Living systems, such as your body or a tree, create themselves. They are not mere assemblages of their parts but are continually growing and changing along with their elements. The German writer and scientist **Goethe** argued that we needed to think very differently about wholes and parts. For Goethe, the whole was something dynamic and living that continually comes into being, "in concrete manifestations". A part, in turn, was a manifestation of the whole, rather than just a component of it. Neither exists without the other. The whole exists through continually manifesting in the parts, and the parts exist as embodiments of the whole. So, in this way, Gestalt is a constant search for integrating our parts into the bigger whole. We do this by making sense of our lives by giving them meaning and purpose, connecting and integrating our human parts into the universe whole.

Eckhart Tolle's book *Practicing the Power of Now*[1] reflects that "The beginning of freedom is the realisation that you are not the possessing entity—the thinker... The moment you start watching the thinker, a higher level of consciousness becomes activated".

People don't remember what you said, they only remember what they thought about what you said, in the silence after you have said it, if you give them their silence. Creating and holding that silent space is one of the core messages in this book. This has always been encapsulated for me by **T. S. Eliot** with the phrase in his poem the *Four Quartets*, "At the still point there the dance is".

---

[1] https://archive.org/stream/PracticingThePowerOfNowEckhartTolle.compressed/Practicing%20 the%20Power%20of%20Now%20-%20Eckhart%20Tolle.compressed#page/n9/mode/2up/search/ watching+the+thinker.

Bibliography

Aiken and **Keller** (2007, Sept), CEO's Role in Leading Transformation. *McKinsey Quarterly*.

Angelou, Maya (1970), *I Know Why the Caged Bird Sings*.

Ann Lewis, Fenman (2005, issue 15 Coach the Coach), *Coaching with the Brain in Mind: Foundations for Practice*.

Argyle, Michael (1994), *The Psychology of Interpersonal Behaviour*.

Ashkanasay, Hartel and **Zerbe** (2000), *Emotions in the Workplace*.

Barrington-Bush, Liam (2013), *Anarchists in the Boardroom*.

Barsh, **Capozzi** and **Davidson** (2008), The Gap Between the Aspirations of Executives To. *McKinsey*.

Beldoch, M. (1964), *Emotional Intelligence*.

Blakey, John (2016), *The Trusted Executive*.

Boehm, Christopher (1999), *Hierarchy in the Forest: The Evolution of Egalitarian Behaviour*.

Bohm, David (1994), *Thought as a System*.

Bond, Michael (2014), *The Power of Others*.

Booz Allen Hamilton (2007), *Annual Study of the World's Largest Corporate R & D Spenders*.

Bossons, Riddell and **Sarain** (2015), *The Neuroscience of Leadership Coaching*.

Branson, Richard (2015), *The Virgin Way How to Listen, Learn and Lead*.

Bresman, H. (2007), *Innovation: Using Externally-Orientated or "X" Teams Can Prove a Winning Strategy*. Insead.

Brockman, John (2013), *Thinking*.

Brooks, David (2011), *The Social Animal*.

Buckingham, Marcus and **Donald Clifton** (2001), *Now Discover Your Strengths*.

© The Editor(s) (if applicable) and The Author(s),
under exclusive license to Springer Nature Switzerland AG 2019
N. Marson, *Leading by Coaching*, https://doi.org/10.1007/978-3-319-76378-1

Chartered Management Institute (2008), *Data on Insurance Sector's Ability to Cope with Uncertain Times.*

Chaskalson, Michael (2014), *The Mindful Workplace.*

Chip and **Dan Heath** (2010), *Switch: How to Change Things When Change Is Hard.*

Ciaramicoli, Arthur (2000), *The Power of Empathy.*

Covey, Stephen R. (2004), *The 8th Habit: From Effectiveness to Greatness.*

Crofts, Neil (2003), *Authentic.*

Crum, Thomas F. (1987), *The Magic of Conflict.*

Cuddy, Amy (2016), *Presence.*

Damasio, Antonio (2000), *The Feeling of What Happens.*

Damasio, Antonio (2005), *Emotion, Reason and the Human Brain.*

De Botton, Alain (2000), *The Consolations of Philosophy.*

de Saint Exupery, Antoine (1942), *The Little Prince.*

Delong, Cabarro and **Lees** (2007), *When Professionals Have to Lead.*

Doz, Yves and **Mikko Kosonen** (2008), *Fast Strategy: How Strategic Agility Will Help You Stay Ahead of the Game.*

Duhigg, Charles (2012), *The Power of Habit.*

Edward de Bono (1985), *Six Thinking Hats.*

Eliot, T. S. (1943), *The Four Quartets.*

Emmens, Ben (2016), *Conscious Collaboration.*

Follmi, Danielle and **Olivier Follmi** (2003), *Buddhist Offerings 365 Days.*

Gelles, David (2015), *Mindful Work.*

George, B. (2003), *Authentic Leadership.*

Gladwell, Malcolm (2006), *Blink, the Power of Thinking Without Thinking.*

Glaser, Judith E. (2014), *Conversational Intelligence.*

Goffee R. and **G. Jones** (2004), *What Makes a Leader?* London Business School and HBR.

Goleman, D. (1995), *Emotional Intelligence.*

Goleman, D. (1998), *Working with Emotional Intelligence.*

Goleman, Daniel (2015), *A Force for Good: The Dalai Lama's Vision for Our World.*

Goleman, Daniel and **The Dalai Lama** (2004), *Destructive Emotions.*

Gonzales, Laurence (2017), *Deep Survival: Who Lives, Who Dies, and Why.*

Green, Charles H., *The Trusted Advisor.*

Greenfield, Susan A. (2000), *The Private Life of the Brain.*

Hall, Edward T. (1959), *The Silent Language.*

Hamel, G. (2007), *The Future of Management.* Harvard.

Hamel, G. (2012), *What Matters Now.*

Handy, Charles (1993), *Understanding Organisations.*

Handy, Charles (1994), *The Age of Paradox.*

Hansen and **Birkinshaw** (2007), *The Innovation Value Chain.* Harvard Business Review.

Harari, Yuval Noah (2011), *Sapiens: A Brief History of Mankind.*

Hawkins, Jeffrey (2004), *On Intelligence.*

Hesselbein and **Cohen** (1999), *Leader to Leader.* The Drucker Foundation.

Hill, Linda A. (2014), *Collective Genius: Why Some Organisations Innovate Time and Again, While Most Cannot.*

His Holiness The Dalai Lama (2008), *The Leader's Way.*

Hofstede, Geert (1991), *Cultures and Organisations: Software of the Mind.*

IBM (2006), *Global CEO Study. Innovate and Their Ability to Execute.*

Joyce, Nohria and **Roberson** (2003), *What (Really) Works.*

Kahneman, Daniel (2011), *Thinking, Fast and Slow.*

Kanter (2006), *Innovation: The Classic Traps.* Harvard Business Review.

Kaplan, R. and **D. Norton** (2007), *Innovation in Strategy Execution Balanced Scorecard.* European Summit.

Keller, Scott and **Colin Price** (2011), *Beyond Performance How Great Organisations Build Ultimate Competitive Advantage.*

Kets de Vries (2002), *Can CEOs Change?* Insead.

Kets de Vries (2006), *The Leader on the Coach.* Insead.

Kline, Nancy (2015), *Time to Think.*

Koole, Wibo (2014), *Mindful Leadership.*

Kotter, John P. (1996), *Leading Change.* Harvard.

Kotter, John P. (2012, Nov), *Change Faster: How to Build Adaptive Genius in Your Organisation.* HBR.

Kreitner, Kinicki and **Buelors** (1989), *Organisational Behaviour.*

Krueger and **Killham** (2007, Apr), *The Innovation Equation.* Gallup Management Journal.

Le Doux, Joseph (1998), *The Emotional Brain.*

Leary-Joyce, John (2014), *The Fertile Void: Gestalt Coaching at Work.*

Levitin, Daniel (2014), *The Organised Mind.*

Lewis, Richard D. (1996), *When Cultures Collide.*

Lieberman, Matthew D. (2013), *Social.*

Maister, D. (2008), *Strategy and the Fat Smoker.*

Marturano, Janice (2014), *Finding the Space to Lead: A Practical Guide to Mindful Leadership.*

Maslow, Abraham (1943), *A Theory of Human Motivation.*

Matthews, Paul (2013), *Informal Learning at Work.*

Matthews, Zeidner and **Roberts** (2007), *The Science of Emotional Intelligence.* Oxford University Press.

Mauborgne, R. (2005), *Blue Ocean Strategy.* Insead.

Maxwell, John C. (1998), *The 21 Irrefutable Laws of Leadership.*

McKinsey (2008), *Global Survey How Companies Approach Innovation.*

MIT Sloan (2008), *Reinventing Your Business Model.*

Muehlfeit, Jan (2017), *The Positive Leader: How Energy and Happiness Fuel Top-Performing Teams.*

Nelson-Jones, Richard (1990), *Relating Skills.*

Nicholson, Nigel (2013), *The "I" of Leadership.* London Business School.

Nordstroir, K. *Emotional Innovation.*
Obama, Barack (2007), *Dreams from My Father.*
Organisations & People (2005, Feb), *Leaders & Values.*
Peltier, Bruce (2011), *Psychology of Executive Coaching.*
Perls, Frederick (1951), *Gestalt Therapy.*
Peters, Steve (2012), *The Chimp Paradox.*
Peters, Tom (2003), *Re-imagine.*
Pettigrew, A. M. (1992), *On Studying Managerial Elites.*
Pink, Daniel (2006), *Whole New Mind—"Right Brain" Thinking.*
Pink, Daniel (2011), *Drive, the Surprising Truth About What Motivates Us.*
Pinker, Stephen (1997), *How the Mind Works.*
Porter, M. (2008, Jan), *The Five Competitive Forces That Shape Strategy.* Harvard and HBR.
Reece and **Walker** (1977), *Teaching Training and Learning.*
Robinson, Ken (2001), *Out of Our Minds.*
Rock, David (2006), *Quiet Leadership.*
Rock, David (2009), *Your Brain at Work.*
Rogers, Carl (1967), *A Way of Being.*
Rosinski, Philippe (2003), *Coaching Across Cultures.*
Sammut, Anton (2016), *Consciousness: The Concept of Mind.*
Sanborn, Mark (2004), *The Fred Factor.*
Sawhney and **Wolcott** (2004, Aug), *Mastering Innovation.* Financial Times.
Schiffer, Frederic (1998), *Of Two Minds.*
Schwartz, Jeffrey M. (2002), *The Mind and The Brain.*
Schon, Donald A. (1990), *Educating the Reflective Practitioner.*
Scott, Susan (2002), *Fierce Conversations.*
Senge, Peter (2005), *Presence.*
Siegel, Daniel (2012), *Pocket Guide to Interpersonal Neurobiology.*
Siegel, Daniel (2017), *Mind: A Journey to the Heart of Being Human.*
Sir Clive Woodward (2004), *Winning!*
Smith, Adam (1759), *The Theory of Moral Sentiments.*
Smith, Simon (2000), *Inner Leadership.*
Solomon (2002), *Working with Difficult People.*
Sprenger, Reinhard K. (2004), *Trust: The Best Way to Manage.*
Sunim, Haemin (2017), *The Things You Can See Only When You Slow Down.*
Steen, R. Grant (2007), *The Evolving Brain.*
Syed, Mathew (2015), *Black Box Thinking.*
Thich Nhat Hanh (1975), *The Miracle of Mindfulness.*
Thomson, Helen (2018), *Unthinkable.*
Tolle, Eckhart (1999), *Practicing the Power of Now.*
Tomorrow's Company (2004), *Restoring Trust: Investment in the 21st Century.*
Trompenaars, Fons (1993), *Riding The Waves of Culture.*

Vaster, V. (1999), *The Art of Networked Thinking—Ideas and Tools for a New Way of Dealing with Complexity.*

von Goethe, Johann Wolfgang (1790), *Theory of the Principles of Botany.*

Weisinger, H. (1998), *Emotional Intelligence at Work.*

West, Lucy, and **Mike Milan** (2001), *The Reflecting Glass: Professional Coaching for Leadership Development.*

Whitmore, John (2002), *Coaching for Performance.*

Winston, Robert (2004), *The Human Mind.*

Yankelovich, Daniel (2001), *The Magic of Dialogue.*

Zaiss, Carl (2002), *True Partnership.*

Index